P9-AGP-269

REVEALING REVEILING

WITHDRAWN

SUNY Series in Middle Eastern Studies
Shahrough Akhavi, EDITOR

REVEALING REVEILING
Islamist Gender Ideology
in Contemporary Egypt

Sherifa Zuhur

State University of New York Press

Cover photo: Student at Cairo University. Reproduced with permission from ABBAS/MAGNUM. The author also gratefully acknowledges the assistance of Margot Schevill and the Austin I. Kelly Foundation.

Published by
State University of New York Press, Albany

©1992 State University of New York

Production by Bernadine Dawes
Marketing by Fran Keneston

For information, address the State University of New York Press,
State University Plaza, Albany, NY 12246

Library of Congress Cataloging-in-Publication Data

Zuhur, Sherifa.
    Revealing reveiling : Islamist gender ideology in contemporary
  Egypt / Sherifa Zuhur.
        p.   cm. — (SUNY series in Middle East studies)
    Includes bibliographical references and index.
    ISBN 0-7914-0927-9 (alk. paper) : $47.50. — ISBN 0-7914-0928-7
  (pbk. : alk. paper) : $15.95
      1. Women—Egypt—Cairo—Attitudes. 2. Women, Muslim—Conduct of
  life. 3. Self perception—Egypt—Cairo.   I. Title. II. Series.
  HQ1793.Z67   1992
  305.42′0962′16—dc20   91-3408
                                                               CIP

10   9   8   7   6   5   4   3   2   1

*To my family and to the city of Cairo, its songs and
its dreams*

CONTENTS

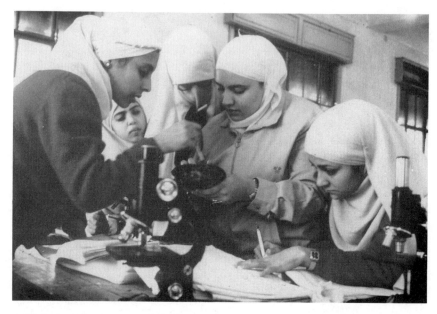

Students wearing the *higab* at Cairo University.
Courtesy of ABBAS/MAGNUM.

ACKNOWLEDGMENTS

I wish first to thank Shahrough Akhavi, series editor for SUNY Press who encouraged me to present this manuscript in book form. His interest persevered and he read patiently through many versions, editing and commenting critically and substantively. Thanks also to Rosalie Robertson and Bernadine Dawes of SUNY Press and all those involved in the copyediting and production processes. I am grateful to the von Grunebaum Center for Near Eastern Studies at UCLA for its support and to the History Faculty of Massachusetts Institute of Technology and Philip Khoury for providing me a subsequent institutional base.

I gratefully acknowledge the support and trust extended by Hagga Zaynab al-Ghazali and all the other individuals who permitted me to interview them, as well as those who helped make these encounters possible including: Hana Ahmad Shawqi, Prof. Ahmad Yusuf, Magdi Ahmad Hussein, Tim Sullivan, Dina Zulfiqar, Ashraf Ramadan, and Yehia Taha.

I also want to thank those who read, edited and commented on early versions of the same work and who have all encouraged me intellectually: Afaf Lutfi al-Sayyid Marsot, Michael Morony, Sondra Hale, George Sabagh, Nikki Keddie. Thanks also to James Schevill and Marina Preussner for reading and editing and to Leonard Binder.

I thank my parents—all four of them, my daughter and my siblings for their enduring support and love and also my friends in America, and in Egypt.

Students wearing *niqab* and *higab* in lab at Cairo University.
Courtesy of ABBAS/MAGNUM.

Chapter One

NEW IMAGES OR CONTINUOUS ARCHETYPES?

Sumaya (a pseudonym) commutes several hours a day by train to attend Cairo University. She is twenty-three years old and one of the best students in her department. On Thursday afternoons and most evenings, she works in a shop with her mother. Sumaya wears Islamic dress, including a face veil (*niqab*) and gloves. She believes that her dream of a more pious society where all women wear Islamic dress will come to pass.

Alham (a pseudonym) has successfully entered a second career in her fifties. She is dismayed by the growing emphasis on a narrowly defined religiosity taking place in urban Egypt at this time. She strongly opposes women who wear Islamic dress, which she finds hideous and degrading. Amina (a pseudonym) is almost twenty-seven years old, and to her mother's concern has rejected several suitors. She would not dream of donning Islamic dress, but defends the historical arguments of the Islamists and criticizes the lax code of moral values found in the West.

How does one analyze these three viewpoints? What elements of their backgrounds, experiences, and motivations are responsible for the varying reactions? These Cairene women, and many others, are reacting to the emergence of new options for women in their society. A new image, or role model, for contemporary Egyptian Muslim women has arisen from the conjuncture of history and sociopolitical pressures. Women now possess multiple avenues to express their identity, including those presented by modern Islamists (usually referred to as Muslim fundamentalists). This book examines the presentation and reception of these options, and considers the processes affecting women under the rubric of gender issues.

Fadwa el-Guindi, in her work on the rise of the Islamists during the 1970s, described a new, growing Islamic ethic reflected by Muslim women.[1] Was that "ethic" really Islamic, or was it a synthesis of a popular understanding of Islam colored by political opposition to the state? In the ten years since this article appeared, numerous works have explored the appeal of the new Islamic groups, but few have described the process of female identification with Islamist ideals in detail.

Much of the recent literature on the Islamic awakening glosses over discussions of gender issues. When the question of women's status is considered, it is often occluded by a host of factors, including ethnocentrism. Social scientists have been more preoccupied with popular attitudes toward

1

authority, tyranny, and the potential for revolt. These issues are embedded in the oppositionist nature of some Islamist groups that sought to counter the secular authority of the state. In the wake of the Iranian revolution, that focus, reflected in governmental research and in the press, was understandable. If women were portrayed at all in materials dealing with Islamic fundamentalism, they appeared as silent appendages or auxiliary members equal neither in accessibility nor in importance to their male counterparts.

Some fossilization has occurred in the study of gender issues in the Middle East, partially due to academic dependence on the written word. Heavily reliant on past scholarship, observers of the region sometimes misrepresented the views of their subjects or failed to fully portray the spirit of studied societies. Scholarship, on the whole, has regarded sources of popular culture, especially oral sources, as interesting but not verifiable. Meanwhile, the literature has exalted the growth of feminism in the Middle East. As a consequence, the condition of Middle Eastern women has been analyzed in global terms of feminism that may be inappropriate to the Egyptian case.

A great deal of background knowledge and interpretive skill is required to explore and utilize written sources on women in Islamic history. Islamic law, another basis for debate on gender issues, is often discussed and taught as if it were observed to the letter and described present circumstances, rather than an ideal human condition. At the same time, we equate women and family law with the forces of traditionalism in the Weberian terms of the 1950s and 1960s (such as patrimonialism). The state has affected gender issues, but often observers describe its effect in antagonistic terms, as a challenge to Muslim ways, as if "Muslim ways" had ever been defined. The arguments for and against female role expansion have consistently been backed by appeals to woman's place in Islamic history. Therefore, we must review that history, and some of the arguments built upon it, in order to see how past events can affect the rights of contemporary women to participate more fully in the public arena.

Some of the methodological problems in assessing the status of Middle Eastern women may be due to an overemphasis on Islam,[2] or alternatively, to what Edward Said has termed an "Orientalist" approach.[3] In the latter instance, the whole area of female status has been an evocative and provocative means to emphasize the difference of the Other since the Victorian era, if not earlier. From Lord Cromer to modern American feminists' expressions, we see that a culture's value may be measured by its treatment of women. The board of directors of the National Organization for Women recently adopted resolutions protesting America's troop buildup in the Gulf that describe Saudi Arabia and Kuwait as "despotic, clan-run monarchies" that "subjugate and systematically oppress women."[4] The Arab Middle East falls short, then, on a scale of humanism when law and history are superficially considered. Perhaps this originally European perspective came from a Victorian consciousness of the lower status of European women, who only began to fight for expanded rights in the later nineteenth century. On the other hand, degrading a civilization that represented high political and economic stakes to the European nations served several purposes—it could divert popular opposition to colonial policies at home, or justify stricter measures abroad.

Middle Eastern as well as Western sources have equated female progress with national development. Themes of the literature have concentrated on female role expansion in the public sphere or measurement of female power. It is still difficult to define the scope and nature of female participation and power because of the incomplete nature of data but also due to flawed methodology. More recent research has addressed women's activities in the private sphere as well as their informal economic activities, and that helps to round out our picture of women's lives.

Since the 1960s (and later on in French sociological and anthropological works), social scientists have encouraged their subjects to describe their own value systems. Val Moghadam emphasized the above theme in her recommendation for a "*verstehende* sociology"— one that would speak from women's experience and perceptions.[5] This trend has been positively expressed in the growing number of oral histories gathered in Egypt, and I, too, intended to draw on that method in this work.

Those watching the development of Middle Eastern studies may have noticed a curious reversal of the study process. The researcher, the "self," generally examined the subjects, the "others." But now the social scientist has been found out; she now comprises the "other" examining the "self." A division occurs between entitled others and colonialist others who propose to examine Middle Eastern women. In suggesting that only the self should examine the self, this new trend challenges many preconceived notions of the value of objective research and questions the appropriateness of outside observation.

In response to this research issue, I should emphasize that I have examined unknown subjects in a familiar environment, for the Middle East, Cairo in particular, was once my home and workplace, inside and outside of academia. The fact that I share many beliefs with my subjects should not render my study less valuable. My conception of Islam is extremely personalized, as are my views on gender issues. These beliefs had no place entering in on the business of identifying my subjects' opinions. It is true, of course, that a subject's views will be affected to some extent by her interaction with a researcher. The new image of woman proffered to the veiled woman (*muhaggabat*) by the Islamists of Egypt is described within all the usual limitations and nuances that stubbornly adhere to the research process.

An Islamic, Historical, or Modern Phenomenon?

One aim of this study is to test the importance of the correlation between socioeconomic background and religiopolitical beliefs. Existing literature, particularly materials dealing with women in earlier periods of Islamic history, and other sociological studies are questioned and are seen to have certain bearing on the development of an Islamist ideology. This study proposes a certain flexibility and adaptability of gender issues in the Egyptian milieu that enables women of differing socioeconomic classes to similarly adopt a new ideology.

Clifford Geertz's categorization of change set forth in *The Interpretation of Cultures* may still be instructive in showing us that our conceptions of change may obstruct portrayals of other cultures.[6] "Evolutionary change," as Geertz defines it, is idealized in other works on female emancipation that hark back to Daniel Lerner's description of the modernization process.[7]

The literature on Middle Eastern women continuously alludes to the pre-existence of matrilinearity, goddess worship, women warriors, and female inheritance patterns in the Arabian Peninsula. These references are made either to defend the position of women in Islam, or to attack Islamic culture as an entity affected by antifemale practices such as seclusion. But Azizah al-Hibri, Jane Smith, and Yvonne Haddad have all described female roles that were less restricted by tribal laws or scripture than were conceptions of women elsewhere in the world. They demonstrate that Islam in and of itself is not anti women, and that Arab tribalism included practices such as matrilocality and matrilinearity that contrasted with the later development of patriarchal practices.[8]

The Islamists, along with other modern writers, state that Muhammad (p.b.u.h.) may be regarded as a champion of women due to his restrictions on female infanticide and polygamy.[9] The Prophet also regulated family interaction in various ways, and *hadith* commenting on the motives for regulation played a role in defining the subsequent rights of women.

The histories of famous women in Islam are important, for they establish a *sunnah* of the Mothers of the Believers.[10] Zaynab al-Ghazali, an ideologue of the moderate Islamists, refers to the Prophet's wives as an appropriate source of emulation for Muslim women. It may be that the more restrictive gender practices of the early Muslim upper classes were drawn on to represent all virtuous women, as W. Montgomery Watt suggests in *Muhammad at Medina*.[11] The women in Muhammad's harem and in other aristocratic harems were likely to have been aware of the neighboring non-Arab elites' customs of veiling and seclusion.[12] The prohibition of existing forms of polyandry, and sanctioning of polygamy, veiling, and seclusion were incorporated in the notion of an Islamic lifestyle, although the original purpose of laws referring to women's clothing, for example, was ambiguous within the developing body of *shari'ah*, Islamic law.[13] The Islamists however, assert that Islam had only positive effects on the lives of female adherents, throughout history, as intended by the Messenger of God.

The works of al-Bukhari reveal that restrictions on women coalesced around themes of ritual purification and the idea that the believer must separate the realm of prayer and the contemplative portion of his consciousness from the sexual distractions of women.[14] Injunctions for women to veil, to guard their virtue,[15] restrictions on travel, or movement through public space, and growing evidence that women did not always obey these restrictions, informs us that economically or politically active women were necessarily resourceful in the face of confining forces. But are the early centuries relevant to the modern discourse of gender?

Modern Egypt is an especially interesting setting for examining gender issues. The early strength of state authority, a complex evolution of civil society, and Egypt's incorporation into the modern world economy are all essential components affecting current arguments over women.[16] The importance of Egypt to the West, and the imprints of British cultural dominance, form the backdrop to the emerging debate on women and to the growth of Egyptian nationalism.[17] Public consciousness of the debate on women has affected the future orientation of religious opposition to gender issues. It is also significant that a tradition of public activism and involvement was inherited by the modern respondents of this study, and that their own mothers may have responded quite differently to the call of public service and private accommodations.

Valerie Hoffman-Ladd presents the essential Islamist conceptions of modesty and segregation.[18] Her analysis of important stances on female roles and functions outlines, in my opinion, an official Islamist theory, or a "leader's ideology." In this book, I have expanded the presentation of that ideology, which considers other gender issues. I have also chosen to contrast it with ordinary women's interpretations.

I will also compare unveiled women with the new Islamic woman. The notions of modesty and segregation that Hoffman-Ladd has presented do not describe the views of all Egyptian women. Sometimes, the Islamists or others writing about them suggest that women who do not espouse Muslim fundamentalist ideals are overly Westernized, "secular" women. Readers should note that Middle Eastern women conceive of and practice their religion in diverse ways but may regard themselves as equally pious Muslims.

Nonacademic treatises by modern champions of the new veiled Islamist woman are supplemented and contrasted with material derived from personal interviews. The writings of Zaynab al-Ghazali and other authors, and magazine and newspaper articles, constantly repeat certain themes of women's roles and rights related in chapter 5. Although many other, similar sources exist, certain works have been emphasized in order to define a coherent moderate position.

Definitions

I spoke recently about the Islamists to a feminist audience, and I remember the troubled expressions and suspicious questions of those unfamiliar with the term *Islamist,* which the French have devised. I hope to make the material clearer to my readers by explaining the following terms.

Gender Issues.

Gender issues refer to a set of controversial themes involving status determinants made on the basis of gender, sex differentiations, or inequality. These include women's roles and status within the family, their position in the workplace, their control over economic resources, their integration into the educational system, their participation in social movements, their political and legal status, and their self-definitions. This term should not be confused with the phrase "the issue of gender" which refers in a general manner to the presence of sex stratification and female disadvantage within society. Gender issues cannot be termed "women's issues," because they involve cross-sex interaction as well as male attitudes and actions, and affect society as a whole.

Self-Image.

Women and men formulate internal portraits, through syzygy, a conjoining process described below. Their inner portraits correspond in some respects to ideal models that they hold unconsciously, as well as consciously, throughout their lives. These inner images may influence women in making decisions on gender issues.

The notion of self-image is found not only in European sources but has been an extremely important concept to the growth of national identity in the third world, particularly in the neocolonial period. Hence, Egyptians or other Africans may consider the term unremarkable, while American social scientists may not be so familiar with the issues involved.

During the processes of self-imaging, women reflect values and specific qualities of femininity that are similar to those of others in their milieu. Sets of moral values, life goals, and cultural orientations are transmitted to women through a variety of sources. Women choose consciously or unconsciously to adopt these values as part of the self-identificative process. Self-imaging is just a step removed from self-conception or self-idealization because it involves the theoretical task of identifying the qualities and capabilities of an imaginary woman who may then be emulated.

Self-imaging involves self-labeling, a conscious action, self-awareness, or sometimes responsiveness to inner pressures, acting within the unconscious. A woman may feel more comfortable with the label of "mother" for example, than with the label of "professional colleague." The reason for her preference may be accessible only to a competent psychologist who might explore her childhood relationship with her own mother or with her children. But she may (or may not) be self-aware enough to act out her preference and continue to "mother" others in the workplace, or her friends or spouse, to the exclusion of other sorts of behavior. Within the parameters of that label she might enact her maternal functions differently in response to the overall image with which she identifies—a virtuous mother, an understanding mother, a challenging mother.

Sawsan el-Messiri states that in Egyptian society, "individuals interact by typification, interpreting their own and one another's behavior according to a process of abstraction based on experience of social reality."[19] The interaction occurs continuously and on many levels.

Transmitters of self-images may be the family, the educational system, literature, religious or popular figures, and the media, including film, television, and radio. Language itself, jokes, poetry, and songs also convey self-images. Popular or intellectual perceptions of women in Islamic history are conductors of self-images as well. The much-discussed issue of authenticity (*asala*) in the Arab world involves the internalization of historical values and their lessons that transmute into portions of self-image.

Historical Models.

Islamic history is the birthplace of female archetypes that correspond to segments of modern consciousness in a manner similar to Jung's discussion of Christ as a Western archetype symbolically representing the self.[20] Jung described the effect of such archetypes on personal consciousness as "syzygy," a conjoining or a "projection making factor" that may influence the recipient to dramatize (or internalize) even mythological events.[21] This explanation of the power of archetypes upon self-image can assist in understanding women's varied motivations for choosing one image over another.

The New Islamic Woman.

The image of the new Islamic woman refers to the internal model of the modern veiled women (*muhaggabat*). These women wear a specific set of garments that they call "Islamic dress" or "lawful dress" (*ziy shar'i*). It should not be confused with traditional forms of the veil worn by lower-class urban women or women earlier in Egyptian history.

I did not refer to this image as the "veiled woman," because its significance goes beyond the issues of veiling and sex separation. But actual survey respondents who related to this image may later be referred to as veiled women, for comparative purposes.

I have also dubbed the new Islamic woman the "virtuous" woman, not because she is more endowed with virtue than her sister, but because her image centers on the piety, modesty, and chastity of its receptors. The new Islamic woman is the subject of analysis because her viewpoint and orientations to gender issues have not always been considered in their cultural and political context.

The Unveiled Woman.

The image of the unveiled woman refers to women who have not adopted the Islamist headcovering, the *higab*, and do not agree with the antisecularist goals of the Islamists. These women come from the lower middle class, the middle class, and the elites. Some of them are lower-class women who no longer identify with the *bint al-balad*, the traditional model for urban lower-class women.

I did not title this image the "modern" woman, because the term "modernity" carries a strong normative connotation, and the unveiled woman might be no more modern than the veiled woman. She may be equally pious and therefore cannot be termed the secular woman. The unveiled woman differs from the new Islamic woman in more solidly supporting women's role in the public sphere, although she is careful to stress women's primary importance as wives and mothers. She may oppose the government, but she does not see the new Islamic groups as the ideal alternative to the current state, although she recognizes their political potential. In contrast to the *bint al-balad*, the unveiled woman may be more constrained in exhibiting her own defenses. For example, she might ignore male harassment in the streets rather than engage in the verbal or even physical reactions of the *bint al-balad*.[22] When at work, or otherwise in public, she wears clothing of European style and does not cover her head. She does not look down on traditional fashions, for at home she may also wear a *galabiyya*, a long robe.

The Bint al-Balad.

Bint al-balad literally means "daughter of the town." She is also known as the *bint al-hitta*, or "daughter of the neighborhood." The *bint al-balad* is an urban lower-class woman who, despite the changes in urban life, still expresses her values and her orientations to gender issues and to other classes of society in a distinct manner.[23] She may wear a *galabiyya*, covered by a black outer dress, and a modesty wrap known as the *malayya laff*. Some women have replaced that costume with a rather long and conservative

Western-style dress and, sometimes, a shawl. She wears a kerchief (*mandil*) over her hair rather than the headcovering of the new Islamic woman. The *bint al-balad* is very religious but may not pray in the mosque regularly, although she observes prayer times at home. She may visit shrines, attend the festivals of the saints, or sometimes participate in an exorcism ceremony known as the *zar*. As demonstrated by respondents of Nayra Attia, Andrea Rugh, el-Messiri's study, and women of my own acquaintance, the *bint al-balad* may conceive of the idealized qualities of men and women in a more disparate and differentiated manner than does the new Islamic woman or the unveiled woman.[24]

The Rural Woman.

The rural woman is known as the peasant woman (*fallaha*) or the villager (*bint al-bandar*). She is not represented in this study, although rural women and their identity codes may be referred to occasionally as a source of contrast. Up to now, the Islamists have not visibly recruited many rural women. The situation may change as rural migrants continue to pour into the cities of Egypt.

In the countryside, women exhibit varied forms of dress that illustrate adherence to the virtue of modesty. Items of their dress and the way they are worn transmit a message that the woman is chaste before marriage and, subsequently, sexually faithful. Andrea Rugh notes that garments may emphasize the female figure, as in waisted styles, or conceal female contours in unwaisted, wider-cut styles,[25] although these choices are dictated by village tradition and do not imply a more lenient or stricter code of morality.

Rural women have always been economically active in Egypt and interpreted their modesty code in a way that freed them for agricultural labor. Since it was impractical to utilize the traditional face veil (*burqa*) while working, they have worn the head kerchief (*mandil*) and a length of black material (*tarha*) covering the *mandil*.

These women cannot afford to share the attitude of those *banat al-balad* who feel that manual labor is "men's work" (despite the fact that some engage in it).[26] Rural women have also been slower to accept the idea that smaller families are beneficial. That attitude can be attributed to the lack of a social security plan to provide for the elderly, and to a need for increased labor on their lands and in their homes.[27] These attitudes may have affected the parents of some of the women in my sample who were from the countryside or from large villages.

Islamic Oppositionism.

The term "Islamic oppositionist" emerges from Afaf Lutfi al-Sayyid Marsot's discussion of protest movements in Egyptian history that "appealed to religious principles as a means of effecting social change."[28] A social group expressing political oppositionism counters the status quo as expressed in the state. Islamic oppositionism may also involve Saad Eddin Ibrahim's definition of fundamentalism: "A return to the purest sources of the religion, a movement to cleanse Islam from all the impurities, heresies and revisionisms which may have influenced its body-intellect as well as its body-practice."[29]

The term "fundamentalism" suggests ahistoricity and looking backward. Although the functions of repurification and revivalism partially define the objectives of the new Islamic social movements, these terms, and the word "fundamentalist," do not explain the tension between the Islamists and the modern state until they are understood as historically sanctioned protest movements. Most, though not all, of the Islamists discussed in this work are oppositionist in a political sense. They may or may not be actively engaged in protest.

Islamic oppositionism is a segment of the Islamic awakening (*sahwat islamiyya*), a phenomenon that includes Islamic opposition but also intellectual preoccupations with religion, increased personal piety, and theoretical linkage between political circumstances and the situation of faith and modernity. Ibrahim also notes that the term "Islamic awakening," is more common in Arabic than *usuliyya,* or derivation from the roots of religion—the Arabic equivalent of fundamentalist.[30]

Jamaᶜat.

In Egypt, the Islamists under discussion are included within what is known as *al-jamaᶜat al-islamiyya,* literally "the Islamic groups." The term *jamaᶜat* conveys overtones of populism and solidarity, as well as political oppositionism.

The Tajdid Movement.

Islamic oppositionism contains the notion of renewal (*tajdid*) of Islamic authenticity (*aṣalah*) and social justice (*ᶜadalah*). *Tajdid* incorporates a call to purify political principles and social mores, and a reconsideration of the body of juridical consensus and precedent (*ijmaᶜ*). Creative and productive thought in the form of *ijtihad,* a source of jurisprudence, may enhance the purified principles of *sharᶜiah* under modern circumstances. Nineteenth-century Egyptian reformers such as Rifaᶜah al-Tahtawi, Mohammed ᶜAbduh, Lutfi al-Sayyid, and Qasim Amin discuss the principles of *tajdid,* as they applied to reform generally, and as it applied to women. The concept of *tajdid* is not strictly modern; it has been recognized as a theoretical principle throughout Islamic history dating back to the Abbasid revolution of the eighth century.

Moderates.

The moderates encompass Islamists who envision a gradual shift from a secular state to an Islamic state. Some, including the Muslim Brotherhood, consider such a transformation to be possible through education. I have also labeled these groups "moderates" with regard to their position on gender issues, although some moderates hold to a more rigid definition of women's role boundaries.

Ibrahim divides Islamic resurgence in Egypt into three main tendencies: "establishment Islam, Sufi Islam, and activist Islam." He further separates activist Muslims into those who are political and those who are apolitical.[31] My use of the term "oppositionism" includes those covered under the category "activist Islam" as well as some members of the other two groups who oppose the secularist state.

The Islamic oppositionists are comprised of two subgroups: the moderates and the radical fringe. These labels lump together Ibrahim's divisions of the "apolitical Muslim Brotherhood" and the "mainstream Muslim Brotherhood" into a moderate grouping.[32] The "moderate oppositionist" label includes some actors and groups outside of the Muslim Brotherhood.

Radical Fringe.

The radical fringe includes the movements who propose swifter and more disruptive means of progression toward an Islamist state. It includes groups who have seceded from Egyptian social life to create their own communities,[33] as well as others who have operated and recruited within the city, schools, and the army. So it encompasses groups like the *Takfir wa al-Higrah*, as well as the *Jihad* members who planned and carried out Sadat's assassination.

Success of a New Female Image

The alternative modes of self-image present arguments questioning the very nature of femininity to women as well as a variety of strategies for approaching gender issues. Some Egyptian women are involved with or sympathetic to the Islamist alternative because they have found the image of a new Islamic woman to be viable in important ways.

Modern Islamists claim to have rejuvenated the meanings of womanhood and femininity by creating a tangible, charismatic image. My personal interviews have revealed the variable degree of female veiling and adherence to the social values of the moderate Islamic groups. Women appear to be genuinely sensitive to their involvement in the image process and can articulate their feelings as well as their ideals.

The moderate oppositionists present a controversy over women's functions in the public and private spheres. They also incorporate arguments on the political and social role of Islam. The Islamic oppositionist message to women has been more successful than was internationally anticipated, because of a number of social, economic, political, and ideological factors. The interaction of these factors is visible in the data and essential to the formation of an alternative image for women. The oppositionist message has gained viability through its association with cultural authenticity, nationalism, and the pursuit of ʿadala, or social justice. It seeks a political, economic, and social leveling in response to a period of increasing and visible inequities.

The oppositionist message to women has gained support through its flexibility in key areas that affect women. Furthermore, women have demonstrated an elasticity in interpreting and applying the Islamist message. That interaction may be an example of the route by which popular ideology reworks official ideology. Social adaptability is also useful to the objectives of an oppositionist social movement.

Certain positions on gender issues have become negotiable rather than fixed, or unmalleable, components of the Islamic message to women. The shift from intrinsic element to negotiable element has taken place despite much argument among the Islamists, and despite ahistoric and immutable characterizations of gender and gender relations.

I believe that women's adaptability is an essential component in the self-image process. Because women enact many roles, the self-image model they adopt must be capable of instantaneous and complete transformation. The self-imaging process should also alleviate some of the emotional stress incurred through enactment of multiple roles.

In this study, I suggest a way in which historical archetypes may reflect a cultural norm of femininity and how that norm may vary and transmute itself through the self-image process. In their idealization of femininity, as women express it, some of the ideal feminine qualities are surprisingly close, or even identical, to those projected to men. The parallels form a cultural declaration of woman as "liberated equal" rather than as "protected dependent," to borrow from Barbara Stowasser.[34] But in areas of self-image, other than idealized definitions of femininity, many women pragmatically aspire to the status of protected dependent, especially younger women. This paradox is fascinating, though not peculiar to Egypt, and may be tied generally to an international economic crisis and dissatisfaction with the achievements of the nation-state.

A key respondent referred to women's attitudes as a lingering of the haramlek/salamlek ideology of the Ottoman period, when elite women remained physically secluded in the harem, despite economic involvements in public life.[35] The idealization of a family woman, a nonworking wife, is a phenomenon to be more attributed to the development of customary law, and non-Arab influences, than to Islamic discourse on women. Marsot's work on elite women of the early twentieth century shows that even after centuries of restrictions, women's work was acceptable when unsalaried.[36] The idea of spiritual recompense for unpaid work (*ajr*) is widespread in the Middle East, but is balanced by a social system of favors or influence.[37]

Explanations of social relations and politics in Egypt usually stem from analyses of the national environment or microcosmic areas within it, or from the international setting. The first group may act to self-criticize, and are designed for internal consumption (there is no sure way to insure that outcome). Foreign policy may be explained entirely on the basis of international and regional pressures rather than national interaction, but in fact a cross-stream of both currents is usually at work.

In Egypt, arguments that attribute the problematic of women and work to interior causes may be based, erroneously, on popular understandings of Islamic or Arab culture and social status, and examples abound in recent and older literature on Middle Eastern women. They may also propose that women are pawns of the state (or of an oppositional social movement). Indeed, many states encourage women to work only when a shortage of unskilled labor exists or if the male labor force is diverted by war or migration. But when unemployment soars and women are entrenched in high-visibility white-collar and service-sector jobs, then they must be discouraged from working. The enemies of female employment utilize similar interior and also exterior arguments that blame the forces of Westernism, Zionism, or neocapitalism for jeopardizing the femininity, dependence, and moral foundation of women, especially working women. Many women have argued against these contentions and recognize the machinations of their critics even when they are couched in an interior discourse.

This study has found that age and social class have an important effect on the receptivity of women to the Islamic message. Egyptians reported that younger women and women of a petit bourgeois or lower-middle-class background were more susceptible to the Islamists, and they were partially correct. Nonetheless, many respondents did not fall into that profile. The appeal of an Islamic image to elite women has to be explained.

Other studies have maintained that the strength of the oppositionists lay in Cairo and in the provincial capitals. On the basis of my present data, I concur. Still, this statement cannot be repeated with any finality until more interviews are conducted outside of Greater Cairo.

The Islamist stance on women allows their members to escape social and economic limitations in a hierarchical society through a visible leveling process and the wearing of a uniform, and by verbally emphasizing social equality. Those unveiled respondents who do not accept Islamist ideology explained the wearing of *higab* in this way. The current situation is more complex. The above formula addresses the predicament of petit bourgeois women who awoke to the strain of social mobility. Unable to acquire the trappings of elite life, they abandoned expensive clothing, hairstyles, and makeup.

Those who argue that *higab* wearers wish to attain social anonymity cannot fully explain the logic of upper-middle-class or elite women who adopted Islamist ideals. The numbers of these women have clearly increased in the last ten years. Unveiled women said that peer or family pressure was responsible for the reverse social induction process. Both are difficult to prove. Nonetheless, some peer pressure was apparent in group interviews, informal conversations, and the respondents' living situations. When veiled women were willing to discuss the responses of their families or friends to their own ideology or appearance, they reported varying reactions. If their relatives or peers reacted negatively, their initial disapproval lessened over time. Unveiled women told me that the veiled women's fathers and brothers were happy with their new Islamic dress, whereas their mothers were up in arms. According to veiled women, familial reactions were not so neatly divided into patterns of male approval and female disapproval.

Most available sources show that the lowest urban classes have not exchanged their own modesty codes of dress and behavior for either the Islamist model or the elite model to any significant degree. The strength of the lower classes' own image system attests to the stronger process of class crystallization in a neocolonialist setting.[38]

Some of the Islamists or their sympathizers call for a new examination of historical sources and for the use of *ijtihad* to reform the position on women. Others are opposed to a critical reexamination of the sources, for it would attack the immutable nature of information that has been granted sacred stature. The inevitably different interpretations of such a review might weaken the impact of a movement attempting to portray itself in as unified a manner as possible. Finally, that sort of endeavor could force a critique of principles that members had accepted blindly. Faith can be more comforting than the acquiring of critical faculties that easily demolish but resurrect with difficulty.

The Islamist groups view women as an integral reproductive and productive core. Their stance resembles other burgeoning social opposition movements. They say that ideally, women's productive functions should be temporary—temporary within her own life (until she has children to raise, or after they are grown) and temporary within the life of the movement (until they create a system that would eliminate the need for female labor outside of certain specified professions). In practice, however, the question of female labor has undergone an ideological juggling. The flexibility and diversity of resulting positions on the issue of women and work accords with the daily reality of government, schools, and hospitals reliant on a female labor pool.

The Islamic ideal of woman is not the antithesis of an elite, secular model of woman, but it is a reaction to it. Still, women identifying with the Islamist model had more in common with the unveiled women than they did with women of another culture, or even with women who identified with *bint al-balad*. Some unveiled women also expressed distress at the ideological, moral, and social conditions in Egypt, echoing certain Islamist criticisms of the status quo. Veiled and unveiled women alike spoke of a loss of culture; a "flattening of mental life,"[39] which leads to an *angst*, or anomie, a commentary on the process of social transformation in a modern society.

Another important issue that emerges in this study is that some Egyptian women believe that female nature is essentially distinct from male nature, a view that diverges from the mainstream Western feminist perspective. Other women, however, would agree with Nabawiyya Musa, a woman activist writing in 1920 who stated:

> None have said that a female cat likes playing and jumping while the male cat is composed and quiet; none have said that a male dog is loyal while a female dog is sly and mean. . . . Allah created women with two eyes, two ears and one tongue like man; and she is capable as he is of performing tasks, although males are physically stronger than females in all species. The male donkey may be stronger and bigger than a female donkey, but does not understand any more than she does.[40]

Most respondents saw the sexes as equally capable, but complementary rather than identical. This perspective is widely held in modern Egyptian society. Nevertheless, even the more conservative respondents felt that women should be given opportunities equal to men, and equality under the law as long as the principles of *shariʿah* were upheld.

Respondents' divisions of human nature into male and female attributes structured their conceptions of femininity. Again, even the more conservative women recognize that some women might be talented in areas that have been dominated by men. They upheld women's freedom to pursue such interests as long as they met their family obligations.

The centrality of woman to the family is their guiding principle. It applies to career women and housewives, veiled and unveiled women, those who support the Islamic *daʿwah*, or call, and those who are unmoved by it. Most women neither desire nor consider a single, unmarried existence outside the family environment to be viable.

Islamist moderates aver that Islam through its living principles can liberate women. As women are a vital part of the mission to reform Muslim society, the Islamic call (*daʿwah*), the moderates have composed an argument for women's religious functions in the public as well as the private spheres. Again, the adherents to other image models debate the sincerity and applicability of these claims.

The Islamists of Egypt are involved in an active, creative effort at image construction for women. We may also note an eliminative, reactive process against other models of imaging and against Western ideals for women. State policies have in some ways encouraged a model of a secular, elite, powerful woman. The Islamists can criticize that model, and it does contain certain inherent contradictions.

Readers should not interpret this study as an explanation of false consciousness permitting women to accept an ideology that limits their parameters and potential. Such an argument would gravely underestimate Egyptian (and other Muslim) women and their complex skills of reading their world and all its possibilities.[41] Instead, this work explains the aspects of the Islamist image that are firmly rooted in the historical experience of the region. Then it deals with the formation of contemporary attitudes that enhance women's self-images and self-confidence within an alternative mode. To begin with, let us consider some of the problems involved in listening to women's expression of their opinions, concerns, and self-image.

Chapter Two

THE PROCESS OF LISTENING

Eleven years ago, I lived in a slightly run-down building in a once-fashionable area of Cairo. Three doormen (*bawaaba*) sat in the foyer of the building, collecting a pound each from the tenants, monthly, for their services. One was a mute; the others made him wash the hall. "But what do they do?" asked American friends. "They don't fix anything, they don't collect your mail, they don't keep out strangers, exactly." "No," I said, "they don't exactly do anything, but they know how to watch, and how to listen; if you wanted to know anything about this street, they would know, if they felt disposed to tell you." When I began this research project, I wondered about how outsiders could listen to culture in the way my *bawaaba* did.

In the fall of 1988, I conducted interviews with a sample group of fifty Cairene women. They answered questions concerning their self-image, perceptions of their environment, assessed the Islamists, and outlined their position on gender. Other women were interviewed as well, outside of the original fifty, and their answers are not reflected in the construction of a social profile, for various reasons. Some of these respondents did not answer all the questions asked in the profile section of the questionnaire. Several of the women were members of the Majlis al-Shura (the Parliament).

I had lived in Egypt before, in poor as well as wealthier areas of Cairo, and worked outside of the capital as well, in smaller cities, Alexandria, and Ismailiyya. All the same, I found the prospect of blind calls to unknown women daunting. Colleagues were somewhat discouraging; they did not understand how interviews meshed with an historical approach, or they pointed out the problems of approaching a politically sensitive topic. Gender issues and many sorts of sociological surveys are considered to be politically touchy and are certainly academically treacherous. My small daughter accompanied me, none too happy with the change from her beloved Los Angeles. I was dismayed and annoyed at a few negative responses to my project, but once I launched into telephoning, many relative strangers arranged interviews for me, contacted respondents, and thought of other friends who might help.

The Interviewing Process

In some cases, questionnaires were handed out to the respondents so they could fill out a short profile section, while I conducted and taped oral interviews. In other cases, the interviews were taped, and the transcribed material was later used to fill in the questionnaires (see appendix A). Questionnaires and interviews included sections dealing with self-definitions, the political and economic environment, personal faith and religious self-conception, attitudes toward employment, cross-sex relations, education, and household management. Respondents were also asked to give their own definitions of femininity as an idealized quality.

Respondents were free to introduce topics or questions of their own interest and did so. The interview method involved eliciting some life-history material and moving rather swiftly to questions about gender issues. The questions were formed around topic groups. Certain questions were added to serve as information checks. The respondents were sometimes impatient with the repeated, albeit restated, questions. Nonetheless, the subtleties in similar questions had to be explained in some detail.

A few respondents disliked the concentration on gender issues that became more and more apparent throughout the interview process. One student claimed that she had been misquoted before, and after several lengthy conversations she asked me to respond to her own eighty-five page survey but wouldn't answer my questionnaire. A local leader of a women's association glanced at the questions and said that they insulted Egyptian women and that she would print her name for me, but not answer a word. Her colleague chastised her for standing in the way of an intellectual endeavor, citing what she knew or guessed of my politics, and quickly rounded up other women to be interviewed. Most of the respondents were comfortable with the topic and were more confident of the "scientific" nature of this research than I was.

The sample was derived from veiled and unveiled women ranging from age twenty to age seventy-eight. This wide age range was very important to the topic, because earlier studies have focused on younger women, often university students.[1] The appeal of the Islamic moderates is said to be more prevalent among the young, but I wanted to test that assumption.

After reviewing findings of the few preceding works dealing with the Islamists, I interviewed some respondents similar to those in the samples of these earlier surveys.[2] Unveiled respondents under thirty were among the first women to agree to be interviewed. I asked them (and many other acquaintances) to try to contact veiled women they knew who would agree to be interviewed. Some students were originally contacted through a professor at a large university. Students and teaching assistants then provided leads to potential respondents, veiled and unveiled. Veiled middle-aged and older veiled women were also interviewed. A friend suggested that I go to shops that sold clothing for veiled women.

The selection of this sample is predicated on the unremarkable notion that age, social class, and educational background have a profound effect on life decisions, attitudes toward gender issues, and self-image. The selection and interpretation of this data does not comprise a profile of "typical urban Egyptian women" or of "typical Islamic activist women." In a society as rich and varied as modern Cairo, it would be extremely difficult to determine who in fact is a typical young or middle-aged person. Interviewing on a vast scale must be done to come up with a satisfactory sociological profile of women who veil within urban society as a whole.

The purpose of constructing a preliminary sociological profile of Islamist women is to try to identify common components in the backgrounds of those who share similar views or exhibit similar behavior. Accordingly the data was reviewed through the categorizations described above: veiled or unveiled; young, middle-aged and older; married and unmarried.

Further open-ended interviews involving issues not included in the questionnaire were conducted with some members of this group, and with unofficial active representatives of the Islamic oppositionist position. Some male representatives of the Islamic groups were interviewed, one at length, Dr. ʿAsam al-ʿAryan.

A number of lower-class women were also interviewed. They made interesting and unsolicited comments on the nature of femininity. These responses of working lower-class women were excluded from the questionnaire because they really do not fit into the veiled or unveiled categories as defined in chapter 1, but instead identify with *bint al-balad*. In 1988 these women were not much affected by the new image of Islamic women discussed in this work.

The longer interviews held with female representatives in the Majlis al-Shura were undertaken to see if their views resembled or diverged from the Islamists' portrayal of state policies on women. I wanted to meet with women representatives who had been allied with Jihan Sadat's position during the previous regime, and also with "veiled" women representatives who seemed to combine elements of the state outlook on women with Islamist ideals. Magdi Ahmad Hussein, of the Socialist-Labor coalition, allied at the time with the Muslim Brotherhood, and nephew of ʿAdil Hussein, provided introductions to some of these women, and others I called without introductions.

All the women in this survey reside in Greater Cairo, although a sizable proportion were born and grew up in other towns and villages. The interviews took place in a variety of Cairene neighborhoods—Imbaba, Giza, Agouza, El-Mohandesin, Zamalak, Shoubra, Sayida Zeinab, Garden City, Masr al-Gadida, Salaam City, and El-Gamaliya. They were conducted in private, in the respondents' flats, rooms, or homes, and in public, in mosques, on university grounds, shops, offices, and at a political party fund-raiser.

Methodological Limitations

Val Moghadam suggests that Middle East women's studies utilize a "methodology predicated upon the centrality of gender."[3] This work may illustrate some of the benefits and pitfalls of that sort of orientation aimed at interpreting the current effects of the Islamist discourse on gender. One could build an image from literary sources, but I hoped to also highlight the discrepancies or successes of an image's transmission and reception, the process of osmosis into women's lives.

Some of my colleagues were most interested in the issue of female activism within the new Islam. However, in trying to devise a methodology predicated on gender rather than power, I included some very apolitical women, who were also salient to the process of self-imaging. Many women do play a very active role within the Islamist groups. Limiting interviews to these activists would have greatly reduced the quality and quantity of the data.

If the Islamist phenomenon is only described at the level of leaders and active adherents, we cannot imagine or recreate the process of rational choice that takes place in the mind of the "average" woman. Second, this sort of limitation, in essence, silences the voices of those average women we need to hear, and allows activist women to speak for all women. I wanted to portray the world of ordinary women, as well as that of extraordinary women.

Other colleagues expressed regret that radical Islamist groups, (the "radical fringe") were not a major focus. On a practical level, many of the radical fringe leaders (who should be described in a more encompassing analysis of new Islamic ideology) are and will remain unavailable to female researchers. Some of these male leaders simply will not meet with women. On the other hand moderate leaders or spokespersons received me cordially during the course of this research.

The moderate spectrum of Islamic oppositionism has been attacked by some as being purely reactive and reactionary. For example, Lafif Lakhdar claims that these groups are devoid of a clear blueprint for an alternative social format. He states that the continuity of Islamic "archaism" is due to the failures of pan-Islam and the Modernists (Muslim reformers of the nineteenth and twentieth centuries) and to a misguided encouragement by the West.[4]

The Islamist moderates are concerned with gender issues and other social issues. Describing their position is valuable even if the historical impetus appears to be antifeminist, and even if a clearly marked blueprint for women's participation in an idealized society has not emerged. Safinaz Qassim, a writer and an outspoken Islamist, reminded me that there are valid reasons for dissension and disagreement on gender issues. The Islamist groups, even the *Ikhwan*, the Muslim Brotherhood, are formally illegal in Egypt. She pointed out that they cannot convene "in conferences and debate the issues of women's status in a formal and structured atmosphere."[5] An unofficial picture of their views may then be more informative.

Analytical Boundaries

Can one consider oneself a feminist and conduct an impartial study? In fact, my own definitions of feminism changed as a result of this research. Can a study be innocent of cultural impositions? No, not completely. Veiled women and unveiled women continuously asserted that Islam and feminism are not incompatible. Since the author agreed with them, it remained to align that assertion with the purposes of contemporary Islamist thought.

Fatna Sabbah's work builds on the idea that Islam ordains the subjugation of man to God and of woman to man.[6] Sabbah's underlying theme cannot be valid, unless one denies the testimony of many believing Muslim women. Some of the young veiled women in the present study agreed with Sabbah's proposition—but not because of Islam's essential propositions. Rather, they believe that female subjugation is the result of historical, cultural, and intellectual misunderstandings.

Sabbah's principle of female subjugation (woman is to man as man is to God) really represents a view of women in the *male* unconscious and does not delve into women's self-conceptions and views of their own sexuality. She claims that "woman is defined by relations to the orgasmic need of the male believer."[7] Her theories did not correspond to my respondents' version of faith or their idealizations of their lives. Sabbah's vision of the Islamic world makes it difficult to accept that in the Middle East, monogamy, family ties, and social support systems may often enhance healthy sexuality. Social interaction in the Middle East may be healthier perhaps than in certain Western contexts.

In conducting this research, I was nonplused by constant Western queries about the sexual repression of Arab Muslim women. Egyptian women of various social classes openly discuss sexual issues. Besides, Egyptian women (along with all other women) have methods of expressing their sexuality that need not involve pursuit of illicit or unrestricted sex. Especially in rural areas and lower-class urban areas, female circumcision continues (legislation forbidding it notwithstanding), as does an emphasis on premarital virginity and a prohibition against extramarital sex. Male dominance exists in Egyptian society as it does in most other modern cultures of the world. However, women may not view themselves as being sexually oppressed. It is essential to convey women's own responses to these issues.

Some readers, Egyptian and American, asked why more male respondents were not interviewed, especially those who wield more power in the Islamic *jamaʿat*. Men's views on women should be studied, but they are not as useful in exploring the issues of self-viewing, self-identification, and self-expression.

Limitations to this work derive in part from the previous scholarship on this topic. Much must be deduced from the impact of recent events in Egypt and secondary assessments of the Islamists' prospects. Some work on the Islamists has been based on Saad Eddin Ibrahim's sound but preliminary study of incarcerated Egyptian male Islamic activists in the late 1970s.[8] Many references and hypotheses in the succeeding literature have been built on the sociological profile constructed in that work, which described men of small-town or rural origin who migrated to Cairo. They were young and of petit bourgeois (or lower middle class) background. Typically, members of these groups were college-educated young adults, led by a man at least a generation older.[9]

The earlier literature gives the impression that the universities are a central recruiting ground for the Islamic moderate groups.[10] The universities are not the only source of recruitment, or even, in terms of numbers, the main source of those adhering to a new Islamic image of women. Universities provide an accessible and acceptable interviewing environment for researchers. Student respondents are familiar with fieldwork and don't mind being recorded in that setting. In contrast, women whom I approached in the mosques or in clothing stores were wary of my intentions and sometimes ill at ease with the tape recorder.

The structure of the university system in Egypt itself predisposed my findings in important ways as well. More women of rural origin took part in interviews I held in dormitories at Cairo University because their home villages or towns are too far from campus for them to commute. Cairo University does not charge the high fees of some other universities, although students have to come up with living expenses and money for books, clothes, and tutoring.

The university environment in Egypt is quite distinct from the urban society surrounding it. The results may be falsely taken to imply that other non-students follow the profile of those university students also described in Zeinab Radwan's study. The press as well as ordinary observers often accord a petit bourgeois derivation to public university students. Students at the American University in Cairo and Egyptian students studying abroad tend to represent the upper and upper-middle classes, as do a certain percentage of students attending Cairo University. The nationalization of education in Egypt has meant that more young people of rural backgrounds and less wealthy means can attend the universities. On the other hand, students without the high scores on their examinations necessary to attend Cairo University can enroll in private universities, such as the American University in Cairo, if they pay the higher fees. More veiled women were interviewed at Cairo University than at the American University in Cairo because of the greater numbers of veiled women attending.

The university linkages of the Islamists are naturally emphasized in Egypt, where students maintain close social ties through the *shilla,* age set, or friend network, and the *dufᶜa,* graduation-year cohorts. Peer-group pressure is very strong in Egypt. However, family pressures are also powerful, especially the perceived need for parental approval, more so than among young adults in the West.

Far more theoretical literature studying Islamic "revivalism" or authenticity exists than concrete sociological surveys such as Ibrahim's.[11] Several studies have clearly drawn on Ibrahim's work, which sought to place these groups in the context of neo-Marxist predictions regarding the social background of "revolutionary" actors. Ibrahim's early findings, Radwan's data, and Mervat Hatem's work[12] are all important but are based on social characterizations of relatively small groups that may or may not extend to the broader Islamist membership.[13]

Ibrahim notes that the Islamic groups he studied had strong support in smaller urban centers.[14] This fact differentiates the Egyptian groups from the Iranian Muslim oppositionists who represented the rising expectations of the petite bourgeoisie and the proletariat in Teheran. In Egypt, the Islamic groups operate in an urban setting, but those members of rural or small-town origins are significant when one considers group formation, contacts, and tactics.[15]

The Islamists appear to be part of an Egyptian petite bourgeoisie through the intervention of the educational system. That statement requires some qualification. They may have acquired petit bourgeois aspirations for material goods or a certain standard of living, but they may not possess the economic means to attain these goals after graduation from university. As Abdallah points out, they may look forward to "uncertain and often bleak prospects, unsuitable and underpaid employment, scarce and extremely expensive housing, costly marriage in a consumer society and . . . the miserable transport system."[16] Their membership in the petite bourgeoisie is tenuous. One can reasonably define a potential oppositionist as a person possessing petit bourgeois expectations but not necessarily matching material resources.

However, another group of Islamic oppositionists exists; they have gotten wealthier in the last ten years and simply do not fit the Marxist paradigm above. Ibrahim includes them in his discussion of "apolitical" Islam.[17] In Cairo, many prosperous small-business owners and entrepreneurs may be seen who adhere to the *Ikhwan's* basic values and are identifiable by their dress and appearance. The moderately or very prosperous status of these Islamists meant that unmet, rising expectations of the petite bourgeoisie were insufficient to explain the "revolutionary" nature of the oppositionist philosophy. Wives, daughters, and fiancées of the prosperous Islamists had adopted the *higab* among these groups, as had some elite women. These trends were significant enough to counter the idea that only petite bourgeois women, or nouveaux riches women (originating from the petite bourgeoisie), were identifying with the values of modesty, segregation, or sex-role contraction. Although unveiled elite women objected to the Islamization of other social groups, or felt that these groups were not acting out of intellectual sincerity, their own explanations of class interaction were unsatisfactory. Class interaction is part of a multicausative process affecting the growth of the Islamists but remains only one intricate step of this process.

The Conundrum of Socioeconomic Status

Class divisions in Egypt are a complex and shifting entity. Class mobility, relations, and divisions in Egypt do not follow many of the paradigms developed in studies of the Western industrialized world, such as Johann Nestroy's comic description of the ambiguous merchant class in nineteenth-century Germany, *Einen Fux will er sich machen,* poised between invention and convention.[18] That is not to say that Egypt is a special case, because historically, class struggle in Egypt is similar to that in other countries of the Third World.

It is essential to note that very rapid economic changes have taken place over the last twenty-five years. Overpopulation and labor migration have gravely affected the social and economic makeup of Egypt. The national economy has also responded to pulls of the world economic system through recessions, currency imbalances, trade deficits, foreign aid, and so on.[19]

These economic pressures have not always resulted in corresponding transfers of social status in Egypt. Hence, class definitions are nuanced and translate into social rights or exclusions, as in marriage or friendship pools or restrictions. Class crystallization is still occurring in Egypt, typified, Landecker tells us, by a large population, a high degree of differential association, cultural differentiation or categorization that affects access to social status, public goods, and sometimes, political participation.[20]

In Egypt, transfers of political and economic power occur but do not always correspond to social expectations of ascribed status. Another aspect of class struggle is the resentment of the disenfranchised and of the newly poor, and the efforts to maintain power and economic control on the part of older and newer elites.

Class interaction is problematic to a consideration of the Islamists, because veiled women do not really constitute one class, one interpretation of religion, or one special interest group. Marxists expect women to behave in accordance with the motivations of their social class. But in Egypt, they may sometimes behave in accordance with the social rather than the economic expectations of their class. That confuses our attempts to unify social theory regarding class.

Problems of Prediction and Structure

Interviews with Islamist leaders generated some predictive material on how policy might be developed to enhance compliance with positions on gender issues. Naturally, deciphering policies of the Islamists is subject to much argument because the groups are formally illegal. The Islamists, their leaders and followers are using *ra'y,* an Islamic juridical classification involving an informed use of personal opinion, to determine gender policies. A great deal of informal debate is in progress, and relevant bits of in-group discussion will be mentioned.

I analyzed the Islamists as if they were evolving a theoretical "state" ideology in order to categorize their opinions. Obviously, the Islamists do not really represent the viewpoint of a state, nor does their ideology parallel that of a legal social movement. But we need to put their views in context. Leaders' ideas should then be separated from those of followers to discuss an "official" or an "unofficial" viewpoint.

The size of the survey, the gaps in previous related research, and the financial and bureaucratic limits placed on the researcher all detracted from the scope of this study. Despite long familiarity with the area, its history, and its language, and previous residence in Cairo, the researcher would nevertheless define herself as a "cultural outsider" to the objects of this study. Notwithstanding, respondents and contacts in Egypt went out of their way to assist my research and constantly made remarks intended to emphasize my cultural proximity to them.

I applied stricter measurements of "insider" status to myself than those defined by the authors of a recent work on this topic, *Arab Women in the Field.*[21] It has long been held that outsider identification is useful in raising the levels of academic objectivity or rationalism in research, and helps to remove emotional ties to the topic. Lately, however, in the field of Middle Eastern women's studies the value of empathy in research has emerged.[22] Researchers have acknowledged a virtue in more closely identifying with the respondents and in permitting one's subjects to utilize their own voices, rather than the narrow portraits emerging from tightly controlled questioning. Nevertheless, the women writing *Arab Women in the Field* are light years away from their subjects, socially and culturally, and in fact, that distance was expected and accepted by their respondents.[23]

My respondents as well were conscious of the differences separating us, and they were curious about my life. They were well aware that the interpretation of their responses was crucial to my career as well as to the research.[24] They showed no resentment of this situation, and tried rather consistently to find points of agreement with me rather than differences. I had to work hard to conceal my views and opinions during the interviewing process, to remain the listener instead of another speaker.

The researcher cannot live the life of her respondents. She is at best briefly immersed culturally, and is always conscious of her "other" existence. She could leave her project if she became seriously ill and can never experience the constancy of milieu that her subjects know. She anticipates her departure from them and is usually removed from their environment during the writing process. She examines a limited portion of the respondents' lives and must conjecture about, or omit, the missing portions of her subjects' experiences. But that does not invalidate the portion of their lives that she can come to know.

Any one of the particular dilemmas of this study could be the subject of further research. Let us now consider the historical background of gender issues in the Egyptian context. A journey back to the creation of woman and man according to Islam introduces historical arguments and female archetypes.

Chapter Three

HER STORY: ARCHETYPES AND ARGUMENTS OF MIDDLE EASTERN WOMEN

The history of Egyptian women is essential to an understanding of the Islamist stance on gender. Past events help explain the emergence of an environment in which women use oppositionist Islam to assuage political and economic alienation. We must also comprehend the linkage of the contemporary intellectual and spiritual environment with the early Muslim community whereby modern citizens search for authenticity, equality, morality, and new solutions for political authority that may extend to gender issues.

To present the context of gender issues in modern Egypt, we may treat the past as a continuum, from the Muslim version of Creation until the present. We will consider major female historical figures, archetypes to Islamic history, in that their names evoke specific gender issues that continue to affect modern debates on women's status. I included figures who were mentioned by the respondents within the interview process in order to authenticate their opinions on gender issues. Many other important historical figures are excluded for the sake of brevity and to try to focus attention on the controversial areas of the female image as described by the Islamists.

Other historians have examined the changes in the status of women over the years as a way of understanding the present environment while describing (or revising) the past. Middle Eastern specialists have been criticized for the determinism inherent in that approach, because it was often misleading. It is still worth examining historical issues that influenced the formulation, discourse, and appeal of the modern Islamic opposition despite the theoretical risks involved. A review of the historical setting is warranted, especially when focusing on gender issues, because Middle Eastern women's history has not often been analyzed as a distinct continuum.[1]

Barbara Stowasser and other historians described the growth of patriarchy as a gradual process in Middle Eastern society. Scholars have tried to identify the ethnic origins of female seclusion or patrilineal inheritance, to ascertain the Arab or non-Arab basis for these practices, or to suggest that development of these customs came about after the first generation of Islam.[2] Azizah Al-Hibri and others believed that the eventual restrictions on women in public life may not have been intended by the Prophet, who initiated many reforms affecting the status of Muslim women in his lifetime.[3] Their work represents a ''women's studies'' approach to the history of women in the

Middle East, in that they characterize the rigidity of interpretations of women's status as a continuous one-way process leading up to the sparking of a feminist movement in Egypt early in the twentieth century. Women's status has always varied, especially with regard to socioeconomic standing. Women transmit culture and sex-role norms to their children and are responsible along with the educational system for their socialization. Women educated their daughters in survival techniques adapted to the degree of patriarchy prevalent in each era. Mothers-in-law established their own dominance over young brides, utilizing the power of age and status along with the patrilineal definitions of influence. Some degree of female support or passive acceptance of the patriarchal order occurred over time, but we do not know if female power existed despite it or because of it. These contradictions are included in the story of women in Egypt, often told as if women were continuously or successively oppressed.

The historical context of women's issues in Egypt also accentuates the aspects of the Islamist outlook on gender that parallel those of other transitional social groups. The Islamists resemble oppositionist social movements in other countries, which typically utilize the reproductive and productive value of female members in accordance with their labor demand. From the industrialized world to the third world, women have experienced expanded sex roles in certain periods, but they were encouraged to return home when economic circumstances altered or when social reeducation policies proved politically costly. The case of women in the United States before and after World War II is an example. So were various policies on women in Mozambique, Cuba, and China,[4] the Stalinist reentrenchment of the Soviet family woman, and the case of Algerian women after the victory of the FLN.[5]

The Islamic oppositionist movement is unique in that it appeals to and attracts women, but provides a very different rationale for female labor than most other oppositionist groups. The key to understanding this enigma may be found in the Islamists' interpretations of gender issues in Islamic history.

Scholars have favored certain themes as they have recounted the story of women in Islamic history. They have emphasized sociopolitical authority and instances where women have held authority over men, challenged male authority, or fought against illegitimate authority of the state.

Morality and family honor was another lively focus, but rarely were pragmatic explanations for gender attitudes proposed. A scholarly preoccupation with the verification of matriarchal or matrilineal groups in pre-Islamic Arabia occurred through the early 1980s. Earlier Western literature up to about the 1970s generally agreed on the existence of a matriarchal order in the *jahiliyyah* (pre-Islamic period). Predecessors of the modern Islamic conservatives and some of the Islamists have contested that work and unilaterally emphasized women's unprotected legal status in the *jahiliyyah*.[6] In the Middle East, non-Islamist scholars have reflected the earlier Western interpretation and found Arabic sources to cite (as in al-Hibri's work), just as Western academics began to reverse themselves on the issue and assumed more conservative arguments. The Islamists are aware of the historiographical record of this argument and use it to their advantage.

The Islamists declare their intent to recapture the spirit of the first generation of Islam. However, when entering the arena of gender issues, they utilize and give credence to the later (thirteenth- or fourteenth-century) arguments, more conservative regarding male dominance, female sexuality, and status. They have rejected the more lenient interpretations of al-ᶜAbbas and al-Tabari regarding these issues and claim that the modern Islamist headcovering, the *higab,* is the self-same *khimar* (a garment referred to in the Qurᵓan) of the first generation of believers. A confusing stance on women emerged where historical values gleaned from later centuries assumed greater importance than the Prophet's own words and actions. Some Islamists do not assent to this historical montage, and call for a deep reanalysis of women's role in Islam.[7]

When the Islamists review the history of Muslims in the Middle East, they strongly identify with the innovative spirit and moral challenge of the first generation of Muslims. They are but one of many *tajdid* (Islamic renewal) movements that have spontaneously emerged throughout the centuries, for the element of *tajdid* is essential to their ideology. When the Islamic oppositionists contemplate and present gender issues, they have incorporated the element of *tajdid* by referring to historical examples of gender issues, which exemplify increased morality to them.

The early women of Islam, especially the wives and descendants of the Prophet, are crucial referents to the oppositionist image of modern women. We will begin with the original woman, Hawwa (a living entity).[8]

Hawwa

The first woman in the world was Hawwa, known as Eve in the Bible. According to the Qurᵓan, the original man and woman were created simultaneously.[9] Woman was not a derivation of man, in this account, nor inferior to him, nor God's afterthought. Hawwa is an entity necessary to Creation itself.[10]

The stories of derivation from Adam come from accounts talking of the connection of woman with a human "rib" in the *hadith,* perhaps due to the influence of literary traditions, or from Christian and Jewish scripture.[11] They say that women in general are like the human rib, which is crooked, or bent, but there is no reference to Adam as the owner of the rib. The crookedness of the rib is viewed as a metaphor for woman's uneven temperament and her wayward, gossipy tendencies.[12] Jane Smith and Yvonne Haddad tell us that in the *hadith* of Ibn ʿAbbas and Ibn Massud, Hawwa *is* created from Adam's rib. Here the name *hawwa,* which does not appear in the Qurʾan, is explained to the angels. It refers to the woman's creation from a living thing, a rib from Adam's left side.[13]

To the Islamists, Hawwa's meaning and status is quite complex. Some of the Islamists call for a reliance on the original source, the Qurʾan, rather than later and more questionable *hadith.* They argue along with the Islamic liberal, Bint al-Shatti, that the Qurʾan affirms the equality of women's spirit in the Creation.[14] Here, Iblis (Satan) directly confronted Adam rather than first approaching Hawwa as in the Bible. Hawwa is therefore innocent of the charges levied against her by later sources in *hadith,* which allude to a previous interaction between Hawwa and Iblis.[15]

Hawwa and Adam ate of the tree of immortality and power and so became equally knowledgeable and powerful. But they were both guilty of disobedience and were condemned to conflict, and to toil for their bread.

> But the devil whispered to him, saying: O Adam! Shall I show thee the tree of immortality and power that wasteth not away? Then they twain ate thereof, so that their shame became apparent unto them, and they began to hide by heaping on themselves some of the leaves of the Garden . . . He said: Go down hence, both of you, one of you a foe unto the other. (Surah Ta Ha, XX: 118–123)

One may interpret that curse to mean that humankind would always turn on itself, condemned to strife and warfare. Or, as some of my respondents maintained, it may explain the continuous tension, if not enmity, between the sexes that replaced the prior harmony of the Garden. The late Mahmoud Mohammed Taha, leader of the Republican Brothers, tells us that the fall of Adam and Eve began both the condition of divorce, and of *al-hijab* (the more complete covering that replaced the previous innocent and less concealed condition of *al-sufur*):

> When Adam and Eve fell through sin and were expelled from paradise, they descended to earth separated, and began to look for each other; Adam looking for Eve, and Eve looking for Adam. After much search, Adam found Eve without really finding her, and Eve found Adam, without really finding him. From that day to the present, each Adam is looking for his Eve, and each Eve is looking for her Adam.[16]

Here the "battle of the sexes" is more a longing for the unspoiled marriage of Paradise, a timeless condition, and a source of the coexistent hostility and affection between the sexes. Hawwa and Adam were disobedient and they both experienced a new emotion, shame, an awareness of their physical beings and sexuality. But their shame is minimally described in the Qurʾan and *hadith* in comparison to the Biblical version.

Other Islamists relied on scholars who depicted Hawwa as a temptress. She supposedly made Adam drink wine and then transmitted Iblis's message. This elaboration found in *hadith* is unlike the Qur'anic version, but as Smith and Haddad mention, al-Tabari and al-Tha'labi include such reports, and al-Razi says it is "not far-fetched."[17] Here, woman has brought a forbidden substance, wine, into the Garden, tainting the original condition of Creation. The episode was then utilized to substantiate man's superior position and woman's culpability for the first betrayal of God's trust.

Hawwa symbolizes reproduction and the sexual division of labor. Hawwa, like all women of creation myths, is a generator of mankind. God's skills were required to shape Adam and Hawwa, but his miraculous human creations are self-propagating. We are told in certain *hadith* that from this time forth Adam toiled and Hawwa cared for him, although the Qur'an says nothing regarding the outcome of the crisis in the Garden. In the Bible, God admonishes the First Couple for their sin and tells Eve she will henceforth bring forth her young in pain.

In *hadith*, Hawwa's sentencing is more severe than in Biblical tradition. She has given Adam wine, and only then does he taste the forbidden fruit. God decrees ten punishments to the intoxicator and disobedient seductress, among them menstruation and pregnancy. These accounts emphasize woman's reproductive value, for they tell us that Hawwa's descendants are to be considered martyrs if they die in childbirth and will be united with their husbands in Paradise. Hawwa is further connected with the taboos surrounding women's menstrual cycle and their ritual purification. In Mecca, it is said that she menstruated, whereupon Adam stamped his foot on the ground and the well, Zamzam, sprang forth. In its waters Hawwa could purify herself.[18] This provides logical grounds for many of the restrictions on women and their participation in prayer, fasting, and pilgrimage. They are based on the concept that the bleeding of the woman, whether through menstruation or childbirth, renders her ritually unclean.

Initially, Hawwa was a symbol of equality of the sexes and of the perfection of the Garden. But she was also transformed from Adam's spiritual and intellectual equal into the temptress, sinner, and impure mother of humankind in the *hadith*.

Khadijah

The story of Khadijah, the first wife of the Prophet, provides a setting for arguments on the status of women in the pre-Islamic era. Khadijah represented the transition of the Meccan woman from one who conformed to pre-Islamic patterns of marriage, inheritance, and control to that of a new believer, and a Muslim wife.

Khadijah's own history, and her prior marriages to Abu Hala al-Tamimi and Utayyik bin ʿAʾidh, reveal evidence of the matrilineal kinship practices discussed by W. Montgomery Watt.[19] Khadijah, a widow, became a wealthy businesswoman and controlled substantial assets when she engaged Muhammad as her steward. In sponsoring and marrying Muhammad, she transformed him from an unconnected, needy member of Meccan society to a wealthy merchant. She provided her husband with more than material blessings. Khadijah, as Muhammad's first convert, also symbolizes the abstract virtues of loyalty, encouragement, faith, and devotion, virtues that are valued in both sexes.

Khadijah chose marriage to Muhammad and proposed to him in accordance with the customs of her time.[20] Modern Arab and Western historians suggest that female independence at the time was connected perhaps to earlier prevailing matrilineal power and uxorilocal marriage.[21]

Goddess worship might have had some connection to female independence in this period. Muhammad's struggle with the worship of the Three Daughters of Allah, al-Lat, Manat, and al-ʿUzzah (whose shrines were just outside of Mecca), resulted in strife between the early Muslims and Meccan devotees of the goddesses.[22] al-ʿUzzah was an especially powerful figure who symbolized the congruence of the feminine spiritual principle along with strength, ferocity, and passion.[23] The monotheism of the emerging Islam required a formal disavowal of the power of these goddesses, which occurred after the episode of the *gharaniq* (known as the Satanic verses, they refer to the three goddesses as swans).[24] The verses Muhammad revealed implied that these goddesses were to be acknowledged along with Allah. Then he retracted the verses, claiming that they came from Iblis rather than the angel Gabriel. The *gharaniq* were obliterated from the collections of the Qurʾan and many Muslims believe that the episode never took place, and may cite alternate commentary.

Watt hypothesizes in the same vein as Robertson Smith that in preIslamic Arabian society "a transition was in progress from a matrilineal system to one that was wholly or largely patrilineal" and that "this transition was linked with the growth of individualism."[25] Muhammad's reforms encouraged the growing strength of the single-family, male-headed household by promoting virilocal (establishing residence with the husband or husband's clan) rather than uxorilocal (primary residence with the wife's clan) practices. The new trends took place at a time when many men had broken away from their own clans by leaving Mecca. They enhanced the mutual dependence of husbands and wives rather than their ties to their individual clans. Khadijah's adoption of her husband's new faith had earlier exemplified the importance of the marriage bond at a time when the surrounding community and Muhammad's own fellow clan members were hostile to him.

Although Muhammad later took many wives, Khadijah was his only spouse during her lifetime. She did not accept any other marriage partners while married to Muhammad. If we assume that their exclusive union was due to emotional attachment or to a mutual agreement, then the Prophet's relationship with Khadijah contrasts with his sanctioning of polygamy and his own behavior in later years. We do not know if their monogamous relationship was intentional, by chance, or due perhaps to Khadijah's maturity and economic power.

Some of Muhammad's later marriages were politically motivated. The female adherence to monandry that he stressed was necessary for the early Muslims in order to anchor their female members to stable households. Many women were widowed in the battles of the early Muslims and their opponents' widows were claimed as well. That meant that women may have outnumbered men for a time, and the polygamous system ensured their support. Women were enjoined to be faithful to their husbands, for that was the only way to require paternal responsibility for offspring. It was also true that the new community had to retain its children, who would be lost if mothers returned to their own clans.[26]

The sources inherited by the Islamists state that Muhammad's new system greatly improved the condition of women in the Muslim age. Female infanticide, which was existent in the Peninsula, was then forbidden.[27] Azizah al-Hibri suggests that the conversion of a barter economy to a money economy was significant to the increasing value of women, who were valued by the groom's family for the large *mahr*, bridewealth, they would bring.[28] But the Qur'an specified that the greater part of the *mahr* should be paid to the bride and that she should retain this money throughout her marriage.

How then, did patriarchy prevail over Khadijah's daughters? Al-Hibri believes that since Arab women were also warriors in the pre-Islamic era,[29] their subjugation was problematic. She suggests that men may have acquired some new technology, weapons, or tools.[30] Men's dominance of long-distance trade may have had some bearing on their growing authority, or on the adoption of the customs of veiling and segregation, which had prevailed elsewhere in the region. Women's economic and social status was not consistent throughout the Peninsula before Islam, and the uneven situation continued, particularly after the Ummayad period, due to the influences of other cultures.

Women's influence in spiritual and political matters also evolved along other routes. The growth of Islam as a spiritual solution in the early centuries did not necessarily mean the immediate devaluation of other belief systems. Goddess worship in Pharaonic Egypt is well documented and affected popular superstitions and beliefs.[31] The goddess Isis was particularly significant. She was associated with a tradition of female power in the Pharaonic period.[32] It is true that these traditions may not have been as strong at the time of the Arab conquest, but we are also told that women in Pharaonic Egypt had the right to choose and divorce their husbands freely.[33] Marriage customs, rites of passage, magic, and healing procedures were influenced by the earlier beliefs. In Egypt, as elsewhere in the Arab world, it is women who usually resort to and officiate over magical or healing ceremonies that derive from earlier beliefs. For example, the Qurʾanic rejection of "the blowers on knots" refers to the female practitioners of Arabian magic that the new Muslim order wished to suppress.[34]

These women-oriented beliefs were important because they competed and coexisted with the development of an official, centralized faith. Beck discusses modern Muslim women's participation in spiritual beliefs and magic as evidence of women's interiorized involvement in popular religion.[35]

The Monophysite church also influenced the spiritual dimension of women. The Virgin remains a powerful figure to the Copts of Egypt. As elsewhere, those who worship her and other saints invoke notions of fertility and *barakah*, or blessedness. Saint worship by Muslim women also involves these concepts and, along with Sufism, is on the rise in modern Egypt. Muslims as well as Copts have reported miraculous sightings of the Virgin Mary that attest to the society-wide phenomenon of growing religiosity and also to the continuing power of that female archetype. Even recently, stories circulated of crosses appearing miraculously on the material of two women's garments in upper Egypt.

Other beliefs affect women, including the practice of female circumcision, which predated Islam throughout the Nile valley. This operation varies in severity and involves notions of ritual cleanliness as well as control over sexuality. Female circumcision is not recommended by Islam, although it has widely occurred in Muslim and African countries dating long before Islam.[36] We don't have sound sources as to where this practice occurred in the Peninsula in pre-Islamic times, although it was prevalent there, in Yemen, and further north in the Syrian desert later on. Some Islamists have revived certain of the thirteenth- and fourteenth-century scholars who declared that female circumcision is an integral part of Islam's stance on women, to the dismay of the feminist-sociologist Fatima Mernissi.[37]

The modern Islamist portrait of Khadijah varies little from that of earlier Muslim historians. Khadijah remains a symbol of the first and loyal wife, who believed in and encouraged her husband's remarkable new orientation. She is therefore a prototype of an ideal mate. Khadijah also embodies the power and wisdom of the middle-aged and older woman in society. She retained the spirit of the pre-Islamic woman and exemplified the influence to be had by a woman of independent financial means.

ʿAʾishah bint Abu Bakr

ʿAʾishah, the "best beloved" of Muhammad's wives, symbolizes the political power of women. She threatened and influenced not only the political leaders of her time, but also the chroniclers and *hadith* collectors of the next few centuries. Furthermore, her life illustrates the existence of class divisions that allowed women of high status, particularly the Prophet's wives, a strong influence on the gender practices of the community. The special restrictions imposed on the "mothers of the believers,"a title granted to the Prophet's wives, included an increased degree of seclusion and changes in dress style.

ᶜAᵓishah was said to be fiery, jealous, witty, and powerful.[38] She sized up her rival co-wives and allied with some of them. She may be seen as a model of a leading wife within the polygynous households of later Muslim rulers.

The patriarchal, centralized political system evolving during early Islam was strengthened by Muhammad's limitations on polygyny, alteration of inheritance patterns, and insistence on the consent of female marriage partners. The Islamists and apologists claim that in the pre-Islamic era, men could marry an infinite number of wives. Therefore the instruction to marry only four wives, and the injunctions to treat these wives equally, implied progress. A great diversity of opinion on the changes in women's status existed even during the early centuries. ᶜAᵓishah was a woman who strongly influenced that range of interpretation, even though the arguments over her actions occurred long after her death.[39]

Two incidents in ᶜAᵓishah's life have special relevance to the self-image process of modern women. The "affair of the slander" took place when ᶜAᵓishah was accused of dallying with Safwan ibn al-Muᵓattal after she was accidentally left behind on a journey. The subsequent scandal and commotion in the community arose from the belief that female chastity reflects on male honor.[40] ᶜAᵓishah was vulnerable, as were other beautiful, young women who might be accused of immodesty and extramarital affairs. But as Muhammad's wife, the honor of the whole community was at stake. Abbott feels that ᶜAᵓishah was not in any position to protest the new rules then imposed on the Prophet's household by way of the Verse of the Curtain,[41] because

> It took a special revelation from heaven to establish ᶜAᵓishah's innocence and restore her to her favored position in Mohammed's harem. The episode passed, but it most probably helped to convince Mohammed and others of the wisdom, under the circumstances, of the practice of seclusion.[42]

Abbott's reasoning contains at least one flaw, for it was clear that some degree of seclusion was already prevalent at the time of this incident. After all, if ᶜAᵓishah had not been carried in a *curtained,* or covered, howdah, her absence might have been noted sooner.

The new verses ordered the Muslims to show some respect for the Prophet's privacy, and restricted contact with or view of his wives. It was fortuitous that limitations were then placed on the abuse of patriarchal control over female virtue, henceforth requiring four eyewitnesses of impeccable morals to an act of fornication in order to convict the accused parties.[43]

Abbott explains the rules that predated the Verse of the Curtain (XXIV:31–32 and XXXIII:59), which applied to all Muslims, women and men, and the later verses directed to the wives of the Prophets, by claiming that the licentious atmosphere of the times required stricter regulations.[44] The Islamists utilize this argument, for they felt that modern conditions exhibit equally low standards of morality, resulting in substance abuse, sex-crimes, and broken families.

Although ordinary women did not have to limit their interaction with unrelated males as did the Prophet's wives, ᶜAᵓishah witnessed increasing restrictions on women after Muhammad's death, particularly during the reign of ᶜUmar. It was reported that ᶜUmar was harsh with his wives, and he tried to keep certain women from praying in the mosque. ᶜUmar said, "We of Quraysh used to dominate (our) women; but when we came among the Ansar, they proved to be a people whose women dominated them; and our women began to copy the habits of the women of the Ansar."[45] Watt states there was little intermarriage between the two groups.[46]

ᶜAᵓishah led the faction of Makhzumite aristocrats within the harem, and stood up to ᶜUmar on occasion. After the Prophet's death, women's participation in the pilgrimage was restricted, although these measures were rescinded at one point for the remaining widows of the Prophet. The various restraints (along with other *hadith*) were employed by later exegetes to forbid women to travel without being chaperoned by a closely related man (a *mahram*).[47] All these restrictions are included in the fifteenth-century texts of Ibn Taymiyya, which have been revived by Islamists inside and outside of Egypt.[48]

During ᶜUmar's rule, ᶜAᵓishah began to be consulted on the Sunnah of the Prophet. According to Ibn Saᶜd, she issued legal judgments (*fatwa*) in this period.[49] Learned women continued to influence Islamic law, although the Islamists claim that women are unsuited to that activity.[50]

Abbott claims that the issue of women's "right to speak and take action in matters of public affairs" was raised by ᶜAᵓishah's interaction with ᶜUthman after the incident of Walid ibn ᶜUqbah's drunken misconduct. ᶜUthman was furious with ᶜAᵓishah's interference in this instance.[51] ᶜAᵓishah's role in the dispute over succession between ᶜAli and Muᶜawiya was even more troubling, not to the men of her time, but to the learned men of Islamic law (*fuqahaᵓ*) of later periods who saw ᶜAᵓishah as a troublemaker *because* of her sex.

ᶜAᵓishah was inextricably drawn into the events of the first *fitnah* (a political and social schism; the word has also referred to the effect of a beautiful woman). She did not support ᶜUthman, but she also opposed ᶜAli. According to Abbott, Umm Salamah (another wife of the Prophet) wrote to ᶜAᵓishah to prevent her from participating in the Battle of the Camel, and her letter implied that ᶜAᵓishah's interference would be unwomanly and unvirtuous.

ᶜAʾishah disregarded this communication,[52] and Abbott portrays her as a mother admonishing her "fighting sons," compelled to step in for the good of the *ummah*.[53]

But others disapproved. It was Abu Bakra who refused to take part in the *fitnah* and who acknowledged ᶜAʾishah's privileged status but stated: "I have heard the Prophet say: "The people who vest power (or the right to rule) in a woman will never know prosperity.""[54]" Mernissi calls this a "misogynist *hadith*," which has long outlived its author and occurs in most Islamist arguments against female political or judicial power. Mernissi argues that Abu Bakra is not a sound source of *hadith*, and that this particular *hadith* should not rightfully have accrued the fame that it did.[55] The Islamists do not question the validity of this *hadith*; many feel that it did not address ᶜAʾishah initially, but say that it applies to ᶜAʾishah's negative effect on that conflict and to the unfitness of other women leaders. For some reason, the roles of the other two leaders of the *fitnah*, Talha and Zubayr, are omitted from this discussion of female interference.

The life of ᶜAʾishah, unlike that of Khadijah, presents a dilemma for the Islamic oppositionists. They revere her as Muhammad's "best beloved." Yet they uphold the later criticisms of ᶜAʾishah by al-Jawzi (thirteenth C.), Baydawi (thirteenth C.), Ibn Taymiyya (d. 1328), and Said al-Afghani (twentieth C.), and base much of their approach to women on the new restrictions implied in the Verse of the Curtain.[56] ᶜAʾishah's female influence is viewed as an integral part of the first *fitnah*, which tore the community apart—when the first community of new believers lost its innocence.

Those who have supported women's activism in political life (including several of the female Islamists) hold that ᶜAʾishah was justified in her political activities because of her status as the Prophet's wife, her intelligence, and her concern for the *ummah*, the Muslim community. Her part in the conflict may legitimately be minimized. Although she was obviously concerned and intervened in conflict forming around the issue of succession, we have no evidence that she was in any way directly responsible for the initiation of this schism. And ᶜAʾishah, mounted on Asker, the camel, in the midst of battle, was not necessarily a consistent fighter for women's rights. We know from Ibn Hanbal that ᶜAʾishah supported ᶜUmar's attempts to keep women out of the mosques.[57] Abbott conjectures that ᶜAʾishah may have been reacting to the growing numbers of foreign slave women. She felt that they lowered the moral tone of the growing empire or otherwise offended ᶜAʾishah's class sensibilities.[58]

ᶜAʾishah represented the value placed on virginity, as she told Muhammad that she was unlike any of his other wives, who had all been previously married.[59] The Islamists interpret these attitudes as part of ᶜAʾishah's approval of customary law (ᶜurf) of the time, or merely indicative of her special relationship to the Prophet. Islamic liberals or feminists might brush aside these contradictions in ʿAʾishah's historical portrait by reminding us that women as well as men enforce the social order and whatever antifemale practices it condones.

Fatimah

The Prophet's daughter, Fatimah invokes the themes of succession, inheritance, and the legitimacy of Islamic rule. Those who supported ʿAli's claim to the Caliphate, and believed that descent through Fatimah should determine future leadership of the community, proposed male rule through a female line. Those who denied ʿAli's (and his son Husayn's) claim either discounted hereditary rule through a daughter, or argued that the Prophet had not intended dynastic rule, or declared that hereditary rule belonged within the clan, but should not necessarily move from parent to child.

Muslims uphold the right of a daughter to inherit, and in the absence of sons, a daughter may inherit instead of a further-removed male relative, according to the Shiʿa (the party of ʿAli). Relations through females, according to the Twelvers (the Jaafari Shiʿa who revere the lineage of the twelve imams), are considered equal to relations through males.[60] That is also true among the Sunni. In fact, maternal relatives may be closer to the family; a son was typically apprenticed to his mother's brother. In many cases, claims of female inheritance are not often pursued, because male kin were responsible for bereaved female relatives and so required compensation.

Fatimah and her offspring evoke respect in direct proportion to their proximity to the Prophet. His female progeny, Fatimah, carried the seed of prophecy and the imamate, according to the Shiʿa. She is associated with her father's righteousness and moral intent according to the Sunni schools as well.

Fatimah assumed strong archetypal power through a cult revering her at the popular level. A common symbol utilized throughout the Middle East is the hand of Fatimah, which bestows blessing and good fortune (barakah).[61] Fatimah may be compared to other female figures whom the people believe to be endowed with magical connections and powers. These include the Black Marias of Southern Europe, imported from Byzantium, and the previously discussed cult of the Virgin in Egypt.

After the Golden Age

Other female "saints," including Sayyida Zaynab, are revered in Egypt and celebrated regularly in a popular reclamation of women's history. There are many shrines to Zaynab, Husayn's sister, who became a symbol of female courage and political responsibility for commanding the remainder of

Husayn's followers after his death. Zaynab was buried in the city on which Cairo was founded.[62]

Sakinah, also the Prophet's granddaughter, was an independent beauty, famous not only for her poetry, sponsorship of the arts, and political loyalties, and, according to Mernissi, for her refusal to submit to male domination. She married five or six husbands and did not permit them to marry any other women while married to her. Sakinah was within her legal rights according to Islam, for she could include such a clause in her marriage contract. She also made "declarations" of extramarital love and was brought before the tribunal for infidelity.[63] More importantly, she opposed the power shifts occurring within the Ummayad dynasty[64] and so became a model for female political oppositionism.

Many other female figures in Islamic history engaged in counsel, mediation, high political intrigue, or other "behind the helm" participation. These included the powerful and effective Queens of Baghdad studied by Abbott: Khaizuran, the mother of Harun al-Rashid, and Zubaidah, Harun's wife and Amin's mother, who sponsored the waterworks of Mecca and participated in the rivalry between Amin and Maʾmun.[65] In Egypt the clever Shajarat al-Durr, a mamluk of Armenian descent, ruled the land in her own name, and co-ruled under two dynasties.[66] One of many powerful women of the Ottoman empire was Roxelana (Khurren), who was said to dominate Suleiman the Magnificent and held influence in her own right, not merely as the mother of a ruler-to-be.

By the premodern period in Egypt, the restrictions over women's access to the public sphere had constricted since the early Muslim era. These limitations did not evolve as a steady linear progression, nor were Muslim women the only ones affected. Christian and Jewish women had been restricted and veiled as well, throughout the years, and their respective legal codes also limited divorce, permitted polygamy in certain periods, or forbade remarriage. Elite women of all groups were subject to greater control than women of other social classes. The rules of seclusion and the Ottoman version of veiling applied mainly to them by the nineteenth century.

Historians often cite Napoleon's invasion of Egypt as the event that catalyzed the forces shaping the modern Egyptian nation. Napoleon's venture into Egypt constituted the first modern physical interference of Western powers in Egyptian affairs. The emergence of industrialization and centralization under Muhammad ʿAli is a more apt point of origin for the modern nation. The new state, and its subsequent decline after Muhammad ʿAli's death, form a background for the arguments on female education and seclusion that emerged at the end of the nineteenth century.

Judith Tucker states that nineteenth-century Egyptian women were sometimes able to circumvent growing restrictions in the public arena and often sought the legal recourse due them.[67] She suggests that Muhammad ʿAli's centralizing statist policies, in conjunction with an economic contraction, eroded the independent base of women in poorer families of the peasantry and the proletariat. Tucker believed that poorer women had fewer resources to fall back on, or personal allies, and that this weakened their position when they sought legal intervention. That portion of her description holds true for poorer women in most eras, but it may be more stoutly established when other court records of those years are examined in detail. Kenneth Cuno has seriously contested Tucker's assessments of economic contraction in that period.[68] We do know that some wealthy women who acted as landholders and tax collecters (*multazimat*) at that time saw their holdings reduced, but the information on other classes is insufficient. It may be misleading to explain the emerging public debate on the need for gender-issue reform in the nineteenth century by referring to a corresponding decline in status for women.

In an era of growing anti-British sentiment, the arguments on gender issues coalesced into two main camps. The first urged reform and innovation of attitudes toward women that had come to be considered "Islamic." The other camp asserted the autonomy of Islamic laws of personal status from state control or influence, and opposed most reform.[69]

Women's education, freedom from extreme social restrictions, and national roles were at the core of the debate over their rightful status. Qasim Amin (1863–1908), a disciple of Muhammad ʿAbduh who upheld the cause of reform in Islam, called for the education of women, an end to veiling and polygamy, and revised divorce laws.

Arguments that originally developed to deny female role expansion were later incorporated into pieces that glorified the housewife.[70] Paradoxically, the same line of argument was found in works extolling the virtues of public service (undertaken by elite women). Islamic conservatives and Islamists reformulated these older arguments of the virtues of the housewife, the family woman, to contract rather than to expand women's roles as the years progressed.

Women's pens and voices carried out the debate as well as male advocates. Beth Baron has discussed the evolution of female self-vocalization through the women's press, which produced articles on gender issues along with stories, news items, and letters. Expressing one's views in print, once an unladylike activity, became acceptable early in the twentieth century.[71]

The nationalist process required women's participation. Simultaneously, many of those advocating a sovereign Egyptian nation declared it the protector of cultural values, including the Muslim family.[72] The female historical archetypes were employable as symbols of the past *and* the future in the arguments of the two camps. But they already held double- or triple-edged meanings, and their malleability only increased.

The debate on female emancipation and the feminist movement was formulated by the elite and the upper bourgeoisie.[73] One of the participants, Huda Sha'rawi, is generally viewed as a symbol of the feminine challenge and potential for expansion of the era.

Huda Sha'rawi

Huda Sha'rawi has symbolized the growth of feminism in Egypt and throughout the Middle Eastern region. As the daughter of the largest landowner in Egypt,[74] she grew up within the harem system, married early, and participated in the national struggle and strikes. Huda eventually became the president of the Wafdist Women's Central Committee, but she is most renowned for having cast off her face veil along with Saiza Nabarawi in 1923.[75]

Margot Badran described Huda's specific historical position and her personal experiences with gender inequality in her family. She explains the conjunction of circumstances that arose at a time when the mature Sha'rawi was free enough of the patriarchal constraints in her life to choose a new path for herself that questioned the previous standards extended to upper-class women.[76]

Huda's memoirs show us that her early life contrasted sharply in content, purpose, and expression with her later years. Badran notes that Sha'rawi's decision to

> record her early, private years was like much of Huda Shaarawi's life, out of the ordinary. Private life, family life, inner feelings and thought were sacrosanct. They were as veiled by convention as women's faces had been. Writing about her life during the harem years was a final unveiling. It can be seen as Huda Shaarawi's final feminist act.[77]

A woman of Huda's background might have had some reservations about "going public," but her memoirs provide an especially tangible picture of the period, and they contrast with the present in essential ways. Huda demonstrated how elite women moved on from the public writing by and about women discussed by Baron and others to public activities on behalf of women.[78] The significance of Sha'rawi's life to this work is twofold. She is remembered as a founder of a feminism that developed from the final stages of the harem system. Does that sort of characterization mark Egyptian feminism from then on?

Chafetz and Dworkin, who try to construct an international model for feminist movements, have described the Egyptian feminist movement as a "first wave" feminism limited to the upper classes, which they termed "incipient and ameliorative" in orientation.[79] Their model does not sufficiently credit some feminist activities in the third world, because they too narrowly define the necessary preconditions to social change and lack enough historical data to pass judgment in other cases. However, they claim with validity that feminist movements involved in the process of nationalism are typically preempted by the survival and institution-building needs of a successful nationalist struggle.[80] This much was true in the Egyptian case, for the harem system of the nineteenth century ended without the extension of political rights to women in the constitution following the 1919 revolution, even to feminist nationalists like Huda Sha'rawi.[81]

We read that the lower- or middle-class woman was not represented by the feminists of the early decades. (It should be remembered that these women were neither veiled nor segregated from men.) Egyptians whom I interviewed subscribed to a general theory that women of less privilege were more imbued with traditional values and reflected the inherently antifeminist positions of Islamic thought. When their social class gained just enough steam through the nationalization of education and other semisocialist policies to experience rising expectations, they reacted by turning "back" to Islam.[82]

Mervat Hatem suggests that the entrenched patriarchal attitudes inherent in the twentieth-century state preempted serious reforms of gender issues. In her view, the state was composed of rationally acting representatives of the elite and upper-middle classes who superimposed their cultural and social outlook onto state policies. Women activists, and others who fought hard for women's rights, were in some ways thwarted by the social underpinnings of the state system but held Islamists and other conservatives responsible.[83]

Huda Sha'rawi is significant to the growing numbers of veiled women in Egypt as a symbol of the Egyptian-Western dialogue on women's status. She can be seen as the model, a grandmother of the modern, elite Egyptian women. But her great-granddaughters have rejected their mothers' ideals. Although they do not condemn Huda for revealing her face, they oppose the process of unveiling, the continuation of coeducation, and women's participation in politics and in the workplace that are credited as effects of Huda's unveiling.

Zeinab Radwan's contemporary veiled respondents felt that the reforms proposed by Qasim Amin (which Huda enacted personally) with regard to unveiling and female seclusion were a grave mistake.[84] Some of the Islamists claim that the early activists for women's rights were unduly influenced by the West. Some have further characterized the growing feminism of women like Huda Sha'rawi as mimicry of the West. Huda Sha'rawi is therefore a dual symbol; to the unveiled women and many men, her memory invokes the quest for political rights on behalf of all citizens of the era; to others, she represented a precipitous female entry into public life.

Many other women participated in the nationalist effort and gained legitimacy on a social level for women's further efforts in the public arena. It is ironic that in the 1970s, feminist principles, such as female role expansion, actually became associated with the state-sponsored elites of the period who delegitimized the early feminists' efforts in some ways. The state's evolution into a more advanced stage of comprador capitalism under Sadat meant that alienated intellectuals and the masses began to regard both the state and the state's commitment to gender reform in a new light. They felt that the elite groups who benefited from their association with the state and most visibly supported female role expansion had lost the sincerity of their nationalism. The "nationalist" ties to gender reform established in the early decades of the twentieth century had changed along with political definitions.

Sarah Graham-Browne points out that nationalism was the key factor in the independent status of feminism in Egypt and formed a contrast to its counterparts in Turkey and Iran, where powerful male leaders created the official reforms of women's status.[85] A modern Egyptian writer disagrees, and writes:

> They are always rights that are given, not rights that are taken. . . . As for our society . . . these rights came because of two or three books written by men earlier this century, because of the struggle of some wives of prominent men and because our governments want the West to look upon them as enlightened.[86]

If we detect a bitter tone here, we should remember that sex-role expansion became most visible in the public sector and that many contradictions arose from it.

As women fought against veiling and polygamy in the 1920s and 1930s, some commentators called for a reinterpretation of the *hadith* literature on women. Writing in Egypt and elsewhere in the Middle East, they utilized the previously described "Islamic images" of women. Nazirah Zein ad-Din, for example, cited from the Qur'an and other *hadith* that showed a theory of male superiority to be untenable. Her argument against the continued practice of polygamy contained an appeal for the use of *ijtihad*, a juridical resource involving reconsideration of previous rulings and a willingness to make conceptual leaps when weighing the alternative sources of *fiqh*.[87] Conservatives, headed by Shaykh al-Ghayalini, attacked her work and accused her of being a *nom de plume* for a group of nine men. Modern Islamists echo the tone of their rebuttals. The exegete and scholar ʿAishah abd al-Rahman, known as Bint al-Shatti, made a similar call for the use of *ijtihad* in analysis of gender issues, many years later.[88]

The women who entered the public arena in the '20s, '30, and '40s and fought to receive higher education were active, independent, and patriotic. They increased the existing options for women, in spite of their elite status, and basically created the social services in Egypt, which legitimized female employment in those fields.[89] Women also entered academia, but not without pressure; Jehan Sadat describes the academic ordeal and harassment that Soheir al-Qalamawi underwent in her master's examination in 1939.[90] Female role expansion continued on through the parliamentary or liberal period and gained ground during the Nasser years.

The Growth of Islamic Opposition

During the second phase of female role expansion, which lasted from 1923 until the 1950s, the Society of the Muslim Brothers (*Ikhwan al-Muslimin*) arose. At a time of intense political struggle between the monarch and his cabinets, the Wafd and the British, the movement was founded by Shaykh Hasan al-Banna (once a member of the *sufi* Order of the Hasafiya Brothers) in Isma'iliyah in 1928. The movement grew rapidly at the grassroots level. Part of its popular appeal was a call for an end to British interference in Egypt's internal affairs. Eventually the movement went underground, and popular support was necessarily less visible.[91] The Muslim Brotherhood proposed social and political alternatives that were more appealing to the masses than the platforms of competing parties and groups to the right and left. These included the neofascists, the socialists, the communists, the Wafd and the various opposition parties.

Marsot suggests that periods of economic depression combined with "political disillusion" produce a popular search for cultural authenticity.[92] She also points out that three protest movements in Egypt—one in the eighteenth century, the Muslim Brotherhood, and the modern Islamic oppositionists—all gained strength during periods of diminished public political participation, multilevel alienation, governmental rigidity, and growing economic inequity and in the "absence of normal safety valves," and "old, stable, cohesive [social and political] groups."[93] Earlier theorists of revolution and modernization postulated similar conditions typically prefacing social or political explosion.[94] As the Wafd failed to outweigh or control the British or the Palace, the Muslim Brotherhood continued to grow. And a sort of "postponed revolution"[95] occurred in Egypt, never truly or bloodily expressing itself in 1952 except for the burning of Cairo, those turning to religious ideals gathered force.

The difficult economic circumstances during World War II fueled social tensions in Egypt. Egyptians living through those years observed that the entrepreneurial class and some skilled blue-collar workers grew wealthy and capitalized on currency shortages.[96] The German military threat and the presence of the foreign troops in Egypt exacerbated feelings of exploitation, as Yusuf Shahin depicted in his film, *Iskandaria Leh?*.[97] During this period of social stress and growing anomie, the Muslim Brotherhood gained support and membership. The Muslim Sisters were one of ten *aqsam*, or sections of the Society. Also aligned with the *Ikhwan* was the Association of Muslim Women.

Zaynab al-Ghazali and the Islamist Women

Zaynab al-Ghazali, who has written and spoken about gender issues for decades, dates her commitment to the Islamist cause back to the foundation of the Association of Muslim Women, which arose some nine years after Hasan al-Banna's establishment of the *Ikhwan* (the Muslim Brotherhood). She worked with that organization and in cooperation with the *Ikhwan*, but made a personal and emotional pledge to the *Ikhwan* leadership in 1948. Due to her experiences, attitudes, and connections with the *Ikhwan*, al-Ghazali may be considered both an idealogue and another historical archetype to the young Egyptian veiled women. She may not be a figure that unveiled middle-class or elite women would consider a role model, but even they have acknowledged her centrality to a moderate Islamist portrayal of gender issues.[98]

Muhammad Shawqi Zaki and Richard Mitchell tell us that earlier, in 1933, the Muslim Sisters were formed out of an Institute for the Mothers of the Believers, established in Isma'iliyah by Hasan al-Banna, which became their first branch. They state that the women's group never attained the popularity of the men's groups. In fact, the Brothers

> admitted . . . that "the Islamic feminist movement", had not been able "to attract the educated type", that too many women had seen the movement as a "return to the *harim*" rather than . . . the only path to "true female emancipation."[99]

Mitchell says that the Sisters were rarely seen in the university campuses, but that they numbered about five thousand at the height of the movement in 1948.[100] Zaynab al-Ghazali dated the Association of Muslim Women back to 1937. That group met independently from 1937 to 1948, when al-Ghazali made a personal pledge to al-Banna. From that point on, her own positions were more closely coordinated with the *Ikhwan* leadership. The Association met under the umbrella of the Society's activities, but it continued to function independently. Al-Ghazali claims that by the time Nasser banned the group in 1964, "the Association of Muslim Women had 119 branches in Egypt. These branches were scattered over the country, in every village and farm and the number of members had reached 3 million women."[101] Colleagues who were familiar with the *Ikhwan* felt that figure was too high, but many sources on the Brotherhood devote little space to female members, associates, or gender ideology, so let us simply enter Hagga Zaynab's version for the record.

The Society's views on women, as iterated by Muhammad al-Ghazali, and by Bahi al-Khuli in the fifties, called for *tajdid*, renewing reform, but in limited doses. They proposed an avoidance of both the "narrow-mindedness" of the East and the moral laxness and individualism of the West. Under the leadership of al-Hudaybi, al-Khuli issued an official statement (*risala*) in which he offered guidelines on women's issues. Although al-Khuli stated that women and men are equal under Islam, he acknowledged a "limited superiority" of the male, based on the male economic responsibility within traditional family arrangements. Therefore, cooperation and consultation between man and woman are required to bring about equality within their relationship. [102]

Birth control was first portrayed as a "negative device," but in later years the Muslim Brothers "conceded that under certain circumstances it [birth control] is permitted to prevent pregnancy, for the Prophet had not opposed *azl* (coitus interruptus). [103] Birth-control devices were more effective than *azl* and could be allowed when the woman's health was in jeopardy. Couples should not use birth control to avoid the social responsibility of childrearing. The West proposed fewer children as an economic solution for the overpopulated societies of the third world, and vigorously pushed for population control policies in Egypt, but Islam sanctions neither childlessness nor asceticism. The Brotherhood proposed instead a recycling of wealth within society through the mechanism of *zakat* (the portion of one's income that should be given to the needy). *Zakat* is considered one of the five pillars of Islam, obligations of all Muslims.

Veiling and Female Modesty

The Brotherhood and other Muslim conservatives felt that an imitation of European ways was responsible for increased mixing of the sexes, resulting in immorality and debauchery. That view was strongly expressed both prior to and following the British evacuation of 1954. They rebuked women for their "nakedness" (more revealing dress) and the permissiveness of both sexes. [104]

During the early years of the new Egyptian regime, Sayyid Qutb held that the sexes could mingle or associate for "logical reasons" and under conditions of necessity. [105] "Decent dress" was to be required, although this did not imply the veil. Indeed, Muhammad al-Ghazali stated:

> We do not think this [the veil] is a very efficient means of precaution and we consider that Muslims have adopted it in a time of weakness and indecision. Training men and women for virtue requires a more comprehensive and positive programme. [106]

I restated this argument for an "inner *hijab*" to Zaynab al-Ghazali and some of the younger veiled women, and they strongly disagreed. Of course the "decent dress" that the Brotherhood of the fifties referred to most probably implied a headcover.

The costume of the early Muslim Sisters was the forerunner of the current *higab* (Islamic covering). It included a white *khimar*, fabric covering the throat in the way a wimple does, along with a headcover. The white headgarb did not derive from the upper-class face veil, the *yashmak*, or the traditional black wrap, the *malayya-laff*. It was not the same as the headscarf worn by the *bint al-balad* and rural women that ties behind the head, not in front of the chin, and does not cover the neck and shoulders. Although spokeswomen like al-Ghazali and other *Ikhwan* members claimed that this covering is identical to what was worn in the first century of Islam, the current version of *higab* is most likely derived from the *sharf shami* (lit., Eastern scarf) a style of headcovering worn in the eastern Arab states during the 1930s and 1940s when women began to substitute the black coat and *sharf* for the earlier face-veil and outer wrap.[107] The Egyptian adoption of this style might reflect the Levantine-Egyptian current affecting women, discussed by Mervat Hatem.[108]

The white color suggests the headwrap of the women of southern Palestine rather than the black-colored traditional outer wraps of indigenous Egyptian modesty fashions.[109] White is the color of the *hajj*, the pilgrimage, and implies purity and cleanliness in the Sisters' garb, as well as a distinction from the lower-class connotations of the black *malaya laff*. The nun-like effect of the Sisters' headgarb (and that of today's Islamists) is evident, and even Egyptian observers have found it disturbing.[110]

Early Islamist Views on Women in Society

Sayyid Qutb, Muhammad al-Ghazali, and Hasan al-Hudaybi held positions on female education that resemble Zaynab al-Ghazali's stance today. Education is necessary but should primarily prepare a woman for her family life. Medicine and teaching are appropriate fields of study for women, but Hudaybi thought that the study of "male topics" such as "law, chemistry, engineering, agriculture" would cause girls to "sacrifice some of their femininity and sensitivity." He proposed separate classes or universities for women.[111] Many modern veiled young respondents still believe certain fields of employment are more suitable for men.

The idealogues differed over the issue of political rights for women. In general, they were to be postponed until all citizens were more educated and religiously faithful. Abd al-Qadir ʿAwda opposed the vote for women, claiming that the vote was not useful because men held a precedent in political leadership.[112] The Azhari position was similar. A campaign for female suffrage had gone on for years, but there was strong male opposition to the vote for women and alarm following an organized women's hunger strike protesting the issue.[113]

The Muslim Brothers felt that polygamy was a necessary option for men whose wives were seriously ill or sterile. According to them, polygamy preserved the institution of marriage, for otherwise men would resort to illicit relationships. These arguments, along with the historical precedent of polygamy, were strong enough to combat reform attempts, for they construed the abolition of polygamy as an attack on the *sunnah* of the Prophet. In the 1950s, the Muslim Brothers suggested that education would eventually mitigate the abuses of polygamy and divorce.

Because the *Ikhwan* stressed the preservation of marriage bonds, they opposed limitations on male prerogatives in divorce and amelioration of women's rights in divorce proceedings. Zaynab al-Ghazali's position has changed little from that stance, and young veiled women often agreed with her. The conservatives, then and now, argue that making divorce easier will merely create more broken families, not more equality between the sexes.

During the Nasser era, the Muslim Brethren and many of the Muslim Sisters were imprisoned or went into voluntary exile. Zaynab al-Ghazali and others who were part of the "secret apparatus" of the *Ikhwan* were incarcerated for many years. She bitterly resents Nasser, as many *Ikhwan* do, and his socialist principles and policies that countered the strength of religious groups in Egypt. The modern Islamists regard Sayyid Qutb as a martyr, and al-Ghazali represents her own prison years as a torturous experience that strengthened her faith.[114] Some of the Brethren went to Saudi Arabia and returned years later. Their daughters were raised in a socially conservative atmosphere and grew up with the notion of an Islamic future. I interviewed several of these second-generation Islamists, who provide an interesting perspective due to their parents' experiences in the Nasser years.

Doria Shafik and the Statist Years

Doria Shafik, founder of the journal and union of the same title, *Bint al-Nil*, was an ardent feminist who exposed some of the contradictions between feminism and statist goals in this period. In 1951, Shafik and a group of women stormed Parliament to the dismay of many conservatives. She and other women held a hunger strike in 1954 and demanded full political rights.[115] After women were granted suffrage in 1956, some were appointed to official positions. Shafik still protested the requirements of education and the formal application for voting. Then she held another strike to protest the growth of dictatorship in Egypt and the Israeli occupation of Palestine. Nasser placed her under house arrest and denounced her as a traitor.[116]

Nasser's treatment of Shafik was indicative of the narrow range of dissent that could be publicly tolerated in a volatile political environment. Shafik may be viewed as an antithesis to the Islamist model for women of the fifties, as well as a symbol of the state's immobility on social reform.

Female political participation remained low, despite the regime's goals of involving more women in politics and utilizing their political franchise. Nasser's plans for social reform did not and could not mirror the Chinese experiment, where women were herded into production and permitted only one child, or penalized. In China, the expansion of sex roles was essentially based on the destruction of historical and religious determinants of women's status. Changes in social consciousness and in the embedded expectations of men were facilitated through compulsory attendance in small consciousness-raising groups. We now know that in China the destruction of patriarchal structures was incomplete, but in Egypt similar social engineering was inconceivable. Islam was still too close to the essence of popular culture, too legitimizing, and too dangerous to grapple with, as the Muslim Brothers' threat to Nasser had proven. If Nasser had tackled legal reform of gender issues immediately and unequivocally, he would have placed himself in an extremely vulnerable political position.

Nasser did not outlaw the veil, or strongly discourage its use as Reza Shah and Atatürk did. Elite women did wear more modest versions of Western fashions. Elizabeth Fernea describes the "new elite" women of the late 1950s buying flowers, giving dinner parties, still able to afford "good" servants.[117] The components of that elite changed by the late 1960s to include those who had advanced in the military and bureaucracy or had made fortunes on the side. Some social mobility occurred in this period, and a new middle class emerged.

Fernea notes that the previous elite's taste and decor were still valued by those who could afford it. She comments that in the Nasserist era both West and East affected Egyptian life and she notes the European pastries that sold alongside the "Syrian" sweets, and an awakened appreciation of Pharaonic art and design.[118] The elites' continued esteem of things Western contrasted with the state policy of Egyptianism, of sponsoring local dance and music, and of reviving traditional crafts and arts forms, a trend that actually predated the Nasserist period.

Lower-class urban women retained their traditional dress. Many could not afford the clothing styles of the elite. Others would not think of adopting them in any case. They found the clothes pretentious, and their neighbors would say they were conceited if they appeared in them.[119] These women did not often move out of the neighborhood (*hitta*), either physically or culturally. Naguib Mahfouz, the Nobel laureate, described one woman's escape from the *hitta* into a life of prostitution in his novel, *Midaq Alley*.[120] He utilizes a popular theme that tragedy may ensue from social transformation.

By the late 1950s, and into the 1960s, some women wore Western dress under the *galabiya*, a sort of compromise between modesty and individual taste. And by the end of the Nasser era, through education and economic policies, women experienced social mobility. Some of my respondents felt that lower-class women who had risen socially in this period were especially susceptible to the Islamist message in the early 1970s.

As land-holdings broke up during the Nasser years, many country women began to migrate to the cities. Some experienced discrimination and crises of faith and identity, as depicted in the film *Li ʿAdam Kifayah ʿAdlihi*.[121] In this story, a young *fallaha* follows her husband into the city only to discover he has married someone else. She initiates a formal complaint, but the bureaucratic system takes away her child, and finally she murders her errant husband. The film offers a special comment on the oppression of rural or migrant women, that it is her peasant characteristics (outspokenness, irritability, stubbornness, and naiveté) that bring on her tragedy, rather than her feminine status or her sound moral position. The city folk are more complex and less principled in the film, but in fact, polygamy has been more prevalent in the countryside.

Urban lower-class women looked down on the rural migrants to the city, considering them hopelessly inferior and *baladi* (a term that means "common," but also "truly of the people").[122] These social tensions were heightened by the emergence of rural villages within urban Cairo, a ruralization that continued during the Sadat years.[123]

Egyptian women entered the workplace steadily, but in far lower percentages of the total labor force than those in Latin America and certain Asian countries.[124] However, there are large numbers of single mothers in Latin America and in the Caribbean, a factor contributing to higher female employment. In the Far East many younger women are employed in low-skilled (and low paid) assembly positions, featuring dormitory living arrangements. Nadia Youssef has commented that "women's rights and status in most developing nations are nationalistically, rather than individualistically, grounded."[125] Women's potential contribution to national development is of course important, but involvement in the workplace may also enhance women's self-assurance, self-esteem, and personal growth. Certainly, the former, rather than the latter, set of goals were behind the Egyptian state's pursuit of a series of laws designed to increase female employment in this period. Youssef suggests that the tension created through this orientation resulted in ambivalent attitudes toward both "development" and "traditional life."[126]

Egyptian women began to enter technical and professional positions in greater numbers than regional statistics might suggest.[127] The upper sector of working women tended to be more educated and more visible, thus perhaps more susceptible to criticism. Nevertheless, women enjoyed greater legal protection on paper than in many Western countries under Law 91 of 1959. This legislation led later to the granting of many benefits unavailable in the United States that, Sullivan notes, "make it more expensive to hire women"—including paid maternity leave, guaranteed job security, and "the right to retire earlier than men."[128] But women's double work load could not adequately be addressed through legislation, and personal and family tensions sometimes resulted.

Following the 1952 revolution, the new Egyptian leaders only had the haziest concept of how their society should grow and change.[129] As they developed a social program by trial and error, the state remained theoretically committed to Qasim Amin and Muhammad ʿAbduh's proposition that a nation could not advance without the advancement of its women.

With the 1967 defeat, an air of despair descended on the people of Egypt. A rash of religiously motivated visions, apparitions, and sightings took place.[130] People needed reassurance that their God had not forgotten them. The burgeoning of the Islamists may be dated from this period, when the defeat at the hands of Israel profoundly shook the confidence and inner faith of the nation.

Women continued to break ground in the workplace and in education. But they were also involved in the growing search for spiritual relief. It was during the early 1970s that the more radical Islamist groups began to organize.[131] Some women became involved in these organizations through marriage or family relationships. Fewer joined independently. Later on, some of the radical fringe groups, such as the *Takfir wal-Higrah* (Repentance and Flight), began to operate as separate counter societies, seceding from the world around them.[132]

The Islamists under Sadat

Sadat, who was more worried about the left than about the Islamists, released many members of the Muslim Brotherhood imprisoned by Nasser. Other former members of the Brotherhood returned from exile abroad. The new leader hoped to use the Islamists to defuse the Nasserist current in the government and cast himself in the media as a highly religious individual.

Sadat eventually reversed many of Nasser's key orientations in foreign and domestic policy. Although the old elites had been disarmed during the Nasserist period, some emigrated, but others remained in Egypt. Some analysts said that the old elites continued their influence economically and politically to some extent.[133] Generally, slight but visible benefits accrued to the lower and lower-middle classes (as compared to their situations years earlier). Nasser's verbal commitment to the little man had contributed to a general aura of egalitarianism, although a new elite within the bureaucracy and the military had arisen under him. When his successor reversed the prevailing economic policies, there was a feeling that Sadat would betray the populist promises of the 1960s—the gap between the haves and have-nots would inevitably widen. These sentiments also encouraged the further growth of Islamic oppositionism. Moderate Islamists were actually funded by certain high officials.[134]

The economic opening of Egypt (the *infitah*) commenced via the policies inaugurated in Laws 43 and, 32 and in the October Paper of 1974. These included measures that would encourage the private investment sector through free trade, joint ventures, free ports, and higher amounts of foreign participation in the economy. Meanwhile the principles of neutralism, self-development, and protection of local production moved back into the shadows.[135]

A new group of financial adventurers made fortunes along with some of the bureaucratic elite and previously established large capitalists. Economists found that the outcome of the economic opening was, indeed, an increasing gap in income distribution.[136] Galal Amin has felt that the new policies were the result of pressure brought to bear on Egypt by external forces also evident in Egypt's new foreign policy and aid orientation.[137] While certain groups were able to take advantage of these policies and were not only content but wealthy, most were hit by inflation on their fixed salaries and frustrated by a new consumerism they could ill afford.

Why is this period important to women? While those on fixed salaries tightened their belts, their wives' salaries became increasingly important. Conversely, others took the view that during such a tough economic period, men needed the jobs occupied by women to support their families. Some men said the women were merely using jobs as pin money, to buy clothes, and forgot that some women supported families as well.

Sadat promised increased democratization but could not deliver it. Citizens called him Baba (Daddy or Papa) Sadat, not out of affection but with resentment. He bridled his opponents and many on the left whom he suspected, until only the Islamists were left to channel opposition to him.[138]

During the Pahlavi period in Iran, the traditional *ta'ziyeh*, or Shi'i passion plays, used a historical metaphor for the present to "sublimate discontent"[139] or to express opposition.[140] 'Ali or Husayn stood for the people, while the tyrant Mu'awiya represented the Shah. In Egypt, Islamic institutions and historical symbols were also used to communicate the people's discontent. Marsot explains:

> as in earlier eras when free speech was forbidden or restricted, the mosque
> became the main forum for opposition. Here people could speak their minds
> in symbolic terms, using references to Muslim heroes as code words indi-
> cating disapproval of corrupt governments and ineffectual rule.[141]

The Islamic opposition strongly disapproved of a settlement with the Israelis following the post-1973 negotiations and the Camp David agreements. They had always spoken out for the Palestinian cause, and when Sadat traveled to Jerusalem, they felt he had betrayed the entire nation—that the principles of self-determination, political autonomy, and Arabism had been sacrificed to the individual vision of one man.[142]

Islamic dress began to spread. Families with strong liberal leanings were shocked when their daughters adopted the new *higab* and sons grew new beards. The symbolic figure of ʿAʾishah legitimized women's participation in Islamic political life since the earliest *fitnah*. But now, the purity of the Mothers of the Believers, the prophet's wives, took on an added significance. Texts of Ibn Taymiyya and others who assessed the character of political tyranny were revived.[143] Modern-day theorists discussed the responses required of good Muslims to tyranny and considered the current implications of *jihad* (holy war).

At first, elite women did not take the new veiled women very seriously. Jokes focused on the *muhaggabat*, or women pointed out inconsistencies in their pious manner. Only in retrospect did figures such as Jihan Sadat reconsider the veiling phenomenon and the Islamist opinions of her, to find them both troubling and ominous.[144]

Elite women themselves were portrayed in a shallow manner in the media, which stressed their Western ties, adventurism, and ambitions. Or they were held up as superwomen who retained an essential femininity while performing as surrogate men. Valerie Hoffman-Ladd illustrates the ambiguities of the ideal "modern woman" by citing a text by Najwah Salih accompanying fashion photographs in *Hawwa*, a popular women's magazine:

> The modern woman is a simple and elegant woman. She knows how to appear full of vitality and energy at all times of day. She is an excellent housewife . . . a society woman, and a mother. This woman always chooses her clothes with care, so they will be appropriate to her lifestyle and in tempo with the spirit of the times in which she lives. . . . She prefers constant change, so she can appear each day in a new image. . . . She always follows the fashion. . . . She never forgets alongside her responsibilities that she is female.[145]

The image created here was quite incongruous with the resources of most Egyptian women.

The media, popular culture, and the state together, constructed an image of the elite woman, a dominant model that, though flawed, played right into the hands of the Islamists, galvanizing disapproval and moral judgments of her. The interaction continued for many years. For example, the protagonist of the film, *al-Marʾah al-Hadidiyah* (The Iron Woman), ruthlessly pursues her husband's killers. She lures them seductively and kills them (a black widow theme) in between her weight-lifting sessions, karate classes, and wild driving. She is finally caught and punished, sending a confusing message to women about the expansion of sex-role barriers—a female avenger cannot be a heroine.[146]

By the late 1970s, female employment had expanded greatly in the private sector, especially in the pink-collar category. Although women entered all areas of employment at a significant rate, female white-collar workers, bank clerks, tour agents, and guides, and other service-sector employees were especially visible. They earned higher salaries, but not higher status, than their male counterparts. Earl Sullivan has described a small group of extremely successful businesswomen who arose during this period. They encountered and understood the social ambivalence toward female role expansion.[147] Probably large numbers of women also entered the informal wage categories at this time. Nadia Hijab and Mervat Hatem have remarked that the nuclear family and Western-style individualism had become more prevalent, and both were negative in certain ways. The extended family system had provided many benefits that were no longer available.[148]

Women who did not work had mixed feelings about female employment. Working women appeared to make more money, but they had more expenses. Employed women were touted by the regime as an abstract sign of progress, but men harassed them at work and on their way to work.

Female conservatism on this issue might be related to class origins. Some lower-class women were proud of husbands who forbade them to work and said their husbands were "real men" who worked hard to take care of them.[149] On the other hand, some of these women might have difficulty finding employment. They may be displacing jealousy of working women through "sour grapes" remarks, for one would never hear working middle-class women complain that their husbands are "not real men."

Labor migration out of Egypt increased, and the remittances formed an important source of income. Women benefited directly and indirectly from "the brain drain" and from labor shortages throughout the employment market. They experienced increased responsibilities and enhanced control over income and time.[150] Women migrated, as well, and their new status outside of the family environment was a source of both income and stress.[151]

Another form of migration occurred: planned settlements of workers and professionals on reclaimed lands. The expectations and experiences of women in one such settlement, Tahaddi, studied by Sukkary-Stolba, showed that settler women achieved various degrees of status and satisfaction depending on their socioeconomic and educational backgrounds.[152]

During the economic opening, the urban poor developed strategies for coping with the dysfunctional aspects of the state system that allowed them to meet some of their expenses and survive. Psychological strategies worked along with the black market, according to Nadia Khouri-Dagher.[153] The examples of groups who profited from the new policies, and migrants who were able to save, allowed even the poor some room for hopes and dreams.[154]

Survival fears were close to the surface, however, and when Sadat acted on the recommendations of the World Bank to cut back on food subsidies, riots broke out. Permanent restructuring required more attention to internal strains. Poor women coped by planning very carefully[155] and participating in neighborhood saving associations. Others broke the rules if need be, acting as *dallalat* (shoppers and purveyors of black-market goods) some days and as ordinary coupon-book users on other days.[156] Middle-class women were affected as well, but inflation struck them harder later in the 1980s.

Sadat encouraged by his wife, extended many legal reforms to women during this period.[157] Significantly, thirty seats in the People's Assembly were reserved for women, although that policy was reversed in 1978. Law 44 of 1979 reformed the laws of personal status, including women's grounds for divorce; rights to alimony, the family residence, and extended custody of children; and related issues. This law was later challenged and rescinded, for it was enacted as a special edict, deviating from normal procedures and review. Reformulation of this law opened up a huge debate over women's status.[158] The Islamists were not the only conservative voices in the battle over personal status reform. Members of the state-approved religious establishment and many secularized men also fought against the legal changes.

Lieutenant Khalid al-Islambouli, a member of the oppositionist group, *Jihad,* assassinated Sadat in 1981. Following this event, the ensuing violence in the provincial cities, Asyut and Mansoura, and the revelation of a hazy plan to destroy the state, all eyes were on the Islamists. Many were rounded up and tried, and many more were arrested later. But political protest expressed through Islamic opposition was certain to rise again. ʿAli Hilal Dessouki has stated: "Islam has replaced Arab nationalism as the ideology of dissent."[159] The strength and gradual institutionalization of the Islamists continued into the term of the new ruler, Hosni Mubarak.

Islamists Enter the 1990s

Mubarak's regime has pursued two policies toward the Islamic oppositionists. The simultaneous use of these policies and the appropriateness of their goals has resulted in part from the shifting power bases within the regime. One approach has employed strict warnings, surveillance, harassment, legal measures, and mass arrests.

As part of the other strategy, Islamist moderates have been invited to participate to some degree within the government; for example, the *Ikhwan* have entered several coalitions in which their members could run for parliamentary seats and exercise some degree of influence according to the state's terms. Islamist services and economic endeavors were basically left to their own devices until 1988, when Islamic "banks" were more strictly regulated, or closed. Television and radio have included more religious programming.

Saad Eddin Ibrahim considers a phase of institutionalization to be a logical progression for the *Ikhwan* as a social movement.[160] The state has permitted more criticism and dissent. That has meant that women may express antisecular views, wear *higab*, or continue to participate in social activities of the Islamists. The Islamists and women among them realize that the regime is intent on its survival and will reemploy the stick rather than the carrot if need be.

The 1985 reforms of the Personal Status Laws took place under Mubarak. Much of the heated debate took place between men opposing the original reforms, and women who wished to retain many features. State support for their effort came from the woman Minister of Social Affairs Amal Othman.[161] A participant, Ingie Roushdie, has felt that many concessions were made to the conservatives that will eventually have to be addressed through legislation.[162]

A surprisingly vehement dialogue on women's right to work continues from this series of arguments. Although veiled and unveiled women joined forces on the reform issues, they still differ over the formulation of female employment and many other issues. Many Egyptian women agree with Amina Shafiq that they do not intend to be restricted to their homes ever again.[163]

The debate over family law is a regional concern; it is not confined to Egypt. But in each case, economic circumstance and the degree of Islamically clothed conservatism are important. How Mubarak will interact with Islamists and proponents of women's rights in the coming decade will depend on the wider national and regional picture. His reassertion of Egypt's Arab relationships may have mollified, but not satisfied, the Islamists. To some degree, the activities of the *Ikhwan* and other Islamist groups elsewhere in the region regarding gender issues affect the Egyptian viewers, just as stories of the Egyptian Islamists, or television programs including veiled women, affect viewers in neighboring countries. And the Islamists' limited impact on foreign policy may actually increase their concentration on gender issues where they have realized substantial results.

Some elements of women's history have continuously provoked debate. There is no general agreement on women's ideal status and designated roles. Nonetheless, many factions have insisted on the incorporation of an authentic and firm Islamic tradition. The sustained use of historical argument by the religious establishment, Islamic liberals, Islamists, working women, and even the state, ensures a multiplicity of options for women. Competing ideologies have developed as a natural outcome of women's history in modern

Egypt and elsewhere in the region. A wealth of possibilities and choices for women has evolved, which may be viewed in the context of other dynamics—the state versus civil society, social class mobility, and economic disintegration and reformation—as has been illustrated in this brief historical review.

Chapter Four

STUDIES OF SELF-IMAGE

Introduction

Women described their lives, their perceptions of gender issues, and their opinions of the Islamists in interviews carried out in Cairo in the fall of 1988. Their responses also illustrate the processes of self-image and syzygy, or what Michel Foucault terms the process of self-formation as an "ethical subject"—an essential dimension of moral action. For a code of moral action is what the Islamists claim to present, and women react variously to it and to the increased religiosity they observe around them.[1]

Women expressed their own sense of history and of *turath* (religiocultural heritage), which they perceive as an inner source of authenticity (*asala*). It was not mere coincidence that they referred to the historical archetypes previously discussed. These women are aware of the debates over seclusion, modesty, and sexual control of women. They feel their own attitudes are supported by the historical precedents they invoke, as well as other contemporary influences in their environment.

In some ways, their problems resemble those of women the world over. They let me know, without complaining, that they work hard and they have less leisure time than men, as is true of most societies. They probably spend more time planning, organizing, and worrying than men do. They tend to have broader and more meaningful social networks in their society than many urban Americans are able to build. They value their family relationships deeply, and good etiquette involves visiting, favor exchanges, and mutual responsibilities that are not always paralleled in Western contexts.

The interviewing process was valuable because women were able to convey a sense of their own rationale, their hopes, doubts, means of expression, and interactions with each other. I tried to be equally sympathetic and non-interventionist during the interview process with veiled and unveiled respondents. In return, respondents were very cooperative, and offered a great deal of unsolicited material. I got a sense of which issues were truly controversial, and which issues might have been overemphasized in the literature or in the media.

The image of the Islamist women is the primary focus of this work. The data basically divides the women into two groups, veiled and unveiled. I hoped to learn whether women could explain the prevailing dominant image conveyed to them, how satisfactorily it performed, how they interpreted the Islamists' code of behavior for women, and whether they felt that the Islamist image of womanhood was moving to usurp the dominant image's position.

Of the fifty women surveyed, 62 percent are veiled (*muhaggabat*); they wear the "modern" version of the *higab* and the *khimar*. Within that category, a variety of costume interpretations exist. Some women wore long skirts with sweaters or jackets. Some of the older women (but none of those under thirty) wore stylish, conservative clothing along with a knit turban (*bonné*). However, they classified themselves as *muhaggabat* when asked. Many of the younger women and some of the older women wore plain, dark-colored, loosely fitting tunics and long skirts. Some of these garments are fitted at the waist, while others hang straight like a loose coat. One woman remarked to a friend of mine that although she had adopted the *higab*, she still wore dresses with a waist, presenting herself as someone who had not completely transformed herself.

There are other ambiguities in the selection and categorization of the respondents. Certain women were described as partial *muhaggabat,* or fad followers, by other women. They wore the headcovering that covered their throat or went down to their shoulders. Below that they wore Western clothing. Quite a few wore rather daring styles—for example, tight pants, short skirts, or open necklines. There were women who also wore such combinations along with full makeup. They also wore brighter colors than other *muhaggabat*, patterned materials, and in some cases a brightly colored or metallic twisted scarf or cord to hold their headcloth in place, bedouin style. Would the true *muhaggabat* please stand up?

Manufacturers of *higab* now market items of Islamic dress in a wider range of models and prices. Certain shops specialize in providing these fashions ready-made, of varying quality and price. Other women sew their own clothes or have a seamstress make them up.

Islamic designer-label gowns, skirts, tunics, and headcoverings were manufactured; pictures of the Yves St. Laurent logo appeared on photographs of the head veil not only in Egypt, but in Iran and in Saudi Arabia.[2] Women may exhibit their economic status or expensive tastes if they choose. That option directly contradicts one of the purposes of wearing Islamic dress, to declare parity among adherents.

Fourteen percent of the veiled women in the group surveyed were *munaqqabat*—that is, they completely cover their faces with a face veil (*niqab*) and often wear gloves as well as the *higab*. This form of Islamic dress was fairly unusual during the 1970s and early 1980s, but growing numbers of women have adopted it.

The other 38 percent of the respondents were unveiled. Some of these women are seriously thinking about wearing *higab*. A few said that they will veil after they get married; another claimed she would put on the *higab* when she was older. Several of the already veiled women declared their intention to put on the *niqab*, the face veil, in the future.

Interviews developed from a questionnaire and were designed to outline a social profile. Respondents were also questioned about their self-definitions, their perceptions of the political and economic environment, their faith, the role of religion, and their attitudes toward employment, the family, education, and household management. Respondents were asked to define femininity or an ideal woman in a very specific manner (see appendix A).

The images of veiled and unveiled women that emerged from this data provide a counterpoint to the literature written about or by the Islamists. However, the respondents' statements only lead to theory if one understands some of the socioeconomic interactions of Cairo.

A separate set of in-depth interviews focused on the political impact of women and gender issues in the current state institutions and in the oppositionist groups. The respondents discussed their conceptions of political and social change, recent legislation, and social attitudes involving gender issues. Respondents volunteered interpretations of what they called "traditional values." They also assessed the interaction of the state and the Islamists.

Sometimes I felt that I was visiting different planets, as I sat in the afternoon in a political leader's resplendent villa, and in the evening, in dark and crowded dormitory rooms in Giza. The most significant factors in polarizing women into groups supporting or fearing the Islamists were varying standards of living and material expectations, age differentials, and contrasts in social background. I have therefore included some statistical information that pertains to the conditions surrounding women.

Young Women

A profile constructed from my respondents shows that the veiled woman under thirty has a two-in-three possibility of coming from outside of Cairo, either from a provincial capital or from a rural area. Women came from very different socioeconomic backgrounds. Typically, the young *muhaggaba* hopes to marry and raise children instead of pursuing a full-time career. She prays, observes the Ramadan fast, hopes to make the pilgrimage (hajj), and talks about Islam's social implications with her peers.

The profile of the unveiled young women varies significantly from that of the *muhaggaba*, as will be seen below and in chapter 6. The major variables showing a correlation to their attitudes toward the Islamists appear to be father's and mother's occupations, place of birth, and career interest.

Geographic Derivation

Three-fourths of the veiled respondents, (75 percent) list one or both parents born outside of Cairo. A large number (65 percent) were not born in Cairo but moved there as young adults, with 54 percent of those under thirty hailing from Lower Egypt, mostly from large provincial cities. Although other Egyptians mentioned that the Islamists were quite strong in Upper Egypt, in fact only about 20 percent of the veiled women or their parents came from Upper Egyptian towns or villages.

Statistics for Egypt indicate that the general population is pyramidically shaped by age group and that rural and urban populations are about equal. Migration to Cairo and to provincial urban centers has been very high, and one could expect a high number of rural-born respondents in any random sample. In this sample, the higher number of rural-born *muhaggabat* appears to be positively correlated with attitudes against paid full-time employment for women.

In this study, many of the *muhaggabat* who came from provincial centers are designated in tables as "rural" born, but they have always lived an urban lifestyle. If the entire sample had been drawn from university students, the rural tilt would have been more pronounced, because students of rural or provincial origins are drawn through the examination system into universities in Cairo.

Age

A high proportion of veiled women in this study, 48 percent, were under twenty-seven and most of these were under twenty-four. The lowest proportion of veiled women were in the group of women aged forty-five and over (see table 4.1). This particular correlation reveals an inverse relationship of aging to veiling.

This study in no way purports to be a reflection of the macrosociety, but if this correlation holds outside this study, then some assumptions could be made regarding a "generation gap" effect. I asked respondents how they

Table 4.1
Age Range of Veiled and Unveiled Women as Percentage of Survey

Age	Veiled Women Frequency	Percentage	Unveiled Women Frequency	Percentage
20–26	24	48	7	14
27–45	3	06	4	08
46 and over	4	08	8	16

explained this trend. Young women answered that since older women often wore very conservative clothing, and sometimes still wore traditional head-coverings, Islamic dress seemed less imperative to them. Elite, unveiled women, particularly academics, felt that aging women were viewed, or regarded themselves, as less of a sexual temptation to strange men, and that the *higab* was therefore less necessary. Older veiled women disagreed with these responses and said that wearing *higab* was a woman's duty, regardless of her age.

An inverse relationship of veiling to age in Egypt is noteworthy because over the years, older women have often dressed in a more conservative manner or worn black, as elsewhere in the Mediterranean.[3] After the earlier debate over the face veil, women replaced the traditional or Turkish-style outer wrap with a coat. Older women continued to dress more conservatively than their daughters, right on through the miniskirt era. But the modern reversal of that trend does not surprise those who are conversant with both the historical debate over female morality and the current Egyptian milieu.[4]

Socioeconomic Background

Of the veiled women, 47 percent of those under thirty, and 78 percent of those over thirty, listed their fathers' employment as a white-collar job. However, a white-collar classification includes some very low-level (and low salaried) public-sector employees (*mawazzaf*).[5] Blue-collar jobs made up 21 percent of their fathers' employment. This grouping included mosque employees, bus drivers (see table 4.2.) and a carpenter (who was not in business

Table 4.2
Father's Occupation

Father's Occupation	Respondent's Age	% of Veiled Women	% of Unveiled Women
White-collar	20–30	47	87
Merchant, craftsmen, and moneylender	" "	16	7
Blue-collar	" "	21	06
Farmers (includes landowners who employ others)	" "	16	0
White-collar	30 and older	78	80
Merchants or craftsmen	" "	17	10
Farmers	" "	05	10

for himself). Merchants, craftsmen, and moneylenders are considered part of the petite bourgeoisie in Egypt. The prevailing theory amongst the older unveiled women interviewed was that the *muhaggabat* were primarily children of the petite bourgeoisie (which *they* defined to include lower-paid white-collar workers).

Sixteen percent of the younger women were children of farmers. All were born and brought up in rural or semirural areas. Only 5 percent of the older women were children of farmers; most had lived in large cities all their lives.

The mothers of veiled women were housewives more often than were the mothers of unveiled women (82 percent as compared to 76 percent) (see table 4.3). Women (veiled and unveiled) whose mothers had worked seemed to gain an enhanced sense of their own value and potential as human beings outside of the home. Seventy-seven percent of the veiled women plan to marry and have children, and do not want to work, even if they now attend college. Other veiled women (33 percent) did not object to a combination of work and marriage. It is very interesting that this group had the same proportion of working mothers as did the unveiled women under thirty.

Table 4.3
Relationship of Respondents with Working Mothers and Career Plans

	Housewife Mothers	Working Mothers	Working or Career Plans	Not-working or Marriage Plans
% unveiled respondents	76	24	54	46
% veiled respondents	82	18	33	77
% total of respondents, veiled and unveiled	75	25	41	59

Veiled women were sometimes defensive in explaining their future goals and expressed their insecurity through the phrasing and volume of their responses and in body language. The women who argued against careers for women used one or more of the following arguments, sometimes by citing *hadith:*

• Women need to be morally protected and kept away from men who would take advantage of them
• Women deserve to be supported economically
• Women's emotionalism, which stems from their hormonal cycle, impedes their job performance

- Women lack *aql* (reason) as compared to men, and so their judgment is not as sound
- Women bond with their children; if they leave their children in childcare, then they are distracted all the time, thinking and worrying about them
- Children need to have their mother close by, others will not care as well for them, they will become disobedient, selfish or demanding without their mothers. (Women said, "A child is a plant, and the mother is both sunshine and water.")

Other women who were just as adamantly against working women disliked the tone of their co-respondents' arguments, although they said that certain arguments were "part of the *shari'ah*" (a debatable point). Some very lively discussions ensued among the respondents.

Middle-Aged and Older Women

A general profile of the women over thirty varies greatly from that of the younger women. Eighty percent of the older *muhaggabat* listed both parents coming from Cairo, while 20 percent listed parents coming from provinces in Upper Egypt or outside Cairo. A higher percentage of both unveiled and veiled older women came from white-collar homes than did the younger women. Not unexpectedly, they also married men of white-collar professions.

Most older women said that their mothers had not worked, but several had been active in charitable organizations. A few of the oldest women were brought up when a lady was not supposed to work for wages, but she would not dishonor her family if she works for *ajr*, or "spiritual reward."[6] Foreign visitors to the region, Edward Lane, and Savary before him, idealized the leisurely life of women in the "hareem." Lane also used the myth of the idle women to deplore the laziness of a subject population.[7] Of course their households did not run themselves, and deft planning and administrative skills were required.[8] The myth, however, lingers on. Because of a strong concern for family honor, some elite women were ambivalent about careers for their daughters, in spite their own unpaid contributions of time and energy.[9]

As a group, the older women were usually better established financially than the younger women. Their position affects their perspectives; collectively, they represented more education and more interpersonal experience than did the younger respondents. These women over thirty have witnessed the importance and intensity of gender issues within their own lives, and their responses reflect their experiences.

Self-Labeling

Although 72 percent of the older women are employed and some of the others work as volunteers, most of them say their primary role is being a parent, wife, or "homemaker" rather than a lawyer, an educator, or an author. All but one of the veiled women over thirty identified themselves as mothers or wives, although most worked or were volunteers. Some of this subgroup felt that women are best suited for traditionally female careers: health care, social services, and teaching.

Women over thirty spoke of their "double day"; they have little time to relax, and without complaining, they talked about how tired they were and described symptoms of stress. But each has developed techniques for time management, and some can count on their own relatives to help. Generally, their husbands do not do any housework, cooking, or childcare, although some will shop for specific items. They supported any state measures, especially those involving childcare, that address women's double work load.

Most of the young women are students, and that is how they label themselves. If they also work, they did not at first volunteer that fact, although some do work part-time or during summers, generally in low-paying jobs as clerks or service personnel. One works as a bank clerk, and two graduate students work as teaching assistants.

Personal Goals

Some of the younger women are ambitious, but most are not entering traditionally male-dominated fields. Most of the women under thirty want to get married, and work until then, or only if they need the income.

Only 23 percent of the young veiled women mentioned career goals. Nine percent of the veiled women thought they might be able to combine marriage and a career. Eighty-one percent of the veiled respondents, and 62 percent of the unveiled respondents under thirty said that combining a family and a career is impossible. In addition to the earlier arguments against female employment, they stated that Islam itself dictates a sexual division of labor in which men bear economic responsibility. They felt that female employment implies a degree of role reversal, which is unsanctioned morally and unacceptable to men socially, and psychologically. The pressures that a husband feels when his wife works would disturb his pride, and destroy marital harmony.

The personal goals of the older women were more varied than those of younger women. These goals ranged from altruistic aims regarding the development of society to hopes for "good" marriages for their children. Many described special projects they hoped to be able to complete. Quite a few had embarked on midlife careers that included ambitious goals after their children had grown up.

Parental Influence

Certain respondents acknowledged that their parents had pressured them in their own career and marriage choices. Others denied parental influence and typically said, "I was free to choose whoever I wanted, but of course, my parents' opinion was important to me."[10]

Parents of many of the younger women had preferred certain fields for their daughters, but under the current examination system their wishes are often irrelevant. A middle-aged veiled woman admitted that she had obeyed her parents' wishes and now felt that she should have pursued art and design instead. Her parents had also wanted her to marry rather young, and she said that she had been too young. Another woman mentioned that when she was growing up, parents expected their daughters to complete their education before getting married. Now, I was told, many of the elite are marrying their daughters off earlier for social and economic benefits.[11] Actually most of the younger women in my study hoped to finish their studies before marriage. In any case, few of the young men they knew could afford to get married, for marriage involves the purchase of a flat, household furniture, appliances, and the wedding expenses.

Parents are still confidantes, and sometimes matchmakers. Daughters want them to approve and bless the men they choose. Some women, who said their marriages were not arranged, had married relatives contacted through the family network. A twenty-one-year-old middle-class unveiled student said:

> My parents have played a very important role; they knew my fiancé and arranged my marriage. Still, they prefer that I continue to work and retain my own personality and goals. Now my fiancé doesn't want me to work, but I'll break the engagement if I get a good job and he won't agree [to her career].

A woman of forty-two with grown children told me:

> It was easy for me, you see, my husband was related to my mother, so I had always seen him, and I knew him. My parents approved of the match because he had a good job, a respectable position in which he could rise to the next level, in time.

Elite women seemed to have had more freedom to choose their marriage partners than lower-middle-class women in my survey within each age grouping. But elite women considered their families' reactions. Olfat Kamel, an unveiled politician and representative in the parliament, described to me her family's debate over her career. It came down to a vote at the dinner table, and her husband and children did not agree with each other. She laughed as she told me that of course she abided "with the majority," as in any democracy, and embarked on her career.[12]

Employment

Generally, employed women stated that their friends and co-workers had been supportive of their careers, as were their families. However, quite a few had put their career plans on hold for many years at the request of their husbands. The same forty-two-year-old woman explained,

> I stayed home with my two boys when they were little, because that's what my husband asked me to do. But when they were old enough to go together to daycare, it was time for me to work and go on with my studies.

When asked what would prevent them from full-time employment, younger veiled women often answered that "full-time work is not appropriate for *women*." Unveiled younger women cited "husband's or fiancé's negative attitudes" or "needs of children" as reasons not to work. Older women said that their husbands had disapproved, but in fact most (80 percent) had gone to work anyway. Older elite women had trusted servants, who had been their own nannies, to take care of their young children. Others had the help of their own parents to provide childcare while they worked.

Most respondents approved of the current state policies that support maternity leaves, equal pay, and childcare at industries and of the gains made through the reforms of the Personal Status Laws.[13] Some younger veiled women disagreed. They claimed that these policies were only necessary because secular laws had not introduced justice or equality. The state had been overly influenced by Western attitudes toward gender. If women would take their family responsibilities seriously, many would leave their current jobs. The ongoing furor over women in the workplace would abate. In any case, if the state (or the Islamists) implemented the *shariʿah*, the Personal Status reforms would not hold. A reevaluation of woman's true social role in an Islamic society would have to be undertaken. A few of these younger women felt that some women took advantage of the current maternity leave policy to hold their positions for years. They felt it would be more fair to co-workers and the departments in general if these women left their jobs and reentered the workforce later on.

Several of the unveiled older women claimed that the drafting and implementation of the reforms of 1985 did not challenge the underlying patriarchal structure strongly enough. For example, legislators and lawyers used the concept and term "alimony of the *mutʿa*" (the woman who is enjoyed) to provide a legal rationale for alimony within the amendments of the Personal

Status Laws. The very notion of "alimony" beyond the three-month waiting period known as the ʿiddah is absent from traditional Islamic family law.[14] Those drafting the law invoked the idea of compensation for sexual services, to satisfy religious leaders who had stridently protested this introduction of alimony, calling it an "innovation" (bidʿah).[15] These women felt that the amendments to the Personal Status Laws should have gone further and made fewer concessions to the conservatives and Islamists (who are strongly represented in the Lawyer's Union and now within Parliament). They also understand that women need to be educated about their new options and that there are problems with enforcement of the reforms. The courts must be willing to more swiftly penalize husbands who disregard the changes in the law.

Another respondent told me that discriminatory hiring practices are still applied to female applicants to the foreign service. Current hiring procedures are officially supposed to discourage discrimination on the basis of sex, and the written examination held by the Foreign Service shields candidates names during the grading process. But the applicants must also undergo a personal interview, which is used as an oral examination. Interviewers inquire if women are married or have marriage plans. They may ask what women applicants would do if they became pregnant or if they would take an assignment around the world, in a war zone, or at a remote location. Would they contract and be happy with a long-distance marriage? Interviewers can say that women's responses show "inappropriate" attitudes for appointment.[16] Administrators in this area regard female candidates as less likely to be stable in the job, and believe that appointing women will cost them more time and money than hiring men.

Other difficulties exist in the realization of equal rights. Several respondents told me how factory owners hire just short of one hundred women employees so that they do not have to provide a childcare facility as ordered by law.

Family and Household

Most of the young veiled women declared that they planned to practice family planning. Women often said that two children were the ideal family size, but sometimes they then said that one must thank God for however many, or few, children He chooses to bestow. One young veiled woman insisted that she wants a lot of children, eight at least. She now teaches and is completing an advanced degree in plant physiology, but she would like instead to pursue Islamic studies and write about children after she marries. This young woman was in charge of the dormitory floor and is four or five years older than the residents. She was more confident and forceful than the younger women, and none of the women contradicted her at length during our discussions. "Good luck," I said sincerely, "I've found it very difficult to write and study while raising a child. Eight children could be quite a challenge!" "But you don't *understand*," she said, "it is women's duty to give our best to the *ummah* (the community of Muslims) and to build an Islamic society."[17]

Younger veiled women asked me what I did with my daughter, who has been in full-time daycare since she was eighteen months old. They understood my situation, but most would not want to use outside childcare themselves, deeming it as foreign as the Wimpie's of Cairo. They deplored the existing state-funded centers and thought that the private centers had inadequate spaces and staff. Working women who use childcare facilities have also complained that they are inadequate and are not free of charge.[18]

However, several young veiled women worked at my daughter's childcare facility in Cairo. It was their job, of course, but they did not agree that outside care generally had ill effects on the children. They saw no conflict between their own religiosity and the service they provide to other working women.

Young women understood that children are a responsibility and an expense, in accordance with arguments for family planning. At the same time they idealize the role of the family. Some of the younger women believed that the national birth control program might be based on a "Western conspiracy" to decimate Muslims. But the knowledge that under inflation, raising extra children impoverishes all of society overrides their suspicions. So their "religiously" derived attitudes are mitigated by the socioeconomic environment.

Some people continue to believe in the importance of having many children, because the state has not developed an adequate social security program.[19] These attitudes were predicted to change when the infant mortality rate declined, and with the improvement of health and medical resources. Now, in the uncertain economic environment, exacerbated by the growing population and lack of resources, parents who live longer must depend on the economic support of their children (see table 4.4). Some children may emigrate, and others will not make enough money to support their parents. One study showed that many of those in resettled areas received help from their children (about 56.6 percent of a fairly large sample, 768), and even in urban areas that was true of 22.4 percent.[20]

I talked to lower-class working women who believed that having more than two children, especially boys, was desirable and even essential under current conditions. Daughters were needed to help with housework and childcare.[21] However, these activities do not directly contribute income, nor can an unemployed wife contribute directly to the family's future security. Yet the wife supports her husband's earning power. These observations help to explain why the Islamists have not excluded the indirect economic value of

Table 4.4
Changes in Health Indicators from 1965 to 1987 in Egypt

	1965	*1987*
Infant mortality per 1,000 births	173	85
Life expectancy	48	61
Population per physician	2,300	790

Source: World Bank, *World Development Report*, (Washington D.C.: World Bank June 1989).

women and children in their ideology. A broad sector of society also separates the economic explanations from the moral explanations of women's reproductive value.

All of the older respondents controlled the household budget, and some paid other bills. Several also employed accountants to deal with financial matters outside the household. All of these women were responsible for housework and childrearing. Their husbands might review their children's homework, attend to their religious education, or play with them for limited periods of time. Most women said they cooperatively made decisions with their husbands regarding their children. Major family decisions were made as partners, including purchases made with the husband's income.

Typically, the lower-class or lower-middle-class husband hands over his paycheck to his wife, reserving a certain amount of spending money for himself. This is not usually true among the elite, who have other incomes or assets besides their salaries. Egyptian women may have greater economic control over spending than women in Western households, where the husband hands out an allowance to his wife, or where two-income couples divide up payments of various expenses.

Both younger and older women spoke of their husbands' expectations of a perfectly managed household, excellent food, attentiveness, and maintenance of their personal "space" (keeping the kids quiet while papa naps or reads his newspapers, for example). Quite a few women complained of their husbands' "Oriental ways" (their term). That meant many things: selfishness, extreme jealousy, controlling behavior, and disregard for their wives' feelings. These women are not silent; they chastise their husbands, but they say that once a man is grown, it is unlikely that he will change.

Perceptions of Environment

When asked "What two things would you change in your life if you could?" many women talked about their social environment. Younger women observe that dating and meeting men unknown to their families is problematic.

Young and older women feel that social interaction in Cairo, in general, is a disintegrating process. They pointed out that social anomie and growing materialism interfered with personal relationships and made people suspicious, rude, materialistic, and concerned only with the external and the superficial. Many mentioned typical urban problems such as traffic, crowding, and fast-paced living. One young woman said that if she could effect any change, it would be ''the transformation of the Oriental man, who looks down on his women.'' Another young unveiled student responded at first, ''But I couldn't change anything, social tradition doesn't permit us to actually alter things.''[22]

Most of the veiled women said they hope for the realization of an Islamic state, or that all other women will wear the *higab*. A smaller number of these young women listed personal goals such as travel or study of a foreign language.

Both veiled and unveiled young women wished that those around them would shoulder more social responsibility. People should be more honest, and care about and help each other when possible. Women felt that the concept of *shahama,* or sincere concern and effort for others, is dying in today's Cairo.

Older women responded by listing both changes that they had not made and changes that they might be able to bring about.

> Instead of the School of Commerce I should have gone into the arts. Secondly I should have married later.
> I want to improve my culture through reading and political participation. [I want] to start an exercise program.
> I hope to see an Islamic society gain strength throughout the country. I intend to spend time with a reading group to discuss religious and social matters.[23]
> I want to change my job to one closer to my home. This way commuting won't take up so much time.[24]

Most respondents answered questions regarding their changing political environment by launching into discussions of the declining economic conditions in Egypt. High inflation, increases in the cost of living, and currency problems affected them and their families directly.

Some respondents spoke of a superficial difference between the Sadat and Mubarak regimes with regard to institutionalized democratization and the prosecution of corruption. Others felt that one could see a meaningful contrast of the two eras in terms of political reorganization and increased freedom for the individual and the press.

One young woman commented on the leaders' performances as public speakers. She said that she and her friends thought Sadat a charismatic and eloquent speaker, while Mubarak was less imposing but more clever. Under Sadat, certain groups and individuals gained an extraordinary measure of illicit wealth. A small segment of society controlled most of the access to public goods. She felt that neither trend had subsided during the political transition. Although some individuals had been investigated, in a crackdown on the corruption of the previous regime, other "crooks" had replaced them. Finally, she pointed out that despite Mubarak's opening up of political criticism and free speech in a let-a-thousand-flowers-bloom current, the regime's internal corruption and problems remained unexposed. She said that "the real story about any Egyptian ruler and his kitchen court emerges only after he dies, when more people are able to speak or write books without fear of reprisals."[25]

Other respondents who were reluctant to answer these questions frankly may have been reacting to the political climate following the "Riyan affair" of 1988. To summarize, one of the largest of the investment sharing companies, known as Islamic Banking ventures, had closed its doors due to a run on assets early in November. Although a run had occurred two years previously with no losses for depositors, this time around the bank claimed that they could not access the invested capital. The wife of Ahmad Riyan, the oldest of the three brothers controlling the company, quickly divorced him, reportedly to retain her own assets and possessions. Then, Ahmad Riyan was found dead early in the morning due to an "accidental overdose" of sleeping pills.[26] The other brothers were jailed. The government promised to recover the depositors' assets but failed. One analyst estimated that a quarter of a million people lost their savings.[27]

The regime was put on the spot. Intellectuals and members of the elite and the upper middle class who opposed the Islamists felt that the state might reclaim both face and control following the Riyan affair. But many of my respondents really did not view either side as hero or villain, and they were fairly cynical about the future. Some feared to speak too frankly about a still-volatile situation. Those who believed that an "Islamic state" was plausible in Egypt held more negative views of the state and its reactions than their co-respondents who disagreed with that proposition. They believed that the government's commitment to secularism had tainted the redistributive functions of the state. They claimed that the regime had been so preoccupied with surveilling and controlling the people, and maintaining the current bureaucratic system, that it had neither planned adequately for cohesive reforms nor considered the potential disaster that the alternative banks, as one of the many solutions of civil society, represented. People had jumped at the chance for a 20 percent return (or higher) on their money, a financial enticement that was difficult to resist. And the debacle, that probably stemmed from the previous stock market crash in the United States, really underlined Egyptian financial linkages with the world system of capitalism.

All of the *muhaggabat*, young and old, believed that Egypt could become an Islamic state. They thought that a civil war or some sort of political and economic disaster would occur if the secular state proved stronger than the Islamists. Several of the veiled women delivered rather sophisticated assessments of the weak points of the Islamists, as did certain older unveiled respondents. They noted the movement's lack of a charismatic leader, or at least unified leadership. They mentioned the lack of careful planning for a future Islamic state with regard to social and economic planning. They felt that adherence to the principles of ʿadala, social justice, and economic redistribution, and an outlawing of usury, was indeed imperative, but that a clearly structured and phased program for reform was required. Some talked about the difficult logistics of applying the principles of *shura*, consultation, that some Islamists called "Islamic democracy," when in fact some hierarchical rigidity exists within the Islamist groups, just as it does in society.

Several of the older and younger veiled respondents said that an Islamic state would *improve* the status of women. Perhaps the phrasing of my question simply incited them to challenge it in response to the international media's claims that the status of women is generally low in Islamic countries. They felt that a reemphasis on the "family woman" (*marʾah usriyah*) and an inclusion of women within the reorganization of society would bring this improvement about.

Another question, "Can Egypt become an Islamic state?" was confusing to the respondents. Women identified Egypt today as an "Islamic state" by virtue of the religion of the majority of its inhabitants and its lengthy Islamic history. I clarified the idea of separation of state and religion, and then the respondents distinguished between the current and idealized religious state. Still, many women considered the nature of the state to be culturally and historically predisposed to a religious form.

On the other hand, 75 percent of the unveiled women felt that Egypt could not become an Islamic state under the direction of the current Islamist groups. Nevertheless, many of the unveiled women saw the Islamists as a substantial threat to the secular state. Thirteen percent of veiled and unveiled women said that veiling would become more widespread if the Islamic groups prevailed over the state. Seven percent said that the status of the Christian minority in Egypt, the Copts, would become more problematic along with that scenario.

Those who were apprehensive of the founding of an Islamic state felt that the current regime was pursuing policies against these groups that were simultaneously too tough and too accommodating. The older unveiled women felt that the state was violating the human rights of its citizens and thereby encouraging antagonism against itself. They said that the state was garnering mass sympathy for the Islamists through the arrests made in 1988.[28] At the same time, they felt that the media was over-emphasizing religiosity; that too much coverage was being given to various elements of Islamic activism. They felt that the government was mistaken in believing that by including Islamic moderates in the system, their aim of transforming the state would successfully be deflected. They referred here in part to the coalitions formed in 1987 and 1988 between the *Ikhwan al-Muslimin* and other minority party factions, and also to the governmental appointments of Islamist individuals.

The younger and generally more apolitical respondents characterized the state as a very powerful and undivided entity. They felt that the government's plans to control the Islamists were clever and well organized, but they predicted an ultimate victory for the Islamists. Some women protested the insufficient freedoms of speech and assembly that the Islamists and their sympathizers possess, referring to the restrictions placed by university officials on the *Ikhwan* and other Islamist groups on campuses. The older women felt that the Islamists had taken over the campuses by sending in mature organizers to recruit students. The younger women view the growing number of student sympathizers with the oppositionists to be an independent phenomenon—the natural outgrowth of a new emphasis on Islam throughout society.

Personal Belief and Self-Image

The two determinants of religiosity most often mentioned by the respondents were the *higab* and a notion of dedication to one's fellow Muslims. The *higab* is felt to be a sign of religious identity and sincere belief by veiled women and by about 40 percent of the unveiled women.

The respondents were asked, "Do you consider yourself a religious person, and why?" The most prevalent answer of those under thirty years old was: "Since I veil, I am religious" or "Because I don't veil yet I am not religious enough." Older women first responded, "Because I believe in God and I try to deal with people in the right way." Younger women were also more likely to define their religiosity in terms of their practice of *salat* (prayer), of reading the Qur°an, and of fasting. Older elite women stressed their attempts to pursue social equity. One woman exhibited some discomfort with this question because she wondered if the question referred to the external signs of faith:

> It depends what you mean by "religious." I don't pray, I don't fast, so if that's what you mean, then I'm not religious. But I have a certain philosophy about religion, which I may find when I go to hell is the wrong one. I have a very broad idea about what a religion is supposed to be and Islam gives me the opportunity to believe in this way. Islam is a *dïn mu°amalah* [a religion of social association and reciprocity]; religion is how you treat people, how you live your life, and in that sense I am religious.[29]

Most of the women said that being a Muslim in the modern age is not a problematic condition. Unveiled women, however, mentioned that the veiled women, especially those completely veiled (*munaqqabat*), must be very uncomfortable in the heat. Veiled women denied their discomforts and said very sternly that they had to satisfy their personal commitment to their faith before all else, for the fires of hell were hotter still.

Other women stated that their faith permits them to acknowledge the dual nature of their religious obligations: to God and to their community. A twenty-year-old unveiled woman expressed the concept by citing a popular saying, which she expanded on, saying:

> You must deal with the world as if you will live forever, but you must conceive of your relationship to God as if you will die tomorrow. You must do both and do them well.[30]

The young veiled women especially wanted to make sure that I understood the immutability of the Islamic message; that they did not approve of reform or amendment to particular historical circumstances. One informant stated:

> To have religion that does not cover life completely is not a sound faith. To change one's faith because circumstances in life change, no, that would mean one isn't a soundly religious person. In what is Islam, when one memorizes the Qur'an and its precepts, there is no change and no alteration. . . . Perhaps that is possible in other religions, but not in Islam.[31]

And another respondent added: "One can't negate the timelessness of the Holy Qur'an." She explained that the Qur'an was designed to apply to all people of every era. Mernissi and others have referred to this type of assertion as a part of the "ahistoricity" of modern Muslims. Mernissi believes that ahistoricity negatively affects Middle Eastern society and its potential for true democratization.[32] The Islamist leaders refer to "the true Islam" when addressing their readers or followers, and adherents defend "the true Islam" from doubt without justifying their separation of *reformable* and *unchangeable* issues. As long as they fail to recognize that the course of time has in fact permitted change in certain areas, the appellation *ahistorical* is apt.

Most of the young veiled women stressed the positive aspects of traditional practices in Egypt regarding women that they rightly or wrongly term "Islamic." Women in all four categories—younger, older, veiled, and unveiled—emphasized a woman's right to retain her name, income, and bridewealth during marriage.[33] Younger women felt that a woman's right to consent to her marriage partner is an essential right within *shariʿah* that family members have sometimes withheld illegitimately in the past. Most young women admitted that there were negative aspects of women's status that were really abuses or misunderstandings of women's rights under the *shariʿah*. For example, men had abused their rights to polygamy and easy divorce.

Young veiled women deliberately shifted questions regarding the "practices" affecting women to subjective attitudes toward women. They spoke of the esteem that the maternal qualities and functions of women are granted in Islamic culture. Others pointed to the wearing of *higab* as a practice that they saw as positive and protective of the woman's reputation, but they emphasized men's reactions to unveiled women. Men immediately labeled women as "attractive, available, and sexually accessible," they said, when they saw women walking unveiled in the street.

A few of the older women, on the other hand, listed other traditional practices that have been falsely termed "Islamic," such as physical abuse of women by their parents and husbands, pursuit of male honor through preserving female sexual chastity by controlling behavior, murdering offending female family members, and so on. Older women felt that the state had attempted to address these behaviors, but that only education could complete this task. Younger women did not bring up these issues at all.

Veiling

The majority of the younger veiled women saw the *higab* as a symbol of change. This change was not only a personal and moral decision, but represented a social sisterhood to them. These veiled women under thirty had been wearing *higab* on the average for seven years. The *munaqqabat* had been wearing the face veil for an average of four years after "graduating" from the ordinary *higab*. I realized that meant that most had been wearing the *higab* in secondary school. Almost all of them said that family members had not convinced them to wear *higab*, but a few admitted that teachers or fellow students in secondary school had encouraged them to begin veiling.

In fact, many of the veiled women said their families hated their *higab* at first and were very upset. Gradually, their parents and siblings became accustomed to the idea and accepted their appearance and new ideas. One elite middle-aged woman said that her mother and siblings did not like it when she began wearing *higab*. Her husband, who is a powerful member of the business elite, was embarrassed by her decision. He told her that she already dressed conservatively, and that she therefore need not adopt *higab*. Now, he is quite proud of her, as are her religiously and socially liberal brothers. Her mother and sisters have begun veiling as well.

Several respondents described their decision as a momentous one, made after a period of introspection. Some decided while abroad that they would veil upon their return. Two young respondents partially attributed their veiling to their extended stays in Saudi Arabia.

Unmarried veiled women are convinced that their husbands will approve of and require the wearing of *higab*. When I related to them the story of a

Muslim man who did not want his wife to wear *higab*, all the younger veiled women felt she should divorce him. I was intrigued. On the one hand, they upheld a woman's right to pursue her own conviction even if her marriage was at stake. On the other hand, they continuously stressed a woman's duty to obey her husband and to put her marriage before all else.

Unveiled women thought that the *higab* had caught on because university students and other working women have been paid to don the *higab* by the *Ikhwan* and other groups. One respondent related the story of a nurse whose salary was 45 L.E. per month. This nurse was approached by agents of the *Ikhwan* and asked to stay at home for the same pay. The woman who told me the story felt certain that it was true, and that other women must also have been paid to quit their jobs and wear *higab*. Despite these stories, there was no evidence that any of the respondents were receiving financial help, tutoring, or supplies provided directly by the Islamists.[34]

The *higab*'s true historical origin did not appear to matter much to its proponents. Veiled women of both age groups held that the style of *higab* that they had adopted was identical to the costume worn by the Muslim women in the Medinan community. I kept pointing out (to their annoyance) that this particular version of *higab*, including the headcovering of plain material, wimple-like covering of the neck, and long garments, does not come from any of the earlier garments for covering, the Ottoman face veil, the *izar* (an outerwear wrap), the *carsaf* (a rectangular cotton or silk wrap or dress), or from traditional Egyptian dress, the Mamluk *thaub*, the *malaya* (an outer wrap), or even from the *burqa* (face veil of folk dress).[35] I asked women if this was the *higab* that was worn in the 1940s by the Muslim Sisters, but many disagreed. Although women did not agree with each other about the origins of dress style, they replied firmly that it covered the appropriate portions of the body as described in the Qur'an.[36] The earliest evidence of a similar form of *higab* that I located was a fourteenth-century Persian representation of the birth of Muhammad, in which four women wear headshawls resembling the modern *higab*.[37] Persian women of that century were also represented with uncovered hair, and nothing quite like this style is represented in the Arab world in the early medieval period.[38]

Unveiled respondents disagreed with the *muhaggabat* that the wearing of *higab* constituted a religious duty (*fard*) for Muslim women. Younger women felt that the *higab* required some moral preparation. Comments included the following: "To wear *higab*, a woman must behave like an angel," or

> After all, one can't take it off again, once you start wearing it, that would be terrible. People would really look down on someone who did that. So, I want to be very secure in my decision before I make it.[39]

Several older women stated that the interpretation of what was actually worn in the first century is open to speculation. They expressed anger and distress at the idea that their hair or arms were considered as sexual objects. They felt that this way of thought presupposed and institutionalized a lack of male self-control. They referred here to the belief that a woman's body or voice is ʿawra (pudendal) and must be concealed.[40] The concept includes the idea that a woman is a source of *fitnah,* or social discord.[41] They disagreed with the Islamist interpretion of both ideas, and claimed that because woman has a soul and intelligence equal to that of a man, she must be regarded as more than a sexual body.

The older women, who considered themselves *muhaggabat* yet wore the chic *bonné* rather than the complete *higab*, were very rather guarded in the way they responded to these questions. To them, the *higab* is important as both a political and a religious symbol. They wished that the *higab* and their own midlife decision to wear it would be understood in the context of solidarity of the community and an exhibition of piety.

Fadwa al-Guindi has suggested that veiling was a response to diminished personal space within a crowded public environment.[42] She has claimed that veiling is a psychological response as well as an economic tactic in times of declining real income and therefore demonstrates that the wearer supports an Islamic code of ethics.[43] Unveiled women in this survey thought that explanation was reasonable, and stressed the fact that veiled women could spend less money on clothing, makeup, and expensive haircare. Despite the evidence of designer-label *higab*, and my own visit to a beauty parlor filled with *muhaggabat*, the unveiled women felt that upper-middle-class *muhaggabat* were exceptions. They thought that veiled women wanted to conceal their class origins.

Veiled women disagreed completely with this economic explanation. They also said that *higab* did not make traveling through public spaces easier for them personally, although they acknowledged that such an assumption was reasonable at a superficial level. It was difficult to understand why the respondents would hedge on this point. I decided that it was because they wished me, as an observer and recorder, to interpret their decision to veil as one based on piety and self-control rather than on practicality and pressure from other men and women.

Unveiled women also tended to explain the *higab* in the same vein as Andrea Rugh:

> In some cases the [new Islamic] dress indicates the wearer's more fundamentalist view of religion; in others it is worn more as the latest fashion, *akhir moda.* In this second group, the same girls who several years ago might have worn a mini-skirt as the latest fashion adopt more modest styles now because they have become popular.[44]

As one might expect, the *muhaggabat* disagreed with this sort of explanation, especially the middle-aged and older women.

Femininity

I asked the respondents to describe the attributes of the ideal woman. Their opinions varied a lot. Many women had difficulty separating moral characteristics from physical characteristics. They tended to describe women's idealized *functions,* rather than idealized characteristics. So, at first, the young veiled women tended to respond in this manner:

> The ideal woman must be religious and have faith in religion.
> She must obey her husband and raise her children well.
> She must veil and carry out all her responsibilities in the home.

The young unveiled women also misunderstood the question but answered in a different way:

> The Muslim woman must present an excellent picture, a total picture. It's possible for her to dress nicely, to appear chic. She can dress in any style she wants to, but she must behave in accordance with the rules of her culture.

> The woman is not meant to be equal to the man. This is a fallacy. She will lose her feminine nature that way.[45]

When pressed further to define that feminine nature, about two-thirds of the young veiled women mentioned the qualities of softness, delicacy, and purity. The other third stressed the quality of wisdom. Only a few of the young women who were from large towns outside of Cairo mentioned the quality of *haya',* or shyness, connected with modesty and demureness, or *istisham,* modesty as shame.[46]

Certain young unveiled women expanded their previous definitions and mentioned the qualities of self-assuredness and resourcefulness. They also spoke of a need for intelligence and ambition without aggressiveness.

Some of the middle-aged and older women also confused the notion of function with that of personality characteristics in their responses. Others also gave me a detailed description of how women should look. Several mentioned that a woman's voice is an essential component of her femininity, and that she should express herself in a soft, nonaggressive, yet clever manner.

Those older women who more swiftly understood the implication of the question, responded that courage and strength of character are the most important qualities for a woman. These women were both veiled and unveiled.

The answers to this question demonstrate that the idealization of the "new, virtuous woman," the *muhaggaba,* is conceived in a holistic manner. The characteristics of shyness, delicacy, and softness are important to the Islamists Hoffman-Ladd covers and form the core of the ideal Muslim woman's femininity.[47] Other Islamists balance these qualities with the resourcefulness, intelligence, and courage that are already valued in other models for the modern Egyptian woman. In addition, she should reincorporate traditional characteristics: hospitality, *shahama*, or gallantry, and modesty, and combine them with a "new" element, a spirit of reform (*islah*).

Conclusions of the Survey Data

One may conclude from the survey data that women respond to an evocation of their own self-image in positive ways. When the young veiled women described their beliefs and goals, they communicated a sense of solidarity and strong support from their peers who shared their orientation.

The state had presented a different ideal model for identification to elite women, particularly in the Sadat period. The elite women regarded the veiled women as an unknown and hostile entity. They interpreted the veiled women's message as an attack on their own individuality. A few of the unveiled women who were active in a political setting were more familiar with the moderate Islamist line. These women tried to deemphasize the presence of a competition of images for women, stressing instead the notion that a great variety of interpretations of self-image was present in Egyptian society and was perfectly acceptable.

The profile of the veiled woman, in contrast to her unveiled counterpart, indicates that women may be predisposed to accept this new image by virtue of their socioeconomic background. In the last sixteen years, major socioeconomic changes have taken place in Egypt, heralded by the policies of the economic opening. The resulting income patterns have been combined with increased external migration, certain labor shortages, and other labor surpluses (especially among the college-educated). Consequently, distribution problems within the economy have restricted socioeconomic mobility except for small and highly visible portions of the population.

Skewed development has affected the population in many ways; it has restricted the allocation of public goods to many while guaranteeing those goods to small groups. Political participation has not been widely realized. Ultimately, even the broadening of the political spectrum has not affected the motivations of the regime, which are restricted by economic pressures and the need for massive doses of foreign aid.

The strange mixture of public and private sector that coexists in Egypt presents the ordinary Egyptian with diversity and disparity in work opportunities and conditions. Many employed in the private sector make higher salaries but enjoy less job security. Groups of self-employed tradesmen or professionals have emigrated to the Gulf; others have realized increased income as they have essentially filled labor shortages. Their increased prosperity has not necessarily been matched by increased respectability.

Those educated and employable through the public sector have not always found jobs, and they have limited avenues for advancement, they suffer from disorganization in their offices or work groups, and price and inflation increases hang over their heads. Hence, men perceive women, who are not a large reported section of the workforce (but are concentrated in certain highly visible areas), to be more threatening in the employment arena than statistics indicate, because the workplace itself has become more tenuous to all. The Islamist emphasis on the "family woman," who does not go out of the home for wage employment, allays the fears of unemployed or underpaid men. The battle over women in the workplace is not merely ideological, or a variance of morality codes; it is based on economic fears and social conceptions of status.

Under current conditions, young adults face a myriad of insecurities. The Islamist appeal has been successful due to the combination of several important factors: domestic economic pressures, political and social frustrations, unresolved contradictions in patterns of gender interaction, and pressures on the extended family system under current conditions. One could expect male unemployment to be an important ingredient. However, total unemployment had not risen much as a percentage of the population from 1981 to 1984, although there was an absolute increase (see tables 4.5 and 4.6). For women with previous job experience unemployment actually dropped by half in 1984 from its previous level in 1978. But unemployed women who have never worked before now make up a higher percentage of the total of unemployed persons never previously employed. That figure indicates that more women are seeking employment than in the past. Statistics show that while 108,500 women sought jobs in 1978 out of a total of 300,800, that number rose in 1984 to 265,000 women seeking their first job out of a total of 702,000.[48]

The composition of female employment tells us that while the total of female workers is still relatively low as compared with other Third World countries or with the West, women now make up sizable percentages of certain work categories. (see table 4.7).

On the basis of these figures, one cannot really say that women have entered the workforce in great enough numbers outside the area of agriculture for employed or unemployed men to view them as an overwhelming threat. That is especially true of the productive sector and in sales and services (where, according to the media and the Islamists, women are so visible that we might have expected them to make up a higher proportion of the labor force). There are some men who have never approved of female employment

Table 4.5
Unemployment of Those with Previous Work Experience by Sex (in thousands)

	1978	1980	1981	1984
Total	53.7	50.0	34.5	54.0
Men	47.0	45.5	32.2	50.1
Women	6.7	4.5	2.3	3.9

Table 4.6
Unemployed Persons not Previously Employed in 1984

Total	% of Population	Men	Women
702,000	5.6	437,000	265,000

Source: Yearbook of Labor Statistics, 1989. (Geneva: International Labor Office, 1989). (The most recent information for Egypt is based on 1984 statistics unfortunately. But we know that by 1989, there were approximately 2.5 million unemployed or about 14.7 percent of a population of 54 million.) Source: Social and Labor Bulletin 3–4 (1989) p. 292.

who have been very vocal in recent years in Egypt. To these observers and many older members of Egyptian society, who lived through an era when elite and upper-middle-class women did not work at all, the relatively small increase in the number of working women appears more like an avalanche. Statistics that measure working women in comparison to other societies matter little to critics of female employment, and their opinions are useful to the Islamists.

Many men no longer make enough money at one job to support their families; their frustrations may be directed at the sector in which they work, at the state, or at male and female co-workers. If the entire economic system could be adequately reorganized, jobs would concentrate work that is now dispersed among labor areas. Then workers might make a decent wage at one job. Or if prices, housing, and other costs were better controlled, the worker might not need a second job. Citizens realize that planning based on that sort of logic is unlikely to emerge, hence their frustration is deflected to the female workers whom they view as a source of competition, although statistically this is not, as yet, borne out.

Table 4.7
Employment by Selected Occupation and Sex

	Total	Men	Women
Occupation			
Professional/technical workers	1,415,100	1,000,000	415,100
Administrative managerial	317,000	273,400	43,600
Clerical and related	1,069,800	764,500	305,300
Sales workers	754,500	624,500	130,000
Service sector	889,900	825,700	64,200
Agricultural	4,717,500	3,743,400	974,100
Production related	2,654,800	2,501,400	153,400

Source: Yearbook of Labor Statistics, 1989 (Geneva: International Labor Office). (Also based on 1984 data.)

Women also believe that female employment has exploded in numbers, and veiled women attest to this view more than unveiled women. The statistics describe real conditions from 1981–88 but may not describe the degree of contact that citizens have with their own setting (or how accurate these figures are four or five years later).

The data in this chapter reflect the young women's acceptance of a new image of women formulated by the Islamists. It may be that their socioeconomic and political insecurities provide the strongest reasons for their acceptance of this image, rather than the newfound piety they claim. However, this hypothesis cannot definitively be proven because this analysis must be based on the verbal evidence presented by the respondents. Most of the *muhaggabat* declared that piety and a new realization of the meaning of Islam were the organizing principles of their lifeviews at this time. Consequently, the success or rewards of the new image are what I suggest, rather than a very clear picture of how women felt before they became *muhaggabat*.

My respondents were capable of varying degrees of introspection and self-criticism. Older women appeared most able to utilize these techniques in their insights on the function and "nature" of women. Younger women more often exhibited a defense that has been called "Third Worldism" in current feminist debate. That is, they considered their definitions of femininity and gender relations inapplicable to and unrelated to definitions created in the First World, where increased female employment has heightened certain gender-related contradictions within society. These women were also convinced of the biologically "correct" or "natural" order of gender and their own role interpretions.

The message of the moderate Islamists is viewed by Egyptians, especially younger women, as a response to social, economic, and political factors beyond their control that limit their personal potential participation within the system. The data indicate that the outlook on gender within Egyptian society seems to be particularly affected by age and experience. Secondarily, class and, to a lesser extent, geographic derivation influence the formulation of gender issues in the context of the respondents' lives.

The following chapter describes the ideal woman who may develop from this new message. This idealized model is very important to my respondents, especially the younger women, who conceive of their life choices as a momentous pursuit of the "right" or the "wrong" path (*sabīl*).

Throughout the interview process, the respondents expressed a wide variety of conceptualizations of an ideal image. The narrower *sabīl* of virtue, which these women propose for their ideal model, contrasts with their own code for moral behavior, their "prescriptive ensemble . . . transmitted in a diffuse manner," to borrow from Foucault again, which provides room for compromise.[49]

Chapter Five

CONSTRUCTION OF THE
VIRTUOUS WOMAN

Historical analysis and a *talfiq* (piecing together) of the respondents' views help us understand the Islamist perspective on gender. Then, the coherence of that perspective in the minds of adherents must be reconstructed in order to fully comprehend its appeal. The views represented in this chapter come from Islamist writings and from personal interviews, including those discussed in chapter 4.

Islamist ideology may be divided into a group of general sociopolitical goals that apply to both sexes, and a set of ideals that target women. Theorists' or leaders' expressions of these goals and ideals vary from those of their followers. Variation is due to specific historical influences in their environment as well as the changing internal needs of the Islamists as a social movement. As might be expected, shadings and variations exist in a comparison of views of men and women within the movement. The interviews indicated that some variations on expressions of goals occur even among those of the same sex, age, and background.

An Iconography of Sources

Several sources of a new ideology for women were drawn on. These included Zaynab al-Ghazali, Safinaz Qassim, ʿUmar al-Tilmisani, Niʿmat Fouad, and ʿAsam al-ʿAryan. The views of Niʿmat Sidqi, the author of *Tabarruj* (lit., illicit display), discussed by Valerie Hoffman-Ladd, have also been included.[1] Sidqi is important because she exemplifies the views of many of the younger, veiled respondents.

Zaynab al-Ghazali is a writer, teacher, and lecturer long associated with the Islamists. She writes both detailed and popular prescriptive literature for modern Muslims. She has also written an autobiographical account of her experiences during the earlier blossoming of the Muslim Brotherhood and Nasser's repression of that movement. Her name, Zaynab, reminds modern Muslims of the story of Zaynab bint ʿAli.[2] This granddaughter of the Prophet was deeply affected by her father ʿAli's death, and then by the death of her brother Hussain at Karbala where her two sons were also killed. Her shrine in Egypt is visited by large numbers of pilgrims, who seek intercession or transmitted *baraka* from her spirit and position as a member of the *ahl al-bayt* (the family of the Prophet). *Zaynab* is one of the most common names in Egypt, and as an historical archetype it denotes virtue, loyalty, and ties to martyrdom.[3]

Zaynab al-Ghazali's life presents some interesting contradictions to the image of a Muslim ideologue. She worked in Huda Sha'rawi's Feminist Union as a young woman, but then founded the Association of Muslim Women in the late 1930s.[4] Her father, a cotton merchant, encouraged that shift, according to al-Ghazali. He was educated in al-Azhar, so she refers to him as Shaykh al-Ghazali al-Jabali, but it is not clear whether he was an *imam* or a freelance scholar.[5] She traces her inspiration in becoming an Islamic leader to her father; yet other respondents told me that her sister was a Communist and her brother, a Wafdist. She is a virulent anti-Nasserist and blames him for the trials and tribulations of the Muslim Brotherhood.[6] At the time of this research, the *Ikhwan* were participating in a coalition, the Islamic Alliance, made up of the Socialist Labor and Liberal parties. Most members are agreed on an externalized gender code that al-Ghazali condones.[7]

She has led an active political life, and married twice. Her dedication to the Islamic cause was a problem in her first marriage, she wrote, but her second husband agreed in writing not to interfere with her mission.[8] Nonetheless, al-Ghazali prescribes complete dedication in married life (to her followers) and insists that women give priority to their families.[9]

Sullivan portrays al-Ghazali as a "rebel against secular society,"[10] and stresses, as she does in her autobiography, her independent status vis-à-vis the Muslim Brethren until 1948, when she made a personal pledge to Hassan al-Banna.[11] He describes al-Ghazali's rejection of the legal charges brought by the Nasserist regime against her and the "secret apparatus" of the Muslim Brotherhood on the basis of their "Islamic illegitimacy."[12]

Ni'mat Fouad, an author and professor, offers another approach to an understanding of the veiled women. As a "moderately" veiled academic, she combines a call for cultural authenticity with an attack on the "carpetbagging" of the Sadat era.[13] She maintains a fairly conservative view on women's ideal status, but she has not spoken of an alliance with any particular Islamist group.[14]

Safinaz Qassim, once a theatre critic living in the United States, returned to Egypt and adopted an Islamist ideology as well as the *higab*. Her views on women and Islam are more defensive and less flexible than those of any other woman in this survey, but they remain complex and intelligently formed.[15] Several other women who contribute to the formulation of an ideology have participated in a coalition between the *Ikhwan* and the Labor party. They have differed with many of the societal goals of the Islamic oppositionists, but have concurred with the positions on gender and have adopted the first stage of the *higab*.[16]

The Broader Context of Gender

The broader societal goals of the Islamists include the integration or re-integration of Islam into the political life of the state. The endeavor involves the rejection of secular law and the establishment and reapplication of *shar'iah*.[17] Some believe that an Islamic caliphate should be reestablished.[18] The reorganization of government might involve a regional coalition or a sort of Muslim federation.

The movement enjoins the state to pursue a foreign policy that would enhance the unity of the Islamic *ummah* prior to the reestablishment of an Islamic caliphate. For example, the Islamists criticize the negotiations with the Israelis, who must eventually, they believe, accede to plans for a Palestinian state. They viewed Sadat's peace with Israel as a treacherous surrender of Palestinians rights, indeed, of all Muslims in the region. Palestinian self-determination and a reclamation of Jerusalem would be part of an Islamist agenda.[19]

On the national level, the Islamists urge attainment of the highest possible degree of social justice (*'adala*) and the minimum degrees of corruption, waste, and material display. *'Adala* may be realized through regulations on spending and a redistribution of wealth through an institutionalization of *zakat*.

The Islamic groups realize they must build an infrastructure capable of supporting the state. Even now, their economic and social-service efforts are directed toward that end through the operation of schools, clinics, banks and investment houses, supermarkets, and retail ventures.[20] These endeavors engender mass support for the movement because they provide "cleaner, cheaper and better service and products" to the public.[21] Despite the Riyan affair, the Islamic investment-banking crisis in the fall of 1988, the leadership felt that the principle of encouraging Islamic investment without usury through alternative institutions was a valid alternative. They assess the Riyan affair (in which 150,000 people are estimated to have lost their savings) as further evidence of a need to curb corruption and the state's inability to perform that function.[22]

If an Islamic state is achieved, and even before, problems of internal opposition will arise. Initially, Zaynab al-Ghazali chose to address this issue in sectarian terms. That is, she assumed that those who would oppose the formation of an Islamic state would be non-Muslims, so she stated that Christians, as *dhimmis* (recognized monotheists), will be accorded their historic rights and responsibilities under the *shari'ah*. Other segments of leadership have acknowledged that political opposition is a serious issue, and one that can hopefully be resolved without a reign of terror. They have stated that education, social acceptance, and support should be extended to all members of society regardless of political or religious ideals.[23]

The Islamists realize that a political shift will not take place without struggle. The superpowers currently dominating world affairs will not, they feel, permit the rise of another Islamic state without resistance. If that was their concern in 1988, how much more true it may now seem in the aftermath of the American response to Saddam Hussein's invasion of Kuwait.

They believe that global forces influenced the fate of the *Ikhwan* in the 1960s long before the advent of the "Islamic" revolution in Iran. Gamal Abdel Nasser issued a decree to dissolve the Association of Muslim Women in 1964. According to Zaynab al-Ghazali, his personal fear of the *Ikhwan* and their allies was not the only factor involved.

> During this time, both Russia and America wrote secret letters to Gamal Abdel Nasser telling him that Zaynab al-Ghazali is working against your movement and is thereby endangering all that you have done to fight the Islamic renaissance.[24]

Al-Ghazali's portrayal of Nasser as an agent of the superpowers is understandably harsh in light of the years she spent in prison. Her perspective is paralleled by other Islamists who say that *all* Arab secular rulers have been dominated by the superpowers at some level. Claims of superpower involvement exemplify the conspiratorial perceptions of an oppositionist worldview. Yet according to al-Ghazali and others, the movement will actually benefit from a period of repression, because bitter experiences keep consciences alive. The unity of those opposing the state or fighting outsiders would be heightened by out-and-out struggle.

Other moderate leaders who did not replicate Zaynab al-Ghazali's depiction of Nasser nevertheless shared a view of an essentially bipolar world. The leadership in general perceived the balance of power to be shifting toward a multipolar distribution of power before the 1991 Gulf war. An Islamic nation or bloc of nations would benefit from that shift, they believed.

Ideological positions on women are related to the movement's survival and organizational needs. Secondly, they reveal the Islamists' agenda for sexual and social control in order to maintain a continuous source of support and a contiguous basis for cultural identity. Their ideological positions are organized in the following categories: The movement's perception of women's appropriate functions; the use of *higab* in order to facilitate female participation; the sexual division of labor and public space; idealized female roles in correspondence with a woman's life cycle; and expressed core notions of femininity.

According to most of the Islamists, Egypt is not overpopulated; that is a myth created by the superpowers. The problem is merely that a redistribution of resources must take place.[25] Neither the superpowers nor the forces of international capitalism wish Egypt to attempt that sort of redistribution, and so we note increasing debt and the maintenance of a dependent aid system.

The Islamic oppositionists believe that large families are threatened by family planning and birth control programs. Secular education will further reduce and weaken Islamic culture, as will Western feminist models, which encourage women to establish goals outside the family.[26] Sometimes these arguments incorporate perceived Christian and Jewish conspiracies against Islam. They also involve "disenchantment" with a Western model of women's status, which they say the Egyptian feminist movement emulated.[27] Islamists who argue in this vein would encourage larger families to increase the size and strength of the *ummah*. For this reason, and according to the *sunnah* of the Prophet, the Muslim home is seen as the basic unit of the Islamic nation. Marriage and family life are the glue that holds society together.

Marriage, Reproduction, and the Higab

Woman serves her God and her *ummah* through marriage and reproduction. She is a further asset to her community when she affirms her position within the nuclear family. She should value her duties to her husband and children more than her own career or other outside goals.[28] Married life can be a virtuous existence. If she can manage to also serve her movement with her husband's consent, so much the better. Women in traditionally female occupations are not instructed to leave their jobs, but they are also admonished to consider their families their first priority. After all, obstetricians, nurses, secretaries, and teachers will be required in an Islamist Egypt as they are in the contemporary system.[29]

Since the family is the basic unit of society, factors that threaten the family must be attacked. Society must not encourage illicit extramarital affairs. Sexual temptation must be controlled through law, the wearing of *higab*, limitations on mixing of the sexes outside the home, peer pressure, and self-policing.[30]

Women are as responsible as men are for the condition of the state and for society as a whole, and so they must be included in the political process. The government should consult women as citizens, and their husbands must consult them individually.[31] Their productive functions are to be controlled but not terminated. *If* they do not abandon family life, they retain the right to work, to participate in the affairs of the movement, and ultimately, then, in the state.

The philosophy does not envision a reorganization of domestic responsibilities.[32] It emphasizes the distinct biological nature of the sexes and presents complementary psychological traits of the sexes as immutable scientific facts. When female characteristics are so distinct from male characteristics, and male strength, logic, and support are so emphasized, exclusion of women from the public affairs of men may result. At one end of the "complementarist'' spectrum, the justification for excluding women is expressed in biological terms (i.e., women were always weaker and more vulnerable due to their childbearing function). On the other end of the spectrum the rationale includes preordained intellectual and material male dominance and is expressed in this translation of Surah IV:34:

> Men are in charge of women, because Allah hath made the one of them to excel the other, and because they spend of their property (for the support of women).[33]

Unveiled women or even other veiled women who disagreed with this interpretation might cite instead:

> Men may be responsible for [protecting] women because Allah hath made one of them more able to provide [dominant] than the other, or *if* they [men] expend of their property for women.[34]

One may support this interpretation on the basis of verse 32 of Surah IV.[35] Al-Ghazali, at one end of that spectrum, asks:

> Should the man carry the responsibility of the woman and the woman carry the responsibility of the man? Should therefore the family, the child and the nation suffer because the woman has lost her way?

And she states:

> It is not a woman president [of state] that is required but tender mothers, faithful wives and considered opinions of women.[36]

While stressing the biological, physiological, and emotional factors that predispose the capabilities and talents of the ''family woman,'' the Islamists do not forget the broader needs of society. In order to promote active female political participation, or to replace male members who may be imprisoned or exiled, female participation is necessarily sanctioned.

The Islamists often use historical examples of women who participated in the public sphere, such as Khadijah, ʿAʾishah, Sakinah, the prophet's descendant, a poetess and patroness of the arts,[37] or Fatimah Zahrah in their arguments. The Islamists acknowledge women's historical and intellectual contributions, but constantly ground women in their family setting. They recognize women's importance in a more egalitarian society that would require expansion of their political and spiritual rights, but contraction of these functions if they interfere with a restructuring of society. Hence al-Ghazali asks:

> When Muhammad came back from al-Ghar and after he was inspired for the first time, who did he return to? Who? Khadijah. The first person to receive Muhammad's message and to give this message to others was Khadijah. . . . Muslim women stood by the Prophet Muhammad from the very first day as soldiers ready to work and produce.[38]

Khadijah is an interesting focus for al-Ghazali's argument. she emphasizes Khadijah's role as confidante and ideal spiritual and marital partner,
rather than her position as an independent businesswoman.

The Islamists utilize the example of ʿAʾishah bint Abu Bakr, who fought
in battle and influenced the community politically, but who also provokes the
following questions. Did ʿAʾishah's status limit the parameters of her behavior, or was the wide scope of her behavior particular only to her special
position as Muhammad's best-beloved wife? Is she a model for all women, or
only for those who seek to emulate the wives of the Prophet? Should all
women try to emulate the veiling and seclusion of the elite Mothers of the
Believers?

In regard to the choice of *higab* versus the *niqab,* or full veil, al-Ghazali
advocated following the examples of the Prophet's wives without formally
requiring imitation from all other women. She stated:

> The veil that covers the face is a *fard* (obligation) for the Prophet's wives,
> who are the mothers of the early believers. As for the other women of the
> Islamic nation, it is optional. It is the choice of the woman to wear it. There
> is no objection to those who wish to follow the example of the Prophet's
> wives and any woman who wishes to abide by the *fard* which guides the
> Muslim woman may do so. The *fard* states that all of the woman's body,
> except for the face and the hands should be covered. The Prophet's wives
> were obliged to answer any person from behind the veil. Whoever wants to
> follow the example of the Prophet's wives may do so because it is a virtue.
> And if a woman wants to rise up to that virtue and follow it, nobody can
> oppose her for doing so, as this is her personal right.

But Al-Ghazali clearly feels that at the minimum, the *higab* is required.

> Today's declining society allows women to wear clothes above their knees,
> so if a woman sits, her thighs show and her private parts show. How can we
> tell a woman who wants to follow the example of the Prophet's wives that
> she is bad and the other one is not? The bad one is the one who uncovers her
> body to show her thighs and legs and breasts and back. This is a bad woman,
> who is rejected by Islam and who is condemned for not abiding by the teach-
> ings of Islam.[40]

The battle lines are drawn clearly. The veiled women who model themselves on the Mothers of the Believers stand across the ring from the "na-
ked" (those who show no more than bare arms at times), immoral, and un-
Islamic contenders. The linkage of faith to modesty is essential to the Islamist
argument.

Al-Ghazali added in the next breath that a very beautiful woman should
cover her face, presumably because such a woman was more likely to encounter male harassment, and she would inadvertently tempt men more
strongly. That observation alters the option of veiling for beautiful women

from a preference to a necessity. Beautiful women may still be modest, but their beauty has its own power that causes men to lose self-control. Mernissi discusses that concept, known as *fitnah*, or the potential for social discord that stems from the viewing of a markedly beautiful woman. All women must conceal the portions of themselves that might invoke *fitnah*, for the components of beauty might be unsettling alone or in concert.[41]

The *higab* and the *niqab* may be adopted at puberty.[42] Al-Ghazali's assistant planned to veil her daughter the following year when she turned nine. Her companions urged her to wait until the girl in question "knows a little" (about her role as a woman and adult gender interaction).[43]

Whenever the "new virtuous woman" participates in productive, administrative, prayer, or political work with men, she must observe traditional restrictions to mixing of the sexes. These restrictions stem from the previously discussed Verse of the Curtain, and from the following verses and their various interpretations.

> O Prophet! Tell thy wives and thy daughters and the women of the believers to draw their cloaks (*jalabibihinna*) close round them [when they go abroad]. That will be better, so that they may be recognized and not annoyed. Allah is ever Forgiving, Merciful.[44]
> (Surah XXXIII, the Clans: 59)

> And tell the believing women to lower their gaze and be modest, and to display of their adornment (*zīnatihinna*) only that which is apparent, and to draw their veils (*khumurihinna*) over their bosoms (*juyubihinna*) and not to reveal their adornment (*zīnatihinna*) save to their own husbands or fathers or husbands' fathers, or their sons of their husbands' sons, or their brothers or their brothers' sons or sisters' sons, or their women, or their slaves or male attendants who lack vigour, or children who know naught of women's nakedness (*'awrat al-nisa'*). And let them not stamp their feet so as to reveal what they hide of their adornment (*zīna*).[45]
> (Surah XXIV, Light: 31)

The ambiguous terms indicated in parentheses have been interpreted by the translator to concord with modern versions of veiling. The custom of veiling most probably derives from borrowed Sasanian and Byzantine customs, but many Muslims, including most of the veiled women in this study, believe that the order to veil is contained in scripture.

Stowasser informs us that it was through the commentaries of Bukhari (d. 870), Tabari (d. 923), Baydawi (d. 1256), and Khafaji (d. 1659) that these verses came to justify increased covering and other restrictions on women's participation in public life.[46]

Al-Hibri claims that these instructions to women blended pre-Islamic taboos on female participation with a post-Islamic reassertion of patriarchy and need to control the sexuality and thus reproduction of the *ummah*.[47] But her assessment does not really help us understand why Egyptian women whose mothers rejected strict interpretations of these verses now firmly accept them.

The Islamist emulation of the wives of the Prophet corresponds to a long tradition of attaching sanctity to the persona of the Prophet. That sanctity is extended to his *sunnah*, his practices and opinions, because he is regarded as *al-insan al-kamil* (the complete, or holistic, man). Many people, scholars and ordinary believers, believe that a similar sanctity and *barakah* extends to the Prophet's wives and descendants, the *ahl al-bayt*, and to companions of the first generation. To believers, Muhammad and the extension of his *barakah* exist in the past, the present, and the future as an archetypal experience. A parallel is Jung's discussion of the Christ child, who stands as an archetypal "child god" who

> represents not only something that existed in the distant past, but also something that exists *now;* that is to say it is not just a vestige but a system functioning in the present whose purpose is to compensate or correct, in a meaningful manner, the inevitable one-sidedness and extravagances of the conscious mind.[48]

Jung, as I mentioned, believed that archetypes influence through syzygy—a process that conjoins illusion and reality. He used the example of Maya, the spinning dancer/goddess who invokes the eternal mother to all egos.[49] One might consider how Muhammad's virtuous image is projected as a prototypical father/husband while his wives, the Mothers of the Believers, are viewed literally as a mother-source and beloved of succeeding generations of Muslims.

Foucault discusses two methods by which history and historical models may affect a believer: through a strong codification, as in the development of the penitential system, or through an "ethics-oriented" morality, based on "forms of subjectivation and the practices of the self." He also suggests that most systems of morality involve both elements, although they could coexist and develop independently.[50] Although the Islamists affirm their position through just such a codification, it is apparent that the second inner ethical construction has to occur for their message to be successful.

By emulating the archetypal figures, and veiling, women also derive blessedness (*barakah*) and spirituality. Perhaps they experience a sort of transferred charisma, in which they firmly believe despite all the scriptural inconsistencies, and despite the fact that Islam has proclaimed Muhammad a prophet, but a man like any other, not an object of adoration.

The Rights to Work and Education

In a simpler, earlier version of her views on women, work, and education, al-Ghazali stated, "We know that Islam considers the body and the voice of woman as ʿawra [pudendal], and we know that women have an overwhelming need for home and family."[51] But arguments for the concealment of women's sexuality are separated from the debates over women's intellectual capabilities and female employment. Some observers linked arguments for women's freedom of movement and participation with those whom Ibrahim calls the "Western emulators."[52] Other thinkers who hoped to "synthesize"[53] the best of Islam and Western thought also encouraged female education and employment. But in an age of intense nationalism, and within the confines of neocolonialism, all three issues became reassociated with the enemies of a reassertion of the unity of religious and political life.

Most of the moderate Islamic ideologues do not proscribe education for women. Al-Ghazali argues that education "should not differentiate between the masculine and feminine sex. For true Islamic knowledge should belong to men and women equally."[54] True wisdom and knowledge can only be pursued by means of education and constant study of the Qurʾan and the *sunnah* of the Prophet.

Other Islamist elements continue the arguments of Talʿat Harb and others who had opposed the opening of public education to women. They had proposed that women study topics that prepared them to be better wives and mothers. Modern versions state that women should be trained in areas other than teaching or health care only in the case of demonstrated financial need. That would apply to a relatively small group of women who had no responsible male relatives.

Others feel that women should only interact with other women: treating, teaching, driving, or otherwise providing services not offered to men. In fact, a certain kind of sex-role expansion has occurred as a result, because women have entered some nontraditional occupations in order to provide services for women. In Cairo, one may now ride in a minibus driven by women that only picks up female passengers. Still others insist that the mixing of the sexes must be prohibited in educational institutions, whether along the lines of the Saudi educational system or by sitting, studying, and socializing separately within coeducational institutions. The veiled women under thirty that were interviewed concurred with this idea. In fact, activist students had tried to impose such regulations for some time at Cairo University, at Ain ash-Shams University, and on other campuses.

The image of the veiled woman idealizes love within marriage. The model contrasts with traditional attitudes toward arranged marriages, which are perceived to inspire security rather than love. This view acknowledges that arranged marriages still exist, and that certainly introductions, matchmaking, and parental approval enter into so-called love marriages inside and outside of the movements.

Men and women are comrades within a movement that presents them with a moral framework. They address each other as "brother" and "sister."

Al-Ghazali suggests that the experience of sharing social goals makes their relationship more rewarding, if they decide to move from a sibling mode to that of husband and wife.[55] Comradeship provides an attractive alternative to the limbo of young adults outside the movement, where the war of the sexes rages, and where young people still encourage each other to hunt, to flaunt, and to taunt. Outside the movement, young men and women express ambivalence and concern over the meaning of morality and even over the value of gender interaction. Within the movement, both sexes share a common cause toward which they may move singly or in partnership.

The strength of the bond previously established as comrades in a social movement carries through courtship into married life.[56] Sharing an ideology creates a basis for common interests that is more binding and enduring than that of married couples outside the new Islam, according to the Islamists.

An Islamic marriage will be more secure, for the wife has more time, energy, and respect for her mate when she focuses on her household rather than seeking self-fulfillment and additional income outside the home. She will never achieve true satisfaction through her career, for a woman has a biological need to create a nest and nurture her loved ones within it. Fulfillment through her interests and talents is possible (consider the example of the Egyptian singer, Umm Kalthoum) but only occurs in rare cases where family life is also pursued as recommended by al-Ghazali.[57] Self-fulfillment, according to the data, was a conscious and stated goal only for a small number of upper-class women over thirty, but it seemed a less important or vague ambition to younger women from a wider socioeconomic base.

Pursuit of her career more often leads a woman to mimic male tactics and attitudes, such as extreme competitiveness, aggressiveness, or male demeanor, in an attempt to gain professional acceptance. The career woman may be morally and intellectually tempted to neglect her marital duties or to indulge in forbidden vices, say the Islamists.[58] Just one cup of tea with a male colleague can lead to just one cigarette, then to just one kiss, and then to an affair. The argument resembles those of American films of the 1960s that warned of the dangers of smoking marijuana: a sort of domino theory.

The working woman brings home extra income, but soon it will be swallowed up to pay for childcare, outfits for work, and transportation expenses. She will either struggle with the double work load that outside employment imposes or pay for servants' wages to do the housework she has no time for.

My respondents' assessments of the costs of outside employment are fairly accurate. In 1988, servants were paid about 5 L.E. per day, private childcare cost 10–14 L.E. per day, and one work outfit could run from 30 L.E. to 60 L.E. Seamstresses' or tailors' fees have gone up, as have the costs of labor-saving devices, such as washing machines. If a woman was employed in the public sector, her fixed wage had not increased along with inflation, and she might receive under 100 L.E. per month. If she worked in the industrial sector, her wages were far lower. If employed as a secretary in the private sector, with excellent skills she might earn 250–300 L.E. If she spoke a foreign language as well, she might make somewhat more, but she was expected to reflect her upscale status in her clothing and appearance.

Matrimony, Harmony, and Mahr

The virtuous woman's decision to refrain from employment will result, according to my interviewees, in enhanced marital harmony. Her husband feels needed and admired and is therefore more likely to reciprocate his wife's devotion. He has fewer grounds for potential suspicion or jealousy as he observes his wife dressing "properly," avoiding contact with men outside the home, and catering to his material, emotional, and sexual needs.

She is not neglected intellectually or as a spiritual partner, for her husband is enjoined to seek her wisdom and advice on every occasion. She is encouraged to pursue her education and will be a more stimulating conversationalist and companion to her mate. She will be a more efficient and economical housewife because she is technically and morally educated, and if she has rejected the emphasis on conspicuous and unnecessary consumption demonstrated by many other women in her milieu. The virtuous woman will be a better teacher and companion for her children, who are, after all, the source of Islamic society of the future.

A husband should seek solace in his wife, as she does in him. The Islamists invoke cultural as well as religious indications of deep respect for the wife. Al-Ghazali says, "In Islam, the husband kisses his wife's hand before he leaves the house."[59]

While observing the tenets of her Islamic marriage, the woman need not fear infidelity, which is not permitted to her husband. Polygamy is not forbidden, but the virtue, faith, education, and trust of the wife will make that option less likely. Those who did not much like the idea of a second wife nevertheless saw the abolition of polygamy in the law to be a rejection of the words of the Qur'an and of the *sunnah* of the Prophet. Those opposed to polygamy stressed the implication of the words "Marry two or three or four but treat them equally," which then state "*and if ye can not,* then marry one."[60] Others reiterated that polygamy had been viable in an historical setting of many widowed women and was justified in the modern period in cases where a wife fell ill, became disabled, or was infertile.[61]

The Islamist viewpoint is divided over the necessity of *mahr,* or bridal payment. Theoretically, *mahr* is deemed an essential part of a woman's property within marriage. All the women interviewed felt that the right to receive this money as their own, to retain control of it and of their own last names during their marriages, was a benefit of the traditional marriage system. In fact, it seemed to them to be a great improvement over the Western advent of community property. On the other hand, younger *muhaggabat* were less likely to agree on the value of *mahr*. They felt that it represented the concept of woman as property and brought her down to the level of a flat or a piece of land. They did not deny the importance of the wife's economic autonomy within Islamic marriage, but felt that bridal payments should be reduced to a token payment.[62] Does anti-materialism confront tradition? One should remember that young men or their families must save to accrue the *mahr*, and if such an obstacle to marriage were removed, these young women might be able to marry several years earlier, or to marry younger partners than they now can. Older moderate leaders also acknowledged the need to mediate the settlement of the *mahr*.

Parental Duties and Interaction

Al-Ghazali writes of Western women who form attachments to their dogs and cats as a way of satisfying their maternal instincts.[63] Other women laughed at that substitution for children and reiterated their feeling that child-bearing and -raising are duties as well as needs. Women's primary function is to impart Islamic values to their children and to faithfully and personally attend to the development of their personality, morality, and spirituality.

While upholding the positive influence of the housewife and emphasizing the beneficial aspects of family life, the Islamists are willing and able to confront less wholesome aspects of traditional family interaction. Moderate leaders acknowledged that children need more of a male presence in their lives.[64] Due to the high rate of labor migration out of Egypt, absent-father households are now more common. Egyptian fathers had typically interacted with their children far less often than mothers did, in any case. Mervat Hatem says that it was the economic and cultural pulls contributing to class definition that caused socially accepted male neglect of children to arise in the middle classes. Egyptian fathers in general play a ''marginal role'' but wield a ''large degree of authority.'' Among the lower classes, the extended family system had prevailed. This system, now slowly changing, has meant wider and less differentiated contact between the child and other female family members. Mothering has not been conducted to the exclusion of other economic activities by the lower classes, but middle-class women have been expected to concentrate on mothering.[65]

Islamist moderates feel that nurturing should be intensive, but that it should not exclude the father. The new Muslim man is encouraged to participate more actively in the raising of his children, who need the love, attention, and discipline of both parents. However, the mother should provide primary childcare during the formative years.

One leader acknowledged that the traditional patterns of parenting have sometimes resulted in authoritarian relationships between parents and children, especially between father and child.[66] Such age and authority preferences are not restricted to men. Mothers-in-law have acquired a reputation for interference and obstructionism with married children and their spouses.[67]

Society's attitudes toward the value and power of older men and women versus that of younger family members have combined with parenting practices to produce passive, yielding, conformist reactions when young people respond to pressure.[68] In other cases, quite severe oedipal reactions to parental authority may be expressed or repressed, to the detriment of individuals and the community as a whole. The moderate Islamist ideology holds that while the Islamic family undergoes a reshaping process, the new, ideal Islamic youth, men, and women will be encouraged by their peers to act in accordance with their consciences, even if this conflicts with established patterns of authority. Because young adults will be more involved in their communities, their new orientation would not merely represent a call for heightened individualism.

Women and Legal Reform

The Islamists claim that legal amendments such as the personal status reforms are not in accordance with Islamic law and have been required only because preceding civil law is inadequate and unequal to the rights *shari'ah* provides.[69] *If* the *shari'ah* were genuinely and intelligently applied, and *if* couples sincerely trusted, consulted, and respected each other, women's rights would be enhanced rather than attenuated.

Moderate leaders differ on the specific changes that a return to the *shari'ah* would make. "Rights" that have been abrogated are male instigation or announcement of divorce and/or second marriage without notification of the wife. Mostly male leaders called for abolition of alimony (called "alimony of the *mut'a*"[70]) or the reinclusion of the *bayt al-ta'ah* practice (where a woman may be restricted to her home by her husband). The personal status reforms and their amendments also permit women to obtain extended custody of their children, and allow the divorced wife to remain in her home or apartment.[71] The Islamists say that any of the above practices (i.e., polygamy, barriers to divorce for women) included within *shari'ah* were designed to discourage divorce, not to abuse women. Furthermore, the initial reforms were brought about in an extralegal manner even according to civil procedure.[72] The amendments are no more "un-Islamic" procedurally than the rest of the secular legal code, but their content is further from established interpretations of *shari'ah* than were earlier civil laws governing gender.

Political Rights, Recruitment, and Restrictions of Hukm

Politically, the Islamic woman is the equal of her male counterpart. She should educate herself politically and avail herself of her rights to vote and be represented and consulted. She is urged to participate in the building of the movement and a future state. Female leadership exists and is important. Women leaders write and speak on gender issues, though not to the exclusion of other issues.

According to al-Ghazali, the true Islamic woman will be realized through pursuit of community unity. The unity of the community must be understood through a concentration on the spiritual and practical gifts of the Qur'an. All rules guiding and shaping Islamic women may ultimately be traced back to this source in conjunction with the *sunnah* of the Prophet and the *hadith*. The new Muslim woman must be aware of the unity of her faith and "the indivisibility" of the affairs of the Muslim state, for:

> Politics are emanated from the Qur'an;
> Social life is emanated from the Qur'an;
> Domestic life is emanated from the Qur'an;
> Individual life is emanated from the Qur'an;
> Community life is emanated from the Qur'an.[73]

Women in various capacities recruit women to the "new" Islamic way of life and hold discussion sections with both new and established adherents.[74] Meetings are not held on university campuses exclusively or officially. Unofficial gatherings also occur, although reading groups are more formally organized.

Women do not hold judicial offices under current Egyptian law. Islamists proscribe such status to women or any high position that involves the exercise of *hukm*, rule through judgment. One theorist argued (as did student respondents) that women's emotions are affected by both her menstrual cycle and her family's intrusion on her powers of concentration.[75] A female head of state would be very controversial, to say the least. When I told respondents that there are women judges in other Muslim countries, in Syria and Yemen for example, they said that these states were not really Muslim or had misunderstood both the letter and the spirit of the *shari'ah*.

Femininity Idealized

The Islamists envision a core of idealized feminine qualities for women to draw on that compose the nature of femininity. These qualities are described to contrast with or in some instances to concord with the social reality they observe.

Valerie Hoffman-Ladd, in analyzing the writings of certain Islamists, stresses the qualities of delicacy and graciousness, or *riqqa,* and shyness considered appropriate for women. One might deduce from the literature that these qualities, in addition to *ihtisham* (shame and deference), form the defining features of femininity to the Islamists.[76] But al-Ghazali stressed the need for *shaja'a,* courage, before all else. Courage is necessitated by other essential qualities of truth, dedication, self-sacrifice, faith, wisdom, and devotion. And courage is also valued in men. Modesty, purity, softness, and maternalism were also stressed, more frequently by adherents than by leaders. Some respondents mentioned the ability to diminish negativity through a cheerful and lighthearted attitude, *khifat dam.* This quality is expressed in clever joking sometimes, prized by the traditional *bint al-balad,* and valued in men, as well.[77]

The conjunction of male and female ideal qualities was striking, especially where the respondents had greatly emphasized gender distinctions in terms of personalities and emotions. Al-Ghazali, however, did not find this particularly significant. She saw that conjunction as the natural outcome of the egalitarian relationship of the sexes in Islam.[78]

In fact, that paralleling of idealized qualities contrasts with social portrayals of male and female characteristics described by Andrea Rugh. Rugh witnessed young Cairene girls play-acting. They portrayed a wife and mother who displayed the traits of self-denial, patience, perseverance, and thrift. The father was portrayed as "aggressive, authoritarian, temperamental" and self-indulgent.[79] One must admit that portrayal of perceived reality leads naturally to parody, distinct, in turn, from idealization. Still, the qualities expressed by these young girls promote expectations of a clear sexual division of personal characteristics rather than a leveling. These characteristics of femininity were also mentioned by Islamist ideologues, with two distinctions. Passivity, or patience without purpose and commitment (associated with a mother image), was not seen to be productive. Secondly, the male qualities Rugh's young girls enacted directly counter the ideals for the father and husband in a new Islamic family.

Are there other important distinctions between the Islamist view of feminine qualities and the views already contained within Egyptian society? Nayra Atiya cites the opinions of a respondent in her work *Khul Khaal:*

Women are more loyal than men. As to being equal with men, this is another matter. Men don't like strong women. Any woman who takes on man's work is permeated with a masculinity that repels men. They like women to be weak. What's the point of a masculine woman? It would be as if a man were married to another man. A woman lawyer, for example, assumes masculine qualities, and a man's appetite is closed for this kind of woman.

> A woman has to be fine and weak. No man likes a he-she. A man loves
> a woman's tears. He loves to see her helpless, and he loves her tears.[80]

With the exception of the last two sentences of this description, a large
number of the veiled respondents of rural or lower-middle-class origin in this
study might agree with these statements.

But the Islamist "theorists" had not stressed weakness, but strength. Cu-
riously, the respondents most opposed to the views of the Islamists also responded that the most important qualities for a woman were courage and
strength of character.[81]

Other shapers of the virtuous image would argue for the inclusion of
ihtisham or *hasham*, shame or modesty linked to self-control. Adherents
stressed this quality more often than their leaders. *Ihtisham* was identified as
a learned rather than inherent quality and one that, as Abu Lughod notes,
implies self-control and the attainment of *aql*, or reason. Abu Lughod's respondents, the Awlad 'Ali, claimed that Egyptians, in contrast to them,
lacked this very quality. She decribes *hasham* as an "internal state" and a
"way of acting" that guides both cross-gender relations and cross-status relations. "The experience is one of discomfort, linked to feelings of shyness,
embarrassment, or shame, and the acts are those of the modesty code, a language of formal self-restraint and effacement."[82]

The concept of *ihtisham* was stressed by the veiled respondents of rural
background and a few of the urban-born women. But other rural-born veiled
women emphasized qualities such as *karama,* generosity, or softness/
delicacy.

Many respondents confused feminine traits and functions with the theoretical components of femininity. Their confusion should inform us that external manifestations of identity are very important to respondents. Both the
essence of a woman's femininity and its expression are seen as a part of a
whole. Not only respondents, but one of the theorists, thought of femininity
in terms of appearance and expression rather than personality traits.[83] A 35-
year-old, elite, veiled married woman answered this way:

> Femininity has two parts. First with regards to appearance, the woman must
> take care of her shape and not become obese. If she wears any sort of
> makeup, it should be lightly and carefully applied and she should make her
> hair attractive even when she veils. She must be delicate, her speech and her
> approach should be somewhat indirect, less aggressive or smoother.[84]

The essence of femininity was far more difficult for respondents to describe
than women's daily functions. But other respondents concurred with the theorists' emphasis on femininity, and indeed one respondent claimed, "What is
inside a woman's head is more important than what is on top of it"—a reference to the inner woman as well as the *higab*.[85]

The ideal qualities of the Islamist woman do not clash with traditional definitions of femininity in the Egyptian context. A clash is avoided because of the breadth of conceptualization of femininity in the construction of the "new virtuous" image. This breadth permits women to believe in the need for simultaneous or situation-appropriate strength and delicacy, courage and shyness.

Fouad Zakaria deplores the fundamentalists' depiction of women's "sentimentality," a synonym for women's emotionalism, as compared to male *aql*, rationalism. He notes that women's sentimentality is a learned phenomenon and is "by no means an essential part of women's nature", however, the Islamists consider it precisely that. He notes that this viewpoint is "not exclusive to the fundamentalists" but does not realize how prevalent the view of "sentimental women" is throughout Egyptian society, and in the rest of the world.[86] Notwithstanding, "sentimentality" was downplayed by two of the Islamist leaders contacted in this research, who instead stressed the role of rationality and intellectual stimulation for women.

The women I interviewed said that the expression of the Islamic woman's femininity is part and parcel of her "nature." That "nature" was a complex and confusing topic, for it involves interpretations of "scientific" findings of varying validity incorporated into arguments over the intended functions of women. For example, Hoffman-Ladd refers to "findings" that revealed that work weakened "women's femininity," even if physical labor was not involved.[87] Working-class women I spoke to found that idea humorous. The university students seemed to believe that truism along with other "scientific" findings they had been exposed to. They told me, for example, that newspapers and studies had shown that women were less productive workers and that working women produced more juvenile delinquents. Yvonne Haddad mentions an *Ikhwan*-influenced article referring to the appearance of a third sex with recessive female genes due to growing numbers of working women.[88]

As Hoffman-Ladd points out, *tabarruj*, or display of the woman's *zina*, or charms,[89] must be avoided in order to protect both the essence and the expression of her femininity. But community control focuses upon display of the expressions of femininity rather than interior control of its essence.

Zakaria holds that using the *higab* to achieve this control introduces a fatal duality of spirit and body into the fundamentalist discourse.[90] He contends that the concealed body is objectified, whereas the Islamists claim that the *higab* permits an entry into a world of the spirit. The concealing process admits (a) that the male sexual impulse cannot be controlled and (b) that a woman's body, revealed or concealed, is far more important than her intellect or spirit.[91] Zakaria also believes that a certain schizophrenia is introduced when the *muhaggaba* must present a pristine, asexual persona to the world and a fully appealing sexual image to her husband.[92] So Zakaria contends that the image of the fundamentalist woman proposes a surface spiritual content, designed to cover over a continuous enslavement to identity through the body. He perceives these and other dualities to be fatal flaws in the rationale of the fundamentalists, which have emerged because they isolate women "from their social, historical and economic contexts and treat them as one sex opposed to the other."[93]

The Islamist women described in this research do not regard these dualities as "fatal flaws.' In fact these sorts of paradoxes are not unique to the Islamist or oppositionist viewpoint, but have existed throughout the world and history, and perhaps they existed in that much-idealized first generation of Islam as well.

Numerous sources have pointed out the male world's reduction of woman to her body.[94] Some unveiled women reflect that the socialization of men is responsible for that preoccupation. In many sources of popular culture, and even in the contemporary Egyptian novel, women were reduced, if not to their bodies, then to their sexual impulses, according to Iqbal Baraka.[95] Surely, the adoption of full *higab* lends a gloss of spirituality to many women when they traverse public space. Denying men the ability to comment on their figures or silencing the "eyes of wolves" gave the younger respondents some satisfaction. Furthermore, the decision to veil brings about some sense of personal power, along with Zakaria's suggested schizophrenia, because veiling is a perfectly acceptable form of self-expression within society at this time.

Segregation of the Sexes?

Al-Ghazali herself has met and discussed religious matters with unexpected male visitors in her home, even at night.[96] Women within Muslim associations are not subject to the strictest of sexual segregation; they were not comfortable with the term "segregation," but preferred "restrictions to mixing" (of the sexes). "It is prohibited in Islam that a man and a woman be together in a closed office" they said. "If the man is not the husband, then he has no right to be alone with a woman." Or, "The devil will be the third [party]."

Al-Ghazali and her staff quickly emphasized the presence of a young male colleague who interacted with us throughout our interview. "He is like our son, our brother in Islam, and there is nothing wrong with sitting and discussing such important issues together," said one of the women present.[97]

Safinaz Qassim, a veiled journalist, responded that she finds it intellectually necessary to meet and communicate with her male colleagues. However, she expressed deep concern that her decision to do so was not in response to any Islamically legislated position. Her personal opinion would have to stand in the meanwhile. Guidance was unavailable except as a ruling varying from jurist to jurist.[98] Another respondent was perfectly satisfied with that route. She said that she seeks out a respected jurist and abides by his individual judgment whenever troubled by an issue of this sort or a moral dilemma.

Regarding the modifications of sex segregation, al-Ghazali noted, "Women are allowed to work with the rules and regulations prescribed by Islam, according to the *shari'ah*." When pressed further regarding this issue, al-Ghazali stated:

> The efficiency and intelligence of the woman is defined in Islam. It is highly appreciated as well. The Prophet used to address both men and women at the same time. The men used to take the front seats, and the women used to take the back seats. All were listening and learning, and everybody was asking questions and discussing issues together. But the women had a special door that they entered from called the "Women's Door." The men, too, entered from a special door and had a special seating area.
>
> The Prophet used to go through the seats of the men till he reached the seats of the women. This meant that nothing separated the men's seats from the women's seats except for a certain amount of space. The Prophet used to go to the women's seats with Bilal in order to collect money for the *fitr* or to ask women about things he needed from them.[99]

So women may be expected to observe sex segregation to the extent of separate seating or praying areas, but need not be restricted to a gallery like Orthodox Jews, to a space separated by a curtain or a wall, nor to a separate room.

Furthermore, women in all the above situations described are to wear the *higab*. The *higab* fulfills many of the requirements of cross-sex interaction. Men are encouraged to treat their women comrades as peers and intellectual equals. Men are better able to concentrate on women's views and input when the *higab* deemphasizes their physical charms.

One may ask, why not instead reeducate men to control their sexual impulses and to regard women as body and spirit united? Al-Ghazali, al-'Aryan, and many of the young Islamist women believe that in time, reeducation will occur, as long as the family remains strong enough to inculcate a stronger sense of moral values in its sons.

Mernissi feels that changing men's attitudes is impossible because Islam presents women as the source of social discord, and because the spiritual needs of Islam, as represented by al-Ghazali (the medieval), required a denial and suppression of female sexuality.[100] Another argument against the potential for reeducating Muslim men is based on the idea that since Islam suppresses the male believer and subjugates him to God, he is bound to suppress women. Man is taught to regard her sexuality as voracious, dangerous, and life-sapping.[101] In a more recent work, Mernissi implies that male reeducation is unlikely because Islam itself is used to deny gender equality within the secular national body due to an ahistoricity in its worldview, which affects the political as well as the social dimensions.[102] In this work, she redefines *fitnah,* or social discord, stating that women's *demand for social change* is deemed *fitnah* within a Muslim society.[103]

Higab: Political or Social Statement?

To the Western eye, the wearing of *higab* may signify an allegiance to a political ideal or a commitment to societal change. The voluntary adoption of *higab* represents much more to women than a badge of an activist. It symbolizes a moral decision that could be taken as a sign of opposition by a government threatened by them or as a sign of support by a government promoting Islamic ideals. The *higab* might be more of a political symbol if it were forbidden, than it is now in Egypt.

Writing in 1984, Yvonne Haddad divides the reasons given by respondents in Egypt, Jordan, Oman, Kuwait, and the United States for wearing the veil into the following categories:

> *Religious*—an act of obedience to the will of God as a consequence of a profound religious experience, which several women referred to as being "born again.";
> *Psychological*—an affirmation of authenticity, a return to the roots, and a rejection of Western norms. (One woman talked about the "end of turmoil' and a "sense of peace.");
> *Political*—a sign of disenchantment with the prevailing political order;
> *Revolutionary*—an identification with the Islamic revolutionary forces that affirm [sic] the necessity of the Islamization of society as the only means of its salvation;
> *Economic*—a sign of affluence, of being a lady of leisure;
> *Cultural*—a public affirmation of allegiance to chastity and modesty, of not being a sex object (especially among unmarried working women);
> *Demographic*—a sign of being urbanized;
> *Practical*—a means of reducing the amount to be spent on clothing. Some respondents claimed that others were receiving money from Libya and Saudi Arabia for the purpose.);
> *Domestic*—a way to keep the peace, since the males in the family insist on it.[104]

Her assessments accorded with my data, although the "economic" category of explanation is problematic. The veiled respondents simply did not offer that sort of explanation for their orientation, and they clearly were not ladies of leisure. Even though I feel strongly that economic factors contributed to the growth of *higab* wearing, they ought to be corroborated in a tangible manner by the women directly involved. Unveiled women would agree that there is an economic explanation for veiling, because they believe veiled women seek to hide their lower-class origins. They combine that category with the motivations in Haddad's "practical" category.

My respondents offered explanations for their veiling included in the "cultural," "religious," and "psychological" categories. The wearing of *higab* to women identifying with an Islamic ideal is a "new" badge of authenticity. One might add to the "psychological" category of motivations the factors of sanctioned independence, that women may licitly counter their families on the veiling issue, and peer pressure. Haddad also mentions the paradox of *higab*-wearing women who reflect their historical archetypes, " 'A'isha, Hafsa and Umm Salama' " in "acquiring an Islamic literacy" but who reject contemporary female roles in the workplace.[105]

In the Islamist ideology of gender, *higab* represents religious commitment *and* a freedom from sexual identification rather than a desexualization. That point is hotly debated by their opponents. Adherents appear to have varying interpretations; the young women after all, are hoping to attract husbands, but in a suitable manner.

Islamist theorists share a great deal of their outlook on women's status with the "establishment conservatives," with the Azharites, and with the arguments of early reformers such as Muhammad ʿAbduh. All three groups consider Islam to be a progressive force for women, designed to enhance their status in the community and in society. However, with regard to the *higab* and the importance of the public sphere to women, the Islamists differ from other theorists in their interpretation of ethical standards that could be applied to women through the application of ʿurf (customary standards). For example, Shaykh Shaltut (a distinguished reformer) cited the verse "The Cow" to illustrate the legal grounds for reforming regulations applying to women: "And women have rights similar to the rights of men over them, according to what is recognized" (as fair). Shaltut states that "combining unchanging ethical standards with local and *contemporary* norms of conduct 'al-ʿurf' is an accepted source of legislation in Islamic *fiqh*" (jurisprudence).[106] But the Islamists want to eliminate the notion of evolutionary law and eradicate contemporary and especially foreign influences if possible.

Social and economic pressures are undeniably strong in today's Egypt. Perhaps they are a more forceful source of motivation than any of the ideological explanations offered in this chapter. One can assume that *all* these elements interact when a woman chooses to identify with the "new, virtuous" model.

The particular social structures of young women, the *shilla*, or friendship-and-influence group, and the *dufʿa* (graduation-year cohorts, especially those in the same field) have contributed to the spread of the *higab*.

Such groups are extremely common and popular in Egypt,[107] and unlike broader mutual-interest groupings, they mean social connections, fallbacks, introductions to mates, favor exchanges, and so on. Young women and men feel an essential need to "belong" inside or outside the family circle.

In many ways, social interaction within the Middle Eastern family generally accentuates women's continuing need for social approval. Nahid Toubia describes how children must be wooed to comply with social imperatives such as circumcision, then integrated through a stage of "intimidation" into an acceptance of sexual and social roles. Finally, they must reimpose the social system on their own children or younger women.[108] This account could very well fit the Egyptian setting. As in Egypt, the process is enacted through the mother-daughter dynamic. The message to the young girl is that individuality is undesirable; approval of her social group is the only proper basis for well-being.

The Islamists know that social identification and solidarity balance out many of the ills of a developing society. Close ties between women are supported by traditional cultural patterns of interaction in urban as well as rural Egypt. These dynamics—solidarity, peer support, and strong group identification—were apparent in the living situations of the young university respondents.

Veiled women may be able to keep their close ties to other women alive through visiting networks, study groups, or prayer groups after marriage, and that may alleviate much of the isolation that they may experience in a semi-nuclear family setting, especially after some years of constant childcare. These dynamics are also noted by the Islamists, not as strategies for recruitment but as arguments for increased community interaction.

Conclusion

The ideological message to women proclaims itself to be made in the spirit of the first generation of Islam. The words of the Qurʾan and the intent of the Prophet are deemed timeless. The construction of this message specifically utilizes archetypal examples of women's expertise, religiosity, political commitment, and social mediation. It does not invoke those historical images that demonstrate female independence of male economic support, because they do not bolster the current argument for the marʾah usriyah (family woman). Many theorists are aware of a distinction between "renewal" and "revival" contained in the tajdid process but do not extend the need for "renewal" to the issues surrounding women, because they feel that Western influences on women's self-values must first be expunged.

The Islamists are well aware that women provide important economic services in the areas of health, education, and administration, and that these services could not survive without them, at present. They seek instead to limit women's participation in the work force, and to stress women's commitment to the family as a religiously sanctioned priority.

The Islamists propose social change on a vast scale that would require mass mobilization. Hence, their message is flexible enough to enlist women in any capacity necessary, at least temporarily. They could incorporate both working women and housewives for some time to come.

The Islamist ideology can be communicated in several versions. One senses a subtle distinction in the message concerning women when the audience is judged to be external or internal to the movement.

It is fair to say that greater flexibility appears to be extended to adherents within practice than within theory. Perhaps a simpler and more rigid image is easier to communicate, and easier to adjust to, than one permitting and requiring many nuances and constant social adjustments. Variations from the ideal are tolerated in the areas of education, family planning, childrearing, and family relations. The result is a positive reception of the image of the new Islamic woman, for she is not made unattainable. The sacrifices that the Islamists ask for are not as great as they might be. Solidarity and community acceptances are proffered even to women who interpret or represent the overall ideal somewhat differently than do their peers. For example, some of the young *muhaggabat* in this study planned to travel, study foreign languages, or pursue "male-dominated" careers. Their friends did not criticize their choices.

The Islamists have divided gender issues into areas of negotiability or immutability in accordance with the pressures in their environment. Issues that are intrinsic in the written expressions of that ideology, such as the eschewing of female employment, are accepted as negotiable issues by adherents. There is also more negotiability of issues according to older respondents than in the views of younger respondents. The veiled women over thirty work and are active; they do not intend to quit their jobs, but they justify themselves by declaring their family roles to be more important. In this way, the image of the Islamic woman proves adaptable to the realities of a generation of women and their experience in Egyptian life.

However, the *higab* and the accompanying notions of sex segregation and modesty are intrinsic to Islamist theory *and* practice. The *higab* has acquired too much symbolic value to be negotiated. It reclaims and incorporates modesty, virtue, and a host of traditional cultural mores into a social and political experiment.

The ideology, like the wearing of *higab*, may be adopted in stages. A woman may already believe in the centrality of her role within the family (which is also contained in all the other images competing for her identification) and gradually come to believe in the Islamists' plans for societal reform. She may already accept restrictions to gender mixing and then discover a sense of her political responsibility. Or she may not; she may remain at that first or second level. She may begin by wearing a plain headscarf and a longer skirt, and then adopt the *higab*.

In so doing, a woman expresses an active belief in the Islamists' conception of the Mothers of the Believers. This conception is highly selective and stresses the virtue of women in relation to the Prophet and his Companions. Women who adopt this conception are not receiving new historical information. Many inaccuracies or questionable interpretations of women's status have been in circulation for centuries and also form part of *turath*, the cultural heritage. Hence, a sense of historical continuity may be a psychological centering force in an uncertain economic and political environment.

Women who are young enough to have read about, but not old enough to have witnessed, the experiments in constitutional liberalism and socialism carried out in Egypt during their parents' (or grandparents') youth are even more insecure in the current environment. They have experienced a different sort of invasion from the West, on commercial, technological, political, and social planes. They have witnessed the Arab denunciation of Egypt following the peace treaty with Israel. They have personally felt the effects of economic dislocation upon their career alternatives, their housing circumstances, and their marriage prospects. They are choosing the change, revision, and redefinition of social goals suggested by the Islamists because no other alternatives seem to be viable.

Young women are especially receptive to this ideology and reflect it because they lack avenues for self-definition and self-expression that some of the older women possess. They reflect the image of the "new" virtuous woman in a different manner than their older counterparts—primarily because they are less experienced, less politicized, and perhaps more needful of a guiding philosophy.

The "virtuous woman" is responsive to past and present, nationalism or regionalism, political and economic imperatives, as well as the promise of social identity. She exhibits socially sanctioned self-determination in her decision to exhibit her orientation through wearing *higab*. She rejects the guiding principles of state policy regarding women over the last thirty-five years. Her rejection implies a relinquishment of the principles of secularism and Western models and ideals in general.

Chapter 6

UNVEILED WOMEN REPLY

Unveiled women also reflect a powerful image to be considered and identified. That image is as meaningful to them as the previously described "virtuous woman" is to the veiled women. Up until 1973 (the year of the Egyptian army's triumphant crossing of the Suez canal to attack Israeli positions), the model of the unveiled woman represented a dominant image for the upper class, the bourgeoisie, and segments of the petite bourgeoisie. Then, slowly, the model and ideology of the new Islamic woman began to challenge the dominance of the earlier image, and it gained momentum over the last decade. The message of the new Islamic woman accompanied a growing level of opposition to the state's official internal and external policies.

The projection of an image to the unveiled woman is also intricately tied to issues of class mobility and social interpretations of economic standing in Egyptian society. The goals of state educational and employment policies simultaneously empowered the image of unveiled women and helped to diffuse it through society. The process, occurred even though it was clear that other sorts of women, the *bint al-balad* and the *fallaha,* never accepted the model of the unveiled woman as a part of their identity code.

The *bint al-balad* will be discussed briefly because her concepts of femininity, faith, and identity provide an interesting counterpoint to the views of other unveiled urban women. First, we must define her counterpart in the *bint al-dhawwat*—literally, a daughter of ownership or rank.

Bint al-Dhawwat

The unveiled woman is a composite of many segments of society. She represents the daughters of the upper and middle classes, but a monolithic aristocracy never emerged in Egypt. Instead, the upper cut of society was always mixed in origin, economic base, social reputation, and political connections. In the nineteenth century, the upper classes were made up of Mamluks and their descendants, the Turco-Circassian aristocracy, but there was also an indigenous Egyptian aristocracy. There were other families who were "Arab" in origin, meaning bedouin, or at least non-Mamluk and non-Turkic. A new agrarian capitalist class developed, forming another segment of the elite.

In modern Egypt, a certain degree of continuity has also characterized the composition of social classes, except for periods during which unlikely groups skyrocketed in wealth and became the *nouveaux riches*. Social tensions emerged from this form of class mobility during the Second World War, cumulatively through the 1960s and during the *infitah* period, the economic opening of the 1970s. As new groups of women technically joined the upper bourgeoisie, the earlier elites did not regard them as social equals. The restrictions on social mobility affected both sexes psychologically and materially, and limited social networking to some degree. Perhaps social mobility can be most strictly measured by social attitudes toward the newly rich, or when those of unequal socioeconomic backgrounds can marry without social approbation.

Women of the *nouveaux riches* in the *infitah* period were not easily assimilated to their new positions and neighborhoods. Their neighbors darkly alluded to their former homes or to their husbands' occupations (as plumbers or other tradesmen, for example). They and their daughters were under some pressure to marry social equals, relatives, or those similar in socioeconomic background.

My respondents upheld the idea that one should marry a social equal if possible. Although men were permitted to marry their Muslim servants or slaves according to Surah IV:25,[1] the reverse was not acceptable for women, according to customary practice. In the modern era, cross-class marriage has been unacceptable for both men and women. *Mésalliance* was a favorite theme of popular culture expressed in poems, books, and films.[2] In practice, such a match could be annulled by the bride's parents only if they had opposed the marriage or if the bride were a minor. The families acted to insure the security and resources of family members, and to allow for future familial support for the individual woman if she were later widowed or divorced.

In fact, men seek women of substance as often as women seek men to support them; both kinds of matches are acceptable as long as the couple's social standings are vaguely equivalent. That equivalence often refers to lineage, occupation, the type and length of education they have received, where they reside, and what sort of social connections they hold.

Some respondents expressed their desire to marry into a "good family," a term that lacks the specific connotations of the Arabic term *ibn al-nas*, closer perhaps to the Spanish *hidalgo*. A girl who wants to marry a "son of the elite" is seeking a man whose lineage is known, respected, and derived from one of several acceptable bases of capital. A *bint nas wa bint asala* is a young lady, "well bred and of good stock," as demonstrated by her family, her actions, and character.[3] To the *bint al-balad* the above phrase implies one set of characteristics, while to the upper-middle-class girl it denotes another group of requirements.[4]

In the modern period, the term *ibn nas* refers to a member of the upper class who is not considered to be part of the *nouveaux riches*. With the land-reform policies in the Nasserist period, old titles were in essence outlawed but not forgotten. Some social scientists described the growth of a second stratum, now considered "upper class," that evolved in the wake of land reform, power aggregation in the bureaucracy, and new patterns of acquiring wealth.[5] The women of these groups were predominantly unveiled, but they could still be distinguished from the women of the earlier elite.

Bint al-dhawwat might not define herself with that phrase, simply as a matter of good manners. One would never call oneself or someone else a pasha's son or daughter, although stating that one is from a good family might imply just that.

The families of the upper-class unveiled women included in the survey arrived at their social position at various points in the last century, or earlier. Many have worked as public activists and volunteers for charitable organizations, as women have done for several generations in Egypt.[6] Many work for a living, due to the recent inflation and the lowered value of pensions, although they might not discuss their circumstances. Others boast about their employment as a sign of their higher education.

The middle-class unveiled women were divided into many subcategories. Some came from families that had declined in earnings but not in status. Many of these women would still be identified as *bint al-dhawwat* by lower-class women, although they did not receive the highest incomes comparatively speaking.

Sawsan el-Messiri describes the *ibn al-dhawwat* through the eyes of the lower class as a kind of foreigner, affected by an emulation of Western culture.[7] She says that the *ibn al-balad* calls the *ibn al-dhawwat* lazy and idle, since he inherits wealth rather than working for it. *Ibn al-dhawwat* is comfortable with *afrangi* (foreign) table manners, and *bint al-dhawwat* cares more about her appearance than her family or the order of her household.[8] We should remember that el-Messiri is discussing stereotypes here, but they are informative.

The *effendi,* on the other hand, represents the white-collar classes and must by virtue of his occupation be more "diplomatic" and "submissive" than one employed outside the bureaucracy.[9] A curious feature of Egyptian society is that the *effendi* now makes a set government salary that may be far lower than that of his social inferiors. The *bint al-balad* considers the female governmental employee to be underpaid, "conceited, superficial and neglectful of her wifely duties."[10] This must also be translated to include the envy she holds for the education of the middle-class woman.[11] The lower-class woman considers the clothes and appearance of the middle-class woman to be expenses not justified by her low salary.

El-Messiri's portraits do not tell us how unveiled women conceive of themselves. I want merely to suggest some aspects of self-view constructed from the interview data in chapter 4.

The unveiled woman is aware of her presence in the modern debate over dress and image systems. At the very least, she recognizes that the environment has changed dramatically when she makes a social statement by *not* veiling.

The unveiled woman represented the debate of a generation gap earlier in the century. Just as many of the veiled women have rebelled, in a sense, against their unveiled mothers, their mothers or grandmothers had rebelled against the dominant female images of their youths. Some of the older unveiled women are aware of the generational dimension of the war of images and discuss it.

Spectrum of Age and Politics

Many more of the unveiled women in this study were older and more experienced than the veiled women. Among younger students, unveiled women seemed to outnumber veiled women in the humanities and social sciences sections of the universities. The reverse was true in the hard sciences, in education, and in the Arabic-language departments. In Cairo, the proportion of veiled to unveiled women varies depending on the neighborhood. The ratios have changed because *muhaggabat* have moved into elite areas such as Heliopolis, Muhandesin, or even Zamalak, while other women have become *muhaggabat* who were already residents.

The unveiled women were generally more politicized and possessed of a civic consciousness than were the veiled women.[12] That fact is related to age, experience, and available time. The veiled university students mainly studied and spent time with their friends. Some of them had been involved in political issues on campus, but they were exceptions to the main group. More of the unveiled students were willing to discuss specific political issues than were the veiled students, but that might be due to the censorship of the Islamists on campus.

The unveiled women held a wider spectrum of political orientations and beliefs, and more of them were politically active in some way. More unveiled women had voted or worked for a political campaign than had veiled women in their age categories. Some were deeply involved in social programs that affected their political views.

Many of the older, unveiled elite women had worked as volunteers for many charitable causes. This work seemed to enhance their political consciousness and their understanding of events and social contradictions surrounding them. Others had been involved in the dispute over the personal status reforms and viewed the relegislation of personal status as a special dilemma.[13]

Older unveiled women in particular had a complex view of the state and its relationship to Islamic opposition. These women have witnessed unique transformations in the social and economic policies of the state. Some had lived through World War II, the revolution of 1952, and the defeat of 1967, which the younger women knew only through books. Perhaps their experiences taught them to recognize the ever-shifting character of Egyptian politics. They know that the Egyptian tolerance for difficulty and inequity is not unlimited. Some had also demonstrated their concern that female participation in politics is still low[14] and were actively involved in campaigns to address that problem.[15]

Elite and middle-class women know that other men and women disapprove of their career and political activities. When Jehan Sadat decided to run for the Minufiyya People's Council, her husband cautioned her, "Whether you run or not is up to you, Jehan. . . . But remember that the more you work outside the home, the more you will be criticized."[16] She understood that part of the problem comes from the sanctioning of patriarchy by public figures, like Qaddhafi, who wrote "To demand equality between them [a woman and a man] in any dirty work which stains her beauty and detracts from her femininity is unjust and cruel."[17]

Sullivan's descriptions of parliamentary women in Egypt cover some of the women I interviewed as well. He states that most entered political life through the special provisions for female representatives enacted in 1979.[18] Still, they have had to succeed "on their own merits," says Sullivan, which include "professional expertise," extensive "political contacts," and experience; sophistication and proficiency in debating in the Arabic language;[19] and the fact that they appear respectable and well-dressed, have normal family lives, and campaign with the support and approval of their husbands.[20] All these qualifications of propriety are essential, but they mean that women are viewed as conformists in many senses, challengers only in their official public personae.

Unveiled Women and the Reproductive Sphere

The unveiled woman also believes that the family is the center of society. Children are desired by all and are seen as the source of continuing life and belief. *Illi khallaf ma maat* is a fairly classless proverb (one who reproduces does not die). Women consider their reproductive role and their duties as nurturer and role model to their children to be paramount, placed before concerns such as marital happiness, public service, or self-fulfillment.

Among the upper and middle classes, children are not needed as an immediate source of economic or household support as they are among the lower classes. In the middle and upper classes, children may inherit a family business or assets. Parents may worry more about their abilities to handle these sort of responsibilities. They may become an important source of financial support in cases of disaster or illness, or perhaps a source of emotional support to elderly parents. In transitional economic periods, when inflation occurs, currency fluctuates greatly, and great fortunes may be won or lost, children are logically regarded as a potential resource.

By the time they were in their late teens or early twenties, the older unveiled women had generally married. They had their children early and began graduate studies or careers after their children entered school. The younger unveiled women were delaying marriage a little longer, due no doubt to the current financial and housing crises.[21] Women who were twenty-five or twenty-six viewed marriage as a fairly inevitable and desirable prospect and thought they were ready to marry. They were considering careers along with the idea that they intended to have children within five years.[22]

The unveiled upper-middle-class and upper-class women came from smaller families and produced fewer children than the veiled women of the petite bourgeoisie. They viewed birth control as essential and as a guarantor of the quality of life for their living children.

Yvonne Haddad and Valerie Hoffman-Ladd discuss material from the *Ikhwan* referring to working women's infertility or reduced reproductive capacity.[23] The older, highly educated unveiled women felt these claims were both ridiculous and malicious, but allowed that such perspectives were not uncommon in widely read media materials.

The Working World

The career woman is deeply embedded in the image of unveiled women. The Qur'an itself supports the right of women to work *and* to gain recompense for their labor. ''And covet not the thing in which God hath made some of you excel others. To men a share (or a fortune) of what they earned and to women a share (or a fortune) of what they earned.''[24] Unveiled women cited this verse and listed examples of women who ruled, or controlled property in their own right, or were consulted for their knowledge, as evidence that women always held roles in addition to the family, in Islam. Khadijah, the Prophet's wife, was often mentioned, as was Umm Salim, who adjudicated over the dispute of Abdullah bin Abbas and Zayd bin Sabat in the first century of Islam.[25] She participated in most of the Prophet's expeditions, as did other women. The unveiled women cited Sitt ul-Mulk, the Fatimid regent who ruled Egypt in the eleventh century, and Shajarat ad-Durr, the Mamluk who ruled in the thirteenth century, as prototypes for twentieth-century women who sought political influence.

The older historical archetypes were referred to more frequently by contemporary women than twentieth-century models such as Huda Sha‘rawi, Nabawiyya Musa, or Doria Shafik. Unveiled women employed historical references mainly to support women's right to work or their equal potential as compared to men, with the same degree of conviction that veiled women had shown when they used historical examples to support veiling, or education for women.

Wafaa Marei points out that women have entered the work force in different sectors and with differing motivations in Egypt. While lower-class women have been recruited into industry, middle- and upper-class women were more apt to have viewed employment as "an ideological commitment for the assertion of rights and independence."[26] Marei implies that women who have viewed wage employment as an individual goal for self-enhancement and self-definition differ from lower-class women who have worked due to economic necessity.[27]

Earlier sex-role expansion broke the ground for Nasserist policies, whereby the public sector controlled and regulated recruitment of women. Although women entered the civil service widely, their entry into fields outside of education, special services, and health care took time and aroused criticism.[28] Their enhanced educational opportunities aided entry into white-collar areas.[29] To this day, women are well represented in the public sector, especially in certain ministries, and in the service sector. Unveiled women are generally aware of the composition of female employment and know that they have fairly good employment opportunities in certain fields.[30] In a sense, they view the state as a sponsor for female employment thus far and the Islamists and Islamic conservatives as opponents of female employment. They also believe that unemployment and underemployment are on the rise. Some of them think that the state may give in to pressure against female employment, should the power configurations within the regime change to any great degree.

Social Control over Sexuality, Veiling, and Segregation

Unveiled women adhere to the idea that both male and female sexuality should be controlled to some degree through the socialization process and individual self-control. But many unveiled women feel that the use of *higab* and sex segregation to regulate male-female interaction is retrogressive and an imposition on their rights as individuals. Women are insulted by suggestions that they are immodest or that they represent sources of temptation at their jobs. Furthermore, they find the Islamist logic discriminatory, for men are not equally exhorted to protect their modesty or to control their sexual impulses.

A young unveiled woman was fairly agitated by our discussion of this issue. She was quite sure that she wanted to pursue a career, and if her husband tried to discourage her, she said she would stand firm. She felt that if her husband could not trust her, she would be happier with someone else.[31]

Another interviewee stated that she was modest and dressed conservatively, and did not feel that she was required by the Qur'an to cover her hair. She mentioned that older women might adopt the *higab* and she might do that later in her life. In fact, another older woman said that she adopted the *higab* after being widowed, when her thoughts turned more to God. Her view is common in other Mediterranean countries, where in the years of menopause and after, women veil more heavily or dress more conservatively. The origin of this concept is not found in the Qur'an, which states: "As for women past the age of cohabiting [with issue resulting], they sin not if they discard their attire [outer] in such a way as not to reveal their *zina*. (Surah xxiv: 60)"[32]

Several young women emphasized the utility of moral standards to act as social controls. For example, they felt that Western crime, drug abuse, and psychological problems were due in part to relaxed sexual standards resulting in single-parent families, split families, and social anomie. They felt that sex must continue to be restricted within marriage, as did their veiled peers. Sexual purity could not be maintained merely with modesty, or by blinding people to visual temptation, they said, but required self-control. A woman who was really aware of the consequences of her actions was safer than one covered from head to toe.

Up until the last five or six years, the unveiled woman has watched the growing use of the *higab* with tolerance. Most of my respondents stated that they respect the choice of other women, but do not wish to have their own freedom of expression, employment, or travel restricted. Gradually, some of the middle-class and upper-class women have recognized that the veiling phenomenon is affecting them. One unveiled woman who has light hair and is quite fair told me:

> I went to the hospital to visit my friend. I was dressed decently, you know. I wore a skirt that was midcalf length and full, but I had on a blouse with short sleeves because it was extremely hot. As I moved to get into the elevator, one of those religious types, with a beard and a long shirt, shouted at me, "How dare you come to our country and insult our religion!" Well, it's my country and my religion, too. How dare he talk to me as if I'm a foreigner!

Women who adopt the *higab* also criticize unveiled women. A sense of social or moral awakening, after all, is what the *muhaggabat* say they are responding to. Women's unveiled status is directly challenged by the Islamists. Covering their bodies signals their moral awakening. Wearers state silently through the *higab*, "I am more modest than you, and you should follow my example." Certain respondents praised their peers who had added the *niqab* for their modesty and "goodness."[33] Veiling spreads within families and among friends and peers, along with a conception of Islamic opposition. In response, a smaller group of unveiled women have become more vocal against the *higab*, for they fear that their own civil rights may eventually be affected.

Similarly, unveiled women oppose the notion of increased sex segregation. There are already areas of sex segregation traditional to Egyptian social intercourse that they are used to and accept. For example, a husband and wife may entertain their friends separately and carry out many recreational activities separately. Women shop together, and the public coffeehouses and many restaurants are places where men congregate and single women would be out of place. That is not the sort of segregation that the unveiled woman finds disturbing. She resists the notion that men and women should be separated at educational institutions, within meetings, or at places of employment. She opposes the idea that women should receive training or education in fields deemed exclusively female—or that women train and intern in fields only to give them up because they cannot work in segregated conditions, or simply to marry.

Unveiled Women and the Family

Woman's natural place is within the family, according to unveiled as well as veiled women. They believe woman's position is a result of her essential nature, which harmonizes and complements the male principle among all living things.[34] They believe that all women have basic needs to love, nurture, and be loved that are best met in a family setting.

The unveiled woman believes herself equal to men with respect to her responsibilities and her rights. This does not mean that she is identical to men, nor does she wish to be treated as if she were. She believes that Islam protects women's status, but notes that non-Islamic traditions have infiltrated *turath* to impose and perpetuate limitations on women's social and political rights.

The unveiled woman conceives of her parental, filial, and marital responsibilities as a religious duty. One respondent was asked how she personally conceived of her faith and lived up to it. She responded:

> I won't do anything that would hurt anybody or offend anyone. I look after my family. I obey my husband and my parents. This is what our religion asks us to do.[35]

Parental approval and the *barakah,* or blessing, derived from it is extremely important to a successful marriage and career in Egypt, even if women engage in some degree of self-denial.[36] Parents often wanted their daughters to pursue certain careers. They encouraged them to take the preparatory courses required, paying for outside tutoring, and discussing the merits of that field with them over the years. Nevertheless, it seems that the modern unveiled woman experienced less parental interference than women of her mother's generation.[37]

According to Safia Mohsen, some women of the upper classes have been able to adopt Western practices such as dating and "marriages for love."[38] Films and the media imply that young people normally date, marry and choose careers freely, too freely. But most of the respondents in this survey did not date or marry without supervision, nor did they choose their course of study without advice. Young women were often allowed to go on group outings, without the supervision of elders, and there might be a special boy they were interested in. Actual solo dates really meant they were seriously involved or engaged.

The unveiled woman who had the influence of an independent, working, socially conscious mother in her life displayed the effects of her mother's outlook. Many of these were upper- and middle-class women, who were, after all, the primary beneficiaries of the state's educational and employment policies in the Nasserist era. Elite women who did not enter the public sector began to enter other areas of employment in the private sector during the economic opening.[39] Living with working mothers convinced these young women that employment outside the home was appropriate and necessary for a modern woman.

Unveiled as well as veiled women are generally involved in complex family interactions.[40] They visit relatives, exchange favors and information, are available for emergencies, and celebrate all sorts of occasions, minor and major, with their families. For those with rural ties, that can mean frequent trips out of Cairo, or many cross-city trips for urbanites.

Unveiled women view their husbands as lifetime partners, whether or not they are entirely compatible. Women, especially women with children, are often reluctant to divorce their husbands or to be divorced. Much social stigma continues to be attached to divorced women, because they generally lose economic power, unless they happen to be wealthy women in their own right. The sexual control of single women who are not virgins supervised by their father's household is very problematic within any patriarchal culture. Widowed women, as well as divorced women, fall in this category, although many widows resolve this issue by living with their grown children. Newly single women lose social status, whether they continue to reside alone[41] or go back to their parents' household, where they may again become dependents. Some of the laws addressed by the personal status reforms may eventually alleviate some of the conditions of, and attitudes toward divorced women, but that may take years.[42] In the meantime, women feel that harmonious relations with their mates are essential to their social and economic security.

Safia Mohsen notes problems in the transition between female role expansion in the public sphere and role transformation within the family. The situation varies according to couples' social and economic backgrounds. Many men, especially those in the lower-middle classes, have experienced growing difficulty in supporting their families but resent their wives' entry into the wage force. Hence:

> Many men express their feelings of insecurity by tightening their grip over the family and by exaggerating the expression of their authority over its members, especially the working wife. Lacking the social backing for their changing roles, some lower-middle-class women put up with the husband's restrictions and thus have accepted family conditions that are the same if not worse than those endured by the less educated generally unemployed women of the past generations.[43]

Their husbands' insecurities may lead to further justifications for wearing the *higab*, although my respondents did not describe these pressures as their impetus for veiling.

Ideally, the unveiled woman wants a man who will take pride in her accomplishments, in or out of the home, and one who delights in her efforts at education or self-education. If, in fact, she settles for a good deal less, paradoxically that may be because she values her family life so highly.

If women have long dominated the running of their households, it is difficult for them to give up that form of control. In my survey, some couples now shared long-term budget planning, while women generally controlled household funds and their salaries.[44] Most of these women stated that their husbands initially disapproved of their careers, and acceded later, but still expected a perfect home and good service within the home. It was hard to deliver that perfection on a tight schedule, sometimes even harder to delegate tasks to others who did them sloppily. One respondent told me that she has a maid, but she never lets her touch the washing machine, so she has to do all the laundry and hang it out herself. It would be even harder to delegate household tasks to an unwilling and inept husband. Mohsen suggests that it is very difficult for women to give up full domestic control. She says that women feel less secure in their "extradomestic environment," and that giving up domestic functions makes them feel "they have lost control over their lives."[45]

Part of the solution lies with the socialization of children. Some of the unveiled women discussed the importance of teaching their sons to cook, to clean, and to understand that their sisters were as important as they were.

The unveiled woman is more likely to approve of outside childcare than the idealized veiled woman. In fact, she may have been able to pay for in-home care, or may have stayed home with her children before embarking on a career. However, some of the female respondents were quite active in fundraising for organizing childcare and had campaigned for childcare issues.[46]

Summary of the Image of the Unveiled Woman

The unveiled woman echoes the veiled woman in calling for continued commitment to the family structure. Her ideal model also requires the husband to be a loving, consultative, faithful partner, but permits women more independence in decision making.

The unveiled woman, like the veiled woman, has high expectations of herself as a mother. She is responsible for the moral fabric of her children, but she does not see herself as a substitute for available public or private education.

The unveiled woman views her participation in the public sphere as a moral, intellectual, or national duty. At the very least, she theoretically approves of working women, even if she does not work herself. Some women feel that they have a patriotic and moral obligation to work as advocates of women's legal rights and improved service to women. Women's public activism is thus an accepted feature of female activity to the unveiled woman.[47]

The image of the unveiled women encompasses a great range of religiosity. The unveiled woman considered the *jawhar*, or essence of her religion, to be more important than the *mazhar*, or exterior practices, although most observe the *mazhar* through regular prayer, fasting during Ramadan, reading of the Qur'an, and so on. The veiled women, on the other hand, believes her *higab* to be part of the *mazhar* of her Islam. The unveiled woman disagrees, but stresses the importance of interpersonal relations and good deeds within Islam.[48]

The two images are now confronting one another. The unveiled woman has considered the sources of veiling and is familiar with the Islamist message. According to my data, she is alarmed by the political gains made by the Islamists, although she may understand the social basis for their demands. The unveiled woman is troubled by the prospect of an Islamic state controlled by the members of current Islamist groups. This is because she is beginning to realize that such a scenario will feature a new dominant image for women, that of the veiled woman. In that case many of the perogatives the unveiled woman has enjoyed may be curtailed.

Some of the unveiled women expressed distaste for certain ideological sources of the veiled woman, particularly the shaykhs, popular writers, and speakers whose knowledge and presentation of scriptural materials is selective, repetitive, erroneous, uncited, or unsophisticated. Some women were contemptuous, yet alarmed, as they described Islamist women and those they believe recruit them. Their tone is affected by their perceptions of women's educational and professional status.[49]

The unveiled woman may support or criticize the current regime, but she believes that to some degree it can protect the legal and social advances made by women in Egypt thus far. She assesses current events in a sophisticated way and therefore envisions a multiplicity of outcomes more readily than do the younger, less politicized veiled women. She may view the competing image of the veiled woman with increasing trepidation as time goes on, unless the Islamist oppositionist groups are somehow diverted or disempowered by the state.

Up to the last eight or nine years, the middle class and the petite bourgeoisie have found the dominant image, the unveiled woman, to be powerful and appealing, and have aspired to her appearance, attributes, and possessions. Their emulation of the unveiled woman is now less apparent as the adoption of the *higab* and the search for a male provider have rationally met the growing economic strains on these groups. The lower-middle classes have been less able to compete for marriage partners, say Mohsen; clothing, makeup, and beauty-parlor fees are too high.[50] The lower-middle classes have had to utilize public transportation, cars are too expensive for many, and therefore their modesty and self-conceptions have been under attack.[51]

Two elements remain problematic in this description of dominant and alternative images. The examples of elite and upper-middle-class women who abandoned their very successful dominant image do not fit into the explanations given above. Some reasons for this trend have been given in chapters 4 and 5. We may also hypothesize that in some instances upper-class and upper-middle-class women have responded to the alternative image, rather than the heretofore dominant image, because they have not felt that their own lives fit the ideal image clearly enough. The trigger may be a domineering husband or parents, reduced economic circumstances, frustrated career expectations, feelings of confusion over conflicting goals, or a general feeling that they lack control over their lives. Hence, adopting the *higab* and the mores of the veiled woman represents an individual and independent decision that really cannot be overruled by their husbands or families. In reshaping their image identification they can safely experience the sensation of publicly sanctioned defiance.

Coda: Bint al-Balad

The *bint al-balad* is another image that has not been much affected either by the dominance of the unveiled woman or the challenge of the veiled woman. She is religious but thus far has adopted neither the *higab* nor the political oppositionism of the Islamists.

The *bint al-balad* has not adopted Western fashions or consumer tastes, as have upper-class unveiled women.[52] She would rather not work in a factory or an office situation, although certain specific work areas within the neighborhood have traditionally belonged to the *bint al-balad*. Many *banat al-balad* conceal the fact that they work as servants, if possible. Their continued concern for family honor and the opinions of their neighbor means that even if they work, they have not crossed the same boundaries as upper-class women and do not fit the Islamist criticisms of working women.

Now the *bint al-balad* is also known as the *bint al-suq*, daughter of the market, for she is frequently employed in a family-owned shop or stall.[53] She may also legitimately open her own marketing operation. The *bint al-balad* is allowed and expected to be outspoken, self-sufficient, ingenious, and full of spunk.

Sometimes a *bint al-balad*, often a widow, may become a *mu'allima* (literally, teacher or master) and employ others, usually men.[54] She might have inherited a husband's or a family's business, a coffeehouse, a butcher's shop, or perhaps a smuggling racket that has survived in the district. Often she employs gangs of toughs to collect protection money and deal with the competition. Women who are strong enough to manipulate these operations are regarded as "men," a phrase that shows that people believe they have relinquished some degree of the feminine qualities of dependence, softness, and delicacy of manner in return for control over their establishments. Of course women who exhibit all the traditional foils, care for their appearance, and are coquettish, may also be ruthless and power hungry, so perhaps the *mu'allima* is not such an exception. We are really entering the territory of ethno-aesthetics here, where shades of gray are infinitely important.

Generally, the *bint al-balad* enjoys her work environment, although she respects a husband who can "feed her."[55] In the home, both sexes know that "*is-sittat byihkumu*," the women rule the roost. Men give a ceremonial impression of authority, but, Unni Wikan notes, they have no idea of exactly what the family owns or consumes.[56]

The *bint al-balad* is uniquely equipped, according to Evelyn Early, to deal with ambivalent attitudes toward gender and gender relations. For example, Early mentions the sexual reluctance that baladi women are "expected to feel. They should hold back, but they should likewise obey their husbands."[57] They may express this ambivalence through oral narrative or in action.[58]

The culture of the *bint al-balad* may be more intact and continuous than that of her upper-and middle-class counterparts, for several reasons. Social mobility has been restricted in Egypt, and in many ways the *banat al-balad* have maintained those restrictions themselves. Economic mobility has not been as limited, and therefore produced even greater social confusion and anomie when economic class mobility has intersected with the effects of social crystallizations.[59] The middle classes were more affected, however, than the lower classes.

The *bint al-balad* has a tradition of feeling comfortable with her own image and self-confident. In the 1920s and 1930s the common man, Masri Effendi, was idealized and became a national symbol. During the Nasser period, while the *effendi* of the bureaucracy actually benefited from state policies, there was an official sponsorship of folk culture. The common man was pictured as the core of Egypt, a source of national pride and Islamic heritage. Plays and stories in colloquial Arabic were written, folk dance was officially sponsored, as were revivals of traditional textile arts. Certain of these traditions belonged to the rural Egyptian, but many belonged to the *ibn al-balad* and strengthened his sense of culture.

Also, during the last seventeen years, the tradesmen in Egypt and other *awlad al-balad,* the craftsmen, butchers, grocers, plumbers, purveyors of fruits and vegetables, hashish merchants, currency speculators, and others have made fortunes. In comparison to the *effendi* class, these groups did very well and experienced great economic, if not social, rewards.[60] Wikan feels that even poorer members of the lower classes acquired goods and are materially better off than in the early 1970s.[61] Others became wealthier after working overseas.

The outcome of these economic currents is mixed. Most *baladi* women have clung to their own self-image; wealth does not change their social standing or pride but enhances their living style. Others who made fortunes during this period, but belong to the lower-middle classes, have been more affected by social ostracization, and some of these women have adopted the veil.

The *bint al-balad* views her modesty as truly Egyptian as well as truly Islamic. She is not likely to exchange her *mandil* and *malayya* for the *higab* unless it is imposed on her by others within society. Those whom I interviewed valued their own interpretations of Islam more than the obscure teachings of a particular shaykh or commentator, or texts they cannot read.

The *bint al-balad* does not go to the mosque to pray, in any case, though she visits shrines and attends *zars* (rituals of exorcism), and the saints' festivals. Much of her social life is already segregated from men: her friendships, participations in weddings, and other community events. Therefore, she does not respond to the Islamists' call for increased separation of the sexes.

The idea of a state run by the Islamists is strange to the *banat al-balad.* Perhaps this is because they feel excluded from the state, and simultaneously are masters at manipulating their benefits within the system. Or perhaps this is because they feel their religion deeply and respect the principles of *shariʿah* within their neighborhood already. It may be difficult for them to imagine exterior imposition of these principles onto their daily life.

Some of the *banat al-balad* who work as servants are the exceptions among this group, having adopted versions of the *khimar,* the headcovering of the *muhaggabat,* worn over their headscarf when they travel between neighborhoods to their jobs. But they really do not display the accompanying increased religiosity shown by other social classes. The meaning of *higab* to them is restricted to a defense of their modesty in the street.

Conclusion

The unveiled women in Egypt respond to a set of images influenced by socioeconomic requirements. Since the socioeconomic bases within Egypt have shifted rapidly within the last twenty years, fluidity and flexibility comparable to that found in the image of the veiled woman is present in the unveiled women's image of self-identification. The model of the unveiled woman does not clash with that of the *bint al-balad*. In fact, many of the upper- and middle-class women take pride in certain qualities prized by the *bint al-balad;* her affection for her origins, her *khifat dam* (light heartedness), her resourcefulness, and especially her *shahama*. *Shahama* is usually translated as "gallantry," or "chivalry," but can mean "big-heartedness." The idealized unveiled woman is ready to help others in need, to direct them and give of herself to an extent that would be unusual in other societies. To these qualities the upper-class women add a keen apprehension of tone, color, and emotion, for they are excellent observers and connoisseurs of their surroundings. They incorporate an impeccable sense of timing, style, and moderation into their repertoire of feminine qualities.

The images of the veiled woman and the unveiled woman do clash, precisely in their interpretations of gender roles, and specifically in their definitions of womanhood. While the veiled women define themselves functionally as believers who are women, the unveiled women define themselves as women who believe, but are quintessentially independent, individualist, and feminine.

Chapter 7

DREAMING THE MYTH, AND VEILING IT

The image of the new virtuous woman has sparked debate within Egyptian society over the proper interpretation of gender issues. The changing goals of young women who have adopted the Islamist perspectives of that image, along with the new Islamic dress, may eventually affect a broad range of social issues.

Gender Orientation

The changing nature of gender issues has proven to be the battleground for existing and emerging interpretations of female nature, functions and morality. The decisions women make regarding the Islamist presentation of gender issues are the most essential part of their ideological framework as *women* adherents or sympathizers. The Islamists are significant as modern Muslims, as political activists, as entrepreneurs, as risk takers, and as class actors, but also as those who shape the next generation.

A Pluralism in Social Identity

A select group of women, who reflect the orientations of many other urban Egyptian women, have found the image of the new virtuous woman applicable to their own lives. If we accept the idea that they made their decision as part of an identity crisis, then it is interesting that the other women who remain unveiled do not appear to be particularly traumatized. They ardently assert their own set of values with regard to gender issues and the idealization of female roles. One should characterize the competition of images for women within Egyptian society as a basic pluralism of gender interpretations.

Far from being static, the situation has responded to political and socioeconomic dynamics within the society. The balance between the competing images is precarious. Tensions have mounted in arguments over female dress, orientation, and employment. Gender-image pluralism may seem socially healthy. In fact, however, women and the competing political forces that shape them may not indefinitely tolerate a battle of images. Competing images may go underground if the Islamists attain political control of the state.

Should this occur, many elements of the new veiled woman might be politically imposed on other women, as we saw happen in Iran.[1] Most respondents, however, felt that the events in Egypt would take their own specific historical form, and that even the issue of Islamic dress differs in these two Middle Eastern contexts.

The Utility of the Self-Image Framework

The veiled women surveyed for this study exhibited strong, developed notions of self-image. They were able to describe their goals theoretically and personally. They anchored themselves through historical allusions to the implications of an idealized image. They then utilized multiple historical archetypes from the Muslim experience to verify the archetype of the self. According to Jung, definition and unification of the psyche are among the functions of image projection. When these processes can be accomplished through the use of archetypes, the individual can then define and differentiate between good and evil, and perceive the balance between them. The archetype permits the individual simultaneously to link with the past and to "*dream the myth onwards* and give it a modern dress."[2]

Jung implies that syzygy, the conjoining process, works in one direction, permitting the self to grow from the historical model, which he illustrates through a discussion of the Christ image and the Western psyche. He asks the alchemists' question, "Is the self a symbol of Christ, or is Christ a symbol of self?" He then answers that the second formula must be true.[3]

The new image of women, like earlier female image models, aids women in visualizing and unifying the various and conflicting portions of their own lives and the morality code they seek to apply to it. Foucault explains the same phenomena in a different way, identifying his concern to be the morality of behaviors:

> One must determine how and with what margins of variation or transgression individuals or groups conduct themselves in reference to a prescriptive system that is explicitly or implicitly operative in their culture, and of which they are more or less aware.[4]

The differences one finds have to do with the "*mode d'assujetissement*", he says—that is, the way individuals conceive of their "relation to the rule," and their conceptions of their obligations to practice the rules.[5] The utility of self-image that accords with an ideal model of behavior is that women are better able to express the rules, in this case, the *shariʿah*, and "subject" themselves to what they believe is expected of them. There are multiple reasons for adherence to any code, and the Islamists are stronger for the unification of these reasons into one impulse.

Women, even young women, already understand how to unify the diverse parts of their daily lives quite effectively. A unified self-image that nonetheless allows for some flexibility aids both young and older *muhaggabat* to adjust their aspirations to their circumstances. Because their model for identification is both modern and historical, it is both more visible and more tangible to them.

The veiled women are not "dreaming the myth" by themselves; they are part of a society-wide movement of men and women. They should be regarded as synthesizers of a historical image, a sociopolitical ideal, and an ongoing physical environment, with all its attending social dynamics.

Accurately or not, the Islamists have developed a specific position on women's status, women's history, and women's ideal functions and nature. The reactions of the rest of society have caused them to modify and adapt certain of their positions.

The "virtuous veiled woman" is distinct from the idealized *bint al-balad* and from the idealized elite, unveiled woman, but all three images are valid for their own adherents and respond to certain shared elements of their cultural history. Therefore, women identifying with these respective images agree on many principles and share many insights and reactions to gender-motivated questions.

Nonetheless, women have fundamentally disagreed on those points that form the less flexible Islamist stances: the state's role in gender issues, dress, and female employment. They have sharply expressed these divisions, which arise to some degree from differences in social origins and from exposure to changing concepts of sex-role expansion.

Female Activism and Oppositionist Islam

A continued public role for women appears likely within the moderate stratum of Islamist activity. If this stratum continues to dominate the wider grouping of Islamists, it may be impossible to curb female activism to the degree that many conservatives or members of the radical fringe would hope for. And yet female activism in the public arena may decline in the future.

ʿAsam al-ʿAryan claims that women have an active role to play in the Islamic movement and has stated: "We do not have to impose the *higab,* in any case, women are adopting it of their own volition."[6] He says the movement must utilize the talents and skills of women in redesigning a society that requires the input and expertise of all of its members. A more concrete determination of the degree of female activism, and how widely the movement accepts it, should be a subject for further research.

A profound gulf exists between al-ʿAryan's and al Ghazali's statements on female activism and the outlook of the young women students. The young women generally adhere to the leaders' views but do not accept the basic notion of political activism for women. They do not recognize the fact that, ironically, the oppositionist status of the Islamists has made female activism more necessary, and therefore, more acceptable, within the universities and outside them. At present, the range of activities within this female activism may include meetings, reading group attendance, participation in public prayers, or recruitment. These activities are socially and politically important because they represent an identification with a set of goals and with an authority outside of the family, the government, or state institutions.

Sources of Oppositionism

Tajdid movements emerge cyclically, and the Islamist groups fit into that categorization. The calls for *tajdid*, (renewal) were hastened by the ideological bankruptcy, the regional stalemate, and the declining economic conditions in Egypt. These forces combined with perceptions of continued exploitation and economic penetration of the country by foreign and foreign-influenced local capital, and have caused social pressures to mount. People have searched for an indigenous, historically authentic, viable alternative. To many, the *Ikhwan* and other Islamist groups have presented the most appealing option.

Some social scientists have proffered hypotheses regarding the societal element most likely to respond to the messages of oppositionist Islam. I have attempted to see where my sample fits into the profile presented by Ibrahim, Guenena, Ansari, and others[7] of the petit bourgeois predilection toward activist Islam. The profile suggested by the veiled respondents was that of a young, educated, rural or urban, petit bourgeois woman. The factors that differentiated veiled women from their unveiled counterparts were age (they were younger overall), father's occupation (a lower percentage of white-collar work), mother's occupation (a higher percentage of housewives), and place of birth (more from rural areas). Although this profile conveniently falls into the pattern described by the existing literature, it was troubling that a paradigm built on it does not explain the adherence of older women, elite women, and daughters of publicly active women. In fact, in a comparison of profiles of veiled women and unveiled women, it is significant that the unveiled women displayed less socioeconomic variation than did the veiled women.

The wider, more flexible profile can be explained in several ways. Peer pressure is an important ingredient, combined with the insecurity of the political and economic environment, that has served to spread the phenomenon of veiling (but not necessarily active opposition to the state) more widely through society. Also, women's motivations for adopting the *higab* seemed to have had more to do with searching for self-esteem and finding a way to display morality than with a conscious economic rationale. Therefore, women of wider socioeconomic origins, who, after all, see each other and move together in the urban environment, are more likely to replicate behavior. Finally, although the veiling phenomenon among younger women may have occurred most rapidly among the girls of the Azhar schools, the extension of the Islamist groups themselves to visible economic niches, and apolitical as well as political activities, has had some influence among older and middle-aged women. Older and middle-aged women are also affected by peer pressure and influenced by the behavior and opinions of younger family members, in some cases. Therefore, the Islamist image is not strictly an illustration of the generation gap.

Social Explanations for Female Identification

A purely social or purely economic explanation is not satisfactory. Women's interactions illustrate nuances of economic and social background within the Egyptian framework. Social mobility occurs in a culturally specific manner in Egypt. The factors that block social mobility have now encountered a culturally determined method of rewriting the rules of the game. The Islamist emphasis on enhanced justice and distribution of public goods is a part of that historically sanctioned *modus operandi.*

Benefits of Identification

Do women acquire heightened social status if they adopt the *higab?* Is that in fact what they are seeking? Instead, they seem concerned primarily with self-esteem as it emerges from association with a morality code. To a lesser degree than in some other Middle Eastern countries, in Egypt one remains linked to the social and economic information provided in one's family name. The social and economic position of the family during one's young adulthood may be even more important. Because of the changed circumstances of the *infitah* period, important shifts in social and economic status occurred. Young women have been particularly vulnerable to the changed circumstances that have affected their ability to compete with their peers for the goods promised by the dominant paradigm of women—marriage, career, a comfortable flat filled with furniture, elegant clothing, and so on.

Far fewer of the respondents of this study actually fit the above explanation than was suggested by previous research. But then, it was a difficult scenario to prove or disprove. Those respondents whom I suspected had been under that sort of competitive pressure explained their altered self-image in moral terms.

The young *muhaggabat* have received approval and criticism for their new orientations. They gained more approval than disapproval from family members. The reverse was true for veiled women of elite backgrounds. The *muhaggabat* attained a heightened freedom of movement provided by the *higab* and were often deemed better marriage material.

The Moral Dimension of Women's History

Yvonne Haddad and others have outlined multicausative factors for women's adopting *higab* or Islamic dress.[8] Yet, Fadwa el-Guindi and Valerie Hoffman-Ladd have described this phenomenon as a moral choice.[9] One may ask to what extent moral values are class-based—or more accurately, to what extent Egyptian women and men perceive moral values or religiosity to be derived from class origin. Is the wearing of *higab* simply a means for middle-class and elite women to reclaim the outward morality still expressed in the dress of lower-class women? Do they believe that the elite has truly become less moral by virtue of their experiences over the last several decades? These questions are presented in the media in Egypt and greatly oversimplified.

Multiple purposes are served by wearing the *higab;* economic choices could conveniently hide behind the moral decision, while an ostensible political choice might mask social pressure. Given the effort I made to encourage the women to form their own explanations, it was significant that all the respondents described moral motivations for adopting the *higab* and minimized any other motivations. Whether the respondents were entirely truthful or not, it means that the moral sphere of decision making is more highly valued than economic or social rationales. The emphasis on the moral importance of a new "virtuous" set of goals and ideals is related to the experience of the Islamic history of women as it has been absorbed and reinterpreted by contemporary women.

It was imperative for oppositionist strains in society to reformulate a definition of virtue in the 1970s and 1980s. Classic interpretations of virtue from the history of Muslim women seemed inapplicable to new and shifting concepts of morality, concepts that were tied not only to the integrity of Muslim women, but to the value of social justice in a widely unequal society.

Consider the display of Western fantasy life and immorality as portrayed in the television programs "Dallas" or "Falconcrest," which are viewed avidly in Egypt. The Islamists responded that these cultural messages attest to the nihilism of the West, where the negation of honor, justice, and family loyalties are enshrined in popular culture. The readoption of virtue, along with loyalty, courage, reform-mindedness, and sincerity, have emphasized historical continuity. Hence, the reexamination of Islamic history is the quest of an entire society to reiterate its worth. Muslims hope to refer to their own *turath*, dissensions and all, without giving in lock, stock, and barrel to the gross materialism and anomie included in the Egyptian version of "Westoxification."[10]

Women have created a new orientation to their community, to their own bodies, and to the veil. They have described a sort of inner revitalization that stands as a metaphor for the spiritual awakening that they believe society has longed for. Since they believe they are enacting the will of Allah, it is instructive to remember Jung's comments:

> All in all, it is not only more advantageous but more "correct" psychologically to explain as the "will of God" the natural forces that appear in us as impulses. In this way we find ourselves living in harmony with the *habitus* of our ancestral psychic life. . . . The existence of this *habitus* proves its viability for if it were not viable, all those who obeyed it would long since have perished of maladaptation.[11]

Women have often made independent decisions that reflect both their perception of their environment and their use of the process of self-conjoining, syzygy. Because historical and socioeconomic factors interact with their decisions at this time, they have attained a valuable tone of authenticity.

The Function of Archetypes

The archetypal presentation of women helps to explain the development of symbolic power and pluralism in gender images today in the Middle East. There are many intriguing arguments over the female characters of Islamic history, each one with its supporters. Even if all of Egyptian society reached the consensus that the *hadith* and the Qur'an should be systematically examined to formulate a position on women's rights and responsibilities, both veiled and unveiled women could find examples to support their case. Those who have argued for continued or reimposed restrictions on women's activities have had an easier time formulating their positions because there are abundant later *hadith* to draw from.

Revisionism, Reaction, and Manipulation

All the parties involved in the debate over women's status have manipulated women's history. Scholars and religious authorities, as well as lay participants, feminists, and antifeminists, have engaged in subsurface polemics and historiographical selectivity. The recent history of women in Egypt also reflects the issues of nationalism, Third Worldism, anti-Westernism, and self-determinism. The Islamists have emphasized the high status of women within Islam and the amelioration of women's condition by the Prophet's edicts. They consistently favor sources that support the *mar'ah usriyah*, the "family women," who will counteract the influences of Westernization, secularization, and excessive materialism upon her offspring.

The Viability of the Virtuous Woman

The new virtuous woman owes a triple allegiance to *Allah,* to the *ummah,* the community of Muslims, and to her family. Theoretically, a woman should satisfy her obligations in these three areas before pursuing a career. Asceticism is not accepted within mainstream Islam and is frowned on socially, as are illicit or unsanctioned sexual relationships. The mothers of tomorrow's believers are ordered to reproduce, and the Islamists view women's productive years as a period when they should have children, even if they do not. According to Nira Yural-Davis, a parallel exists in Israel with the policies that limited female access to contraception or abortion in order to foster the births of soldier-children.[12]

The Islamist recommendations for the virtuous woman aim at improvement of her married life, not only for her own sake but for the moral and material benefit of her husband. Women's economic dependency on men is of paramount importance to their argument. In light of the harsh economic circumstances in Cairo today, that approach does not seem entirely rational. When the lives of working women are more closely examined, however, the argument gains some credence. The economic benefits of employment to working women with children may not be great, due to the costs of clothing, transportation, and childcare. Since most employed women are not quitting the jobs they already hold, we should remember that those who make lower salaries derive other benefits from these jobs. For example, they receive free medical care, pension plans, and a certain amount of maternity leave with pay. They benefit psychologically from work, and their status within the family is different if they contribute wages.

The Islamists have also argued that working women threaten the morality and productivity of society. Popular views appear to uphold these statements, which are not supported by any reliable studies or statistics. The decrial of working women derives from society's stress and immobility in the face of eroding trust, justice, and equal opportunities. All this combines with the notion that some men are losing jobs to women. Although available statistics paint quite a different picture, the strength of popular perceptions is nonetheless more sweeping and substantial than the abstract picture of shifting employment patterns.

Femininity

The Islamists' description of female qualities is ambivalent but fascinating. They paint a dual portrait of woman: independent and equal, in every sense but the biological, to her mate, yet delicate, soft, and reliant on her husband and her social network. This duality is reflected by the other two models of women considered in this work—the unveiled woman and the *bint al-balad*—and is therefore assumed to be an integral part of an Egyptian position on femininity. The Islamists add the notion of reform-mindedness and inner morality to the already existent formulations of delicacy, courage, loyalty, and modesty.

Flexibility

The image of the new veiled woman is less flexible than that of her unveiled counterpart. Limited flexibility is permitted within theoretical descriptions of the image, but more tolerance is extended in real life. Presumably that is because strength, clearly identifiable characteristics and guidelines, and a narrowing of choices are useful to new adherents of any social movement. Members allow for more flexibility in the behavior of other members than they express to outsiders, because this social group is still expanding and hopes to incorporate as many members as possible. Identification with a new image is deliberately facilitated.

Flexibility is not extended into the future; that is, veiled women conceive of all women as eventually donning the veil and of the future Islamization of all of secular society. The symbolic value of the new veiled woman, the *muhaggaba,* is that she is both "veilee" and "veilor." She has taken an independent decision to veil which is unchallengeable in the historical context she has chosen. The unveiled woman will continue to resist her, utilizing all the weapons of her secular and religious experience that she can muster. This clash of female images is not merely a cycle of fashion; it is a war about political, social and moral conceptions.

The veiled ʿAʾishahs, Fatimahs, Zaynabs, and Khadijahs of modern-day Cairo are synthesizers of a new tradition, conscious or newly awakened warriors within a new battle for the state. They are potential producers of value, thought, and moral reform. Yet to the degree that they are exclusively devoted mothers of future Muslim citizens, their contribution to a new state or growing social movement will be circumscribed by their time and energy, and the ambivalent Islamist attitudes toward reform of gender issues. To answer that observation, Islamist theorists point to the Western woman's failure to achieve her lofty composite models, Supercareerwoman and Supermom. The ideal model that they propose also combines conflicting goals and outlooks and is more modest in overall expectations. But when one considers the forces shaping those female historical archetypes and the longing for a viable solution to the complex dilemmas of Egypt today, one wonders whether their new model is indeed more modest, or simply more hopeful.

APPENDIX A

Questionnaire and Interview Format
(Translation)

Note: These question "sets" were divided (i.e., asked out of order) in the interviews so that respondents could provide confirmation, elaboration, or amendment of their initial responses.

Notice of Consent: I hereby give my consent to be interviewed by Sherifa Zuhur this _____ day of _____, 1988. I understand that the results of this interview will be integrated into Ms. Zuhur's dissertation or other publications as she sees fit. I understand that I will remain anonymous or referred to by initials only in order to keep the confidence of this interview.

Questionnaire and Interview Format

Section 1

Name _____ Age _____ Occupation _____

or Field of Study _____

Length of Employment _____ City/Neighborhood of

Residence _____ Birthplace _____

Parent's Birthplace: father _____ mother _____

Parent's Occupations: mother _____

father _____

Husbands/Sons/Daughter's Occupations _____

_____

_____

135

Section 2

1. What do you spend the most time and energy doing: your job/ being a parent/homemaker/public or charitable activities/ studying?

2. Which role do you receive the most satisfaction from?

3. What are your own personal goals?

4. If you could change two aspects of your life, what would you change and how?

5. How did your parent (s) affect or influence (a) your marriage, (b) your field of study, (c) your career? [One form of this question was asked to housewives, students, or working women.]

6. What reactions have your experienced from co-workers, employers, friends, parents, or children regarding your decision to work/stay home/engage in political activities/participate in group meetings? [Women often discussed their spouses' reactions, which were addressed in a separate question, #11.]

7a. What has helped you combine work and family life?

  b. Do you intend to work full time when you finish your studies? If not, what would prevent you from considering (full-time) employment?

8. Can you explain why some people, some religious people, disapprove of working women?

9. Are the current state policies on women, including maternity leave, child-care, equal pay, and personal status reforms, beneficial? Are they enforced successfully? Do they need modifications?

10a. How many children do you have, and how have you provided childcare?

  b. How many children do you think you would like to have?

11. Have you resolved employment with your husband, and how? or Have you discussed employment with your husband/fiancé?

Section 3

12. Do you consider yourself to be a religious person? Why?

13. How do you fulfill the requirements of your faith (as you interpret them) and live up to religious values in the circumstances and pressures of modern life?

14. What things or practices do you identify with traditional or modern interpretations of Islam that are positive or negative toward women?

15.a. How do you feel about the *muhaggabat*? Do you have family or friends who are veiling?

  b. Why did you choose to wear *higab*?

16. Does wearing of the *higab* affect you at work or when you commute or within the university?

17. What do you hope for in a future mate/future son-in-law/daughter-in-law?

Section 4

18. What has changed the most in the last eight years? (if comfortable with the above) What do you see as the difference between the Sadat era and the Mubarak era?

19. How has the economic situation affected you personally?

20. Are the *jamaʿat*, the Islamic groups, a threat to the state?

21. Could Egypt become an Islamic state? What would this mean to women?

22. What is the future of the *jamaʿat* if the secular state remains stronger?

Section 5 (married women only)
1. What are your husband's responsibilities at home, and what are yours?
2. Are there specific things he does or likes to do with the kids?
3. Who deals with household expenses?
4. What do you do with your earnings (yours and his)? Who decides on purchases/savings/investments?

Section 6 (all)
23. What are the qualities that make a woman feminine, and explain these to me?
24. Is there anything you wish to add? Have I forgotten to ask something that you feel is important? Or do you have any questions?

APPENDIX B

Note: Three women did not provide enough of the profile section to be included in these figures.

Selected Characteristics of Sample

Variables	Frequency	Percentage distribution
Age groups		
19–24	29	61.7
25–34	2	4.3
35–44	4	8.5
45–54	3	6.4
55–64	7	14.9
65 +	2	4.3
Total	47	100.00
Veiling:		
Muhaggaba	20	42.5
Munaqqaba	6	12.8
Unveiled	21	44.7
Total	47	100.00
Student status		
Students or graduate students	29	61.7
Nonstudents	18	39.3
Place of birth		
Cairo Metropolitan area	30	63.9
Other	17	36.1
Total	47	100.00

Selected Cross-Variables

Veiled and both parents born in Cairo metropolitan area	6	24.2
Veiled and one or both parents born outside of Cairo	20	76.8
Total veiled sample and one or two parents born outside of Cairo	26	100.00
Veiled with mothers who worked outside the home	4	10.4
Veiled with mothers who did not work outside the home	22	89.6
Total	26	100.00
Unveiled with mothers who worked outside the home (or did extensive volunteer work)	7	33.4
Unveiled with mothers who did not work outside the home	14	66.6

139

| Total | | | | 21 | 100.00 |

Note: These data are derived from the profile, collected from *Section 1* of questionnaire.

Preliminary Table of Personal Data
(Initials have been altered)

(V-*muhaggaba;* VM-*munaqqaba*) Emplco-*muwazzaf* (white collar category but of varying income), s-son d-daughter h-husband

Res.	Age	Birth/Res	Par. Birthplace	F Occ.	M Occ.
A. M.	20	Agouza/Agouza	Cairo Cairo	Engineer	Housewife
A S.	20	Shoubra/Shoubra	Cairo Alex	Dir. Broadc.	Teacher, Art Acad.
Na	20	Halwan/Cairo	Cairo Cairo	Teacher	Housewife
Ni V	20	Qanatar/Qana	Qana Qana.	Dir. Prod. co.	Housewife
No	20	Giza/Dokki	Cairo Cairo	Engineer	Doctor
Ri V	20	Tanta/Cair.	Tanta Tanta	Judge	Supervisor
F V	20	Matariya/C.U.	Mat. Mat.	Emplco	Teacher/ Azhar
ʿU	20	Shoubra/Haram	Fayoum Cairo	Gen. mgr.	Teacher sec.
Am A V	21	Shibina al Qums/ CU	S Q S Q	(Dead)em- plco	Housewife
Am B V	21	Kafr al Zayt/CU	Kafr Kafr	Merchant	Housewife
Am K	21	Cair/Hel.	Minufiya Minya	Lawyer	Form.social worker
Ay	21	Cairo/Hel	Up.Eg Cairo	Jeweler	Housewife
I A V	21	Bassioun,Gharbiya	B G B G	Merchant	Housewife
La V	21	Fayoum/CU	Fay Fay	Emplco	Housewife
Lu V	21	Mansoura/CU	Mans. Mans. Sanafa	Farmer	Housewife
Ch V	22	Cairo/Abbasiya	Dakhl. Cairo	Lawyer/co	Engl. teacher
Ha V	22	Mansoura/CU	Mans. Mans.	Moneylender	Housewife
Mo V	22	Zagazig/CU	Zag Zag	Mosque empl.	Housewife
Nag VM	22	Mansoura/CU Abu al-Kabir	Mans. Mans.	Farmer	Housewife
Nih VM	22	Sharqiya/CU	AK AK	Teacher	Housewife
Ri2 V	22	Fayoum/CU Abu al-Kabir	Fay Fay	Emplco	Housewife
F VM	22	Sharqiya/CU	AK AK	Farmer	Housewife
AM M.	23	Cairo/Abbasiya	Cairo Cairo	Mgr.insur.	Housewife
AZ V	23	Cairo/CU	Fayoum Cairo	Emplco	Housewife

Hu V	23	Assiut/CU	Assiut As-siut	Busworker	Housewife
Khe V	23	Baheira/CU	Baheira Ba-heira	Carpenter	Housewife
Sab VM	23	Salam City/SC	Cairo Cairo	Mosque emp.	Shopclerk (owner)
Nah V	24	Tah/Cairo	Cairo Cairo	Teacher	Housewife
Ne V	24	Cairo/CU	Tanta Cairo	Emplco.	Housewife
F	26	Cairo/Cairo	Jaffa Jaffa	Dead	Vol. Red Cresc.
S VM	26	Giza/CU	Giza Giza (village area)	Farmer	Housewife
Am V	35	Giza/Giza urban	Minia Assiut	Co. exec.	Housewife
N V	38	Cairo/Cairo	Cairo Cairo	Teacher	Housewife
M	42	Cairo/Hel.	Cairo England	Professor	Housewife/ designer
Na	42	Cairo/Hel.	Cairo Cairo	Mgr.Min.	Housewife
Ha V	46	Cairo/Cairo	Cairo Cairo	Mgr.co.	Housewife
Sa V	48	Cairo/Hel	Cairo Cairo	s. M.D.	Housewife
Am	53	Cairo/Cairo	Cairo Cairo	S.d.students	Housewife/ volunteer
D	55	Cairo/Cairo	Cairo Cairo	Min.pos.	Housewife
G	56	Cairo/Aguz	Cairo Matar	H/minister	
R	62	Cairo/Cairo	Cairo Cairo		Housewife
A VS	62	Cairo/Cairo	Cairo Alex	Businessman	Housewife
L	60-63	Jaffa/Cairo	Jaffa Jaffa	Landowner	Housewife
S	62	Cairo/Cairo	Egypt Egypt	Merchant	Housewife
D	60s	Cairo/Hel.	Cairo Cairo		Housewife
N	67	Cairo/Garden C.	Cairo Cairo		
L VM/	69	Cairo/Cairo	Up.E Cairo	Landowner	Housewife

Attitudinal Samples
Personal Goals

	Of total sample
Hoping to marry, not to work	46%
	Of those under 30
Hope to marry, no full-time career plans	67%
Hope for career	33%

	Of those veiled and under 30	*Of those Unveiled and under 30*
Want to marry and stay home and veil or continue veiling	68%	12%

	Of those veiled and under 30	*Of those unveiled and under 30*
Spoke of career goals	22%	75%
Want to combine career and marriage	10%	

	Of total sample
Feel that Egypt could become an Islamic state	71%
Feel that Egypt should not or could not become an Islamic state	29%
Think Islamic groups haven't yet accrued sufficient political pressure or adequate leadership to achieve that goal	4%
Feel that widespread veiling will result	13%
Believe the Christian minority must be addressed	7%
Believe the above scenario will be a disaster for women	8%

	Of those veiled	*Of those unveiled*
Egypt could or should become an Islamic state	100%	22%
Egypt should not become an Islamic state		78%

NOTES

Chapter 1: New Images or Continuous Archetypes?

1. Fadwa el-Guindi, "Veiling Infitah with Social Ethic: Egypt's Contemporary Islamic Movement," *Social Problems* 28, no. 4 (April 1981), pp. 465–85.

2. Mai Ghoussoub accused Middle Eastern feminists of continuing Islamic apologetics and therefore assenting to women's continued oppression, in "Women in the Arab World," *The New Left Review* 161 (1987), pp. 17–18. Judith Tucker argues that the emphasis on Islam in Middle Eastern studies has left investigation into the development of women, the state, and social class lacking. Judith Tucker, "Problems in the Historiography of Women in the Middle East: The Case of Nineteenth-Century Egypt," *International Journal of Middle East Studies* 15 (1983), pp. 321–36.

3. Edward Said, *Orientalism* (New York: Pantheon Books, 1978).

4. Executive Board of the National Organization for Women, Resolutions on Women in Combat and Equality for Women in the Persian Gulf (16 September 1990); and on The Status of Women in Saudi Arabia and Kuwait and Troop Build-Up in the Persian Gulf (18 November 1990, Washington D.C.). Objections are raised against defending a country that practices "gender apartheid" and about special restrictions placed on American women in the military, including shorts and blouses to be worn while swimming. Another resolution was made in November following the driving demonstration enacted by twenty-four Saudi women.

5. Val Moghadam, "Problems in Middle Eastern Women's Studies: The View from Marxist-Feminist Sociology" (Paper presented to the Middle East Studies Association, Beverly Hills, California, November 1988), p. 9.

6. Clifford Geertz, *The Interpretation of Cultures* (New York: Basic Books, 1973).

7. Daniel Lerner, *The Passing of Traditional Society* (Glencoe, Ill.: The Free Press, 1958). Evolutionary conceptualization is also utilized by Wafaa Abou Negm Marei, "Female Emancipation and Changing Political Leadership: A Study of Five Arab Countries," Ph.D. diss., Rutgers University, 1978.

143

8. Azizah al-Hibri, "A Study of Islamic Herstory: Or How Did We Ever Get Into This Mess?," *Women's Studies International Forum* 5, no. 2 (1982), pp. 207–19; Jane Smith, "The Experience of Muslim Women: Considerations of Power and Authority," in *The Islamic Impact,* eds. Yvonne Haddad, Byron Haines, and Ellison Findley (Syracuse, N.Y.: Syracuse University Press, 1984); Jane Smith and Yvonne Haddad, "Eve: Islamic Image of Woman," *Women's Studies International Forum* 5, no. 2 (1982), pp. 135–44.

9. al-Hibri, "Herstory"; Muhammad Bahonar, "Islam and Women's Rights," *al-Tawhid* 1, no. 2 (1984), pp. 155–165.

10. As in Masud-ul-Hasan's nonannotated sketches of eighty-two famous Muslim women, *Daughters of Islam* (Lahore, Pakistan: Hazrat Data Ganj Baksh Academy, n.d.).

11. W. Montgomery Watt, *Muhammad at Medina* (Oxford: Oxford University Press, 1981).

12. Nabiah Abbott, *Aishah The Beloved of Mohammed* (London: Al Saqi Books, 1985 reprinting), p. 24–25.

13. Based in part on the verse:

O Prophet! Tell thy wives and thy daughters and the women of the believers to draw their garments close round them (when they go abroad). That will be better, so that they may be recognized and not annoyed. Allah is Forgiving, Merciful. (Qur²an, The Clans, Surah XXXIII:59).

This verse is often employed by the Islamists and others to verify the need for women to dress modestly, or veil in public. There are several problems in this verse. First of all we don't know what sort of garments are referred to. The translators usually render this word as "cloaks" and add the phrase "when they go abroad" so as to interpret outdoor modesty garb. But some sources referred to, such as Mawdudi through Abu Da²ud, are quite dubious. Mawdudi, for example, gives a discription of the appearance of women in the *jahilliyah,* but we know he did not read other Arabic sources. The garment referred to might have been an inner robe, or material to be draped as skirts. There is some evidence that women's legs were exposed; *hadith* inform us that women who fought in battle were wounded in the legs. The phrase "that would be better" is unclear—we don't know what sort of specific annoyance Muslim women (and the Prophet's wives) were encountering.

14. al-Bukhari, *Sahih al-Bukhari,* vols. 1, 3–7, ed. Muhammad Khan (Gujranwala Catt., Pakistan, 1971) vol. 2, ed. Muhammad Khan (Chicago: Kazi Publications, 1977).

15. *Zina,* according to various translators, refers to women's physical charms, their sexuality or their sexual virtue, or simply adornment of some

kind. Certain religious authorities of the Middle Ages believed that the *zina* of the woman rendered her entire body pudendal, or *ʿawra*. It was the *zina* that the woman must conceal, according to the following verse:

> And tell the believing women to lower their gaze and be modest, and to display of their *zina* only that which is apparent and to draw their *khumurihinna* ["veils" in trans.] over their breast pockets ["breasts" in trans.], and not to reveal their *zina* save to their own husbands or fathers or husbands' fathers, or their sons, or their brothers or their brothers' sons or sisters' sons, or their women, or their slaves, or male attendants who lack vigour, or children who know naught of women's *ʿawra* [translated incompletely as "nakedness"]. And let them not stamp their feet so as to reveal what they hide of their adornment. (Qurʾan iv: 30–31)

The verse is used to define the areas of woman's body that might kindle sexual desire. Only male relatives barred from sexual union through incest and marriage regulations might see these women clothed in their indoor garments. This meaning was constructed by use of various *hadith*, some sounder than others, because in the original verse the delineation of *zina* is rather vague. For a lengthy and polemical discussion, see Fatima Mernissi, *Beyond the Veil: Male-Female Dynamics in a Modern Muslim Society* (Cambridge: Cambridge University Press, 1975), or the latest reprinting, 1987.

16. Afaf Lutfi al-Sayyid Marsot, *Egypt in the Reign of Muhammad Ali* (Cambridge: Cambridge University Press, 1984); Charles Issawi, *The Economic History of the Middle East 1800–1914* (Chicago: University of Chicago Press, 1966), and *An Economic History of the Middle East and North Africa* (New York: Columbia University Press, 1982); Judith Tucker, *Women in Nineteenth-Century Egypt* (Cairo: American University in Cairo Press, 1986).

17. Alexander Scholch, *Egypt for the Egyptians! The Socio-political Crisis in Egypt 1876–1882* (London: Ithaca Press, 1981). Earl of Cromer [Lord Cromer], *Modern Egypt,* vols. 1 and 2 (London: MacMillan and Co., Limited, 1908); Peter Mansfield, *The British in Egypt* (Holt, Rinehart & Winston, 1972); Tariq al-Bishri, *Harakah al-Siyasiyah fi Misr 1945–1952* (Cairo: al-Hayaʾ al-Misriyah lil-Kitab, 1972).

18. Valerie Hoffman-Ladd, "Polemics on the Modesty and Segregation of Women in Contemporary Egypt," *International Journal of Middle East Studies* 19, no. 1 (February 1987).

19. Sawsan El-Messiri, "Self-Images of Traditional Urban Women in Cairo," in *Women in the Muslim World,* eds. Lois Beck and Nikki Keddie (Cambridge: Harvard University Press, 1978), p. 523.

20. C. G. Jung, *Psyche and Symbol,* ed. Violet S. de Lazlo (New York: Anchor Books, 1958), p. 35.

21. Ibid.

22. El-Messiri, "Self-Images," pp. 534–35.

23. El-Messiri, "Self-Images"; Sawsan El-Messiri, *Ibn al-Balad: A Conception of Egyptian Identity* (Leiden: E. J. Brill, 1978).

24. Nayra Atiya, *Khul-Khaal: Five Egyptian Women Tell Their Stories* (Syracuse, N.Y.: Syracuse University Press, 1982), pp. 37, 53, 73; Andrea Rugh, "Women and Work: Strategies and Choices in a Lower-Class Quarter of Cairo," in *Women and the Family of the Middle East*, ed. E. Fernea (Austin, Tex.: University of Texas Press, 1985), p. 276.

25. Andrea Rugh, *Reveal and Conceal: Dress in Contemporary Egypt* (Cairo: The American University in Cairo Press, 1986).

26. El-Messiri, "Self-Images," pp. 535–36. A man who does not fully support his wife economically is "described as 'one who is fed by his wife'. . . . The ideal husband . . . enables his wife to be a 'lady' (*sitt*), a nonworking woman. . . . "; Andrea Rugh, "Women and Work," pp. 276–77. On the other hand, see Barbara Lethem Ibrahim, "Cairo's Factory Women," in *Women in the Family,* ed. E. Fernea, p. 296.

27. Helmy Tadros, *Social Security and the Family in Egypt,* Cairo Papers in Social Science, vol. 7, monograph 1 (Cairo: The American University in Cairo, March 1984).

28. Afaf Lutfi al-Sayyid Marsot, *Protest Movements and Religious Undercurrents in Egypt: Past and Present,* Center for Contemporary Arab Studies, Occasional Papers Series (Washington, D.C.: Georgetown University, March 1984), p. 2.

29. Saad Eddin Ibrahim, "Egypt's Islamic Activism in the 1980s," *Third World Quarterly* 10, no. 2 (April 1988), p. 632.

30. Ibid., pp. 640–53.

31. Ibid.

32. Ibid.

33. Ibid.

34. Barbara Stowasser, "Liberated Equal or Protected Dependent? Contemporary Religious Paradigms on Women's Status in Islam," *Arab Studies Quarterly* 9. no. 3 (Summer 1987).

35. Personal interview with Ingie Roushdie, analyst and journalist, Arab Federation of Lawyers, member of the Ad Hoc Women's Status Research Group, held in Cairo, 30 November 1988.

36. Afaf Lutfi al-Sayyid Marsot, "The Revolutionary Gentlewoman in Egypt," in *Women in the Muslim World*, ed. Lois Beck and Nikki Keddie (Cambridge: Harvard University Press, 1978) pp. 270–71.

37. Willy Jansen, " 'God Will Pay in Heaven,' Women and Wages in Algeria" (Paper presented to the Middle East Studies Association, Baltimore, November 1987).

38. A model of the class-crystallization process based on Indian society is described by Werner S. Landecker, *Class Crystalization* (New Brunswick, N.J.: Rutgers University Press, 1981). Egypt has historically been a strongly hierarchical society as well. This paradigm will be described at greater length in chapter 2, et passim.

39. Personal interview with Djenane Sirry, Cairo, 22 November 1988. Personal interview with Ingie Roushdie, Cairo, 30 November 1988. Present also in the remarks of three of the other women interviewed in Cairo on 29 November and 6 December 1988.

40. Nabawiyya Musa, *Al-Marʾah wal-ʿAmal* (Alexandria: al-Matbaʿah al-Wataniyah, 1920), p. 23; also cited in Marei, "Female Emancipation," and Changing Political Leadership: A Study of Five Arab Countries," diss., Department of Political Science, Rutgers University, 1978, p. 76.

41. Sherifa Zuhur, "Why False Consciousness?" (Paper presented to the Berkshire Conference in Women's History, Rutgers University, New Brunswick, New Jersey, 9 June 1990).

Chapter 2: The Process of Listening

1. Zeinab Radwan, "Bahth al-Hijab bayn al-Jamiʿat," (Cairo: The National Center for Sociological and Criminological Research, 1982); ʿAliyah Reda Rafee, "The Students' Islamic Movement: A Study of the Veil," master's thesis, The American University in Cairo, 1983; Nemat Guenena, *The 'Jihad,' An 'Islamic Alternative' in Egypt, Cairo Papers in Social Science*, vol. 9, monograph 2 (Cairo: The American University in Cairo Press, 1986), appendix 1.

2. Radwan, "Bahth al-Hijab"; Rafee, "The Students Islamic Movement; Guenena, *The 'Jihad'*. Guenena discusses adherents in their late twenties but all are men, except for a discussion of women in the appendix.

3. Val Moghadam, "Problems in Middle East Women's Studies: The View from Marxist-Feminist Sociology" (Paper presented to the Middle East Studies Association, Beverly Hills, California, November 1988).

4. Lafif Lakhdar, "Why the Reversion to Islamic Archaism?," *Forbidden Agendas* (London: Al-Saqi, 1984), p. 293.

5. Telephone interview with Safinaz Qassim, Cairo, 5 December 1988. Ms. Qassim, a noted veiled writer, journalist, and critic, refused to arrange a personal interview as she was "boycotting" Americans. Nevertheless, she discussed my topic with me at some length and made several insightful comments.

6. Fatnah Sabbah, *Women in the Muslim Unconscious* (New York: Pergamon Press, 1984).

7. Ibid., p. 117.

8. Saad Eddin Ibrahim, "Anatomy of Egypt's Militant Groups: Methodological Note and Preliminary Findings," *International Journal of Middle East Studies* 12 (1981), pp. 423–53.

9. Ibid.

10. Radwan, "Bahth al-Hijab"; Rafee, "The Students Islamic Movement"; Ibrahim, "Anatomy of Egypt's Militant Groups"; less so in Saad Eddin Ibrahim, "Egypt's Islamic Activism in the 1980s," *Third World Quarterly* 10, no. 2 (April 1988), pp. 652–57.

11. Or in those above, Radwan, "Bahth al-Hijab"; Rafee, "The Students Movement's Ibrahim, "Anatomy," Ibrahim, "Egypt's Islamic Activism"; Guenena, "The 'Jihad'."

12. Mervat Hatem, "Egypt's Middle Class in Crisis: The Sexual Division of Labor," *Middle East Journal* 42, no. 3 (Summer 1988).

13. Ibrahim, "Anatomy."

14. Ibid.

15. Ibrahim, "Egypt's Islamic Activism."

16. Ahmad Abdallah, *The Student Movement and National Politics in Egypt, 1923–1973*, (London: Al Saqi Books, 1985), p. 231.

17. Ibrahim, "Egypt's Islamic Activism."

18. Johann Nestroy wrote a play, *Einen Fux will er sich machen* which was later adapted into "On the Razzle, and "Hello Dolly."

19. Immanuel Wallerstein, "The Rise and Future Demise of the World Capitalist System: Concepts for Comparative Analysis," in *The Capitalist World Economy,* ed. Immanuel Wallerstein (New York: Cambridge University Press, 1979).

20. Werner Landecker, *Class Crystallization*. (New Brunswick: Rutgers University Press, 1981). This work discusses the limitations on social mobility in a Third World society where social status and economic status are not necessarily equivalent. The study was developed from a model of Indian society, but the conditions under which class mobility crystallizes are mirrored in Egypt. They result in a low rate of social change and rank differentiation.

21. Soraya al-Torki and Camillia El-Solh, eds., *Arab Women in the Field: Studying Your Own Society* (Syracuse, N.Y.: Syracuse University Press, 1988).

22. As in the presentation delivered by Afaf Mahfouz on the uses of "empathy," in a Middle Eastern Women's Studies panel presentation to the Middle East Studies Association, Beverly Hills, California, November 3, 1988.

23. Soheir Morsy, "Fieldwork in My Homeland. Toward the Demise of Anthropology's Distinctive-Other Hegemonic Tradition," in *Arab Women in the Field*, ed. Al-Torki and El-Solh, p. 89.

24. Ibid., p. 83, where Morsy states: "For their part, the villagers were well aware that I would be the primary beneficiary of the information I collected in their village. They knew that I would use this information to become a *doktora*."

Chapter 3: Her Story: Archetypes and Arguments of Middle Eastern Women

1. One exception is Azizah al-Hibri, "A Study of Islamic Herstory. Or How Did We Get into This Mess," *Women's Studies International Forum*, 5, No. 2 (1982), pp. 207–221.

2. Ibid.; Jane Smith and Yvonne Haddad, "Eve: Islamic Image of Woman," *Women's Studies International Forum* 5, no. 2 (1982), pp. 135–44; Barbara Stowasser, "The Status of Women in Early Islam," in *Muslim Women*, ed. Freda Hussein (London: Croom Helm, 1984).

3. al-Hibri, "A Study of Islamic Herstory"; ʿAʾisha Abd al-Rahman, *al-Mafhum al-Islami li Tahrir al-Marʾah* (Cairo: Umm Durman, 1967).

4. Phyllis Andors, *The Unfinished Liberation of Chinese Women 1949–1980* (Bloomington: Indiana University Press, 1983); Janet S. Chafetz and Anthony G. Dworkin, *Female Revolt: Women's Movements in World and Historical Perspective* (Totowa, N.J.: Rowman & Allenheld, 1986), pp. 87, 137–40. Espousal of feminist issues added to recruitment and party commitment of women in the C.C.P. in China. But party survival, rather than women's

issues, was always the deepest concern of the leadership. This has also been true of the Palestinian women's movement and progressive parties in Central America, Africa, and even in Cuba, where serious social programs failed to address male-female relations within the family.

5. Sheila Rowbotham, *Women, Resistance, and Revolution: A History of Women and Revolution in the Modern World* (New York: Vintage Books, 1974), chapter 6; Marie-Aimée Hélie-Lucas, "Women, Nationalism, and Religion in the Algerian Liberation Struggle," in *Opening the Gates: A Century of Arab Feminist Writing,* ed. Margot Badran and Miriam Cooke (Bloomington: Indiana University Press, 1990), pp. 105–14; Monique Gadant, "Fatima, Ouardia, and Malika, Contemporary Algerian Women," in *Women of the Mediterranean,* ed. Monique Gadant (London: Zed Books, 1984), pp. 15–43; Juliet Minces, "Women in Algeria," in *Women in the Muslim World,* eds. Lois Beck and Nikki Keddie (Cambridge, Mass: Harvard University Press, 1978). The backsliding into prerevolutionary attitudes, incomplete social transformation, and problems of cultural identity are also reported by Bouthaina Shaaban, when discussing Algerian (and Syrian) women, in *Both Right and Left Handed: Arab Women Talk About Their Lives* (London: The Women's Press, 1988), pp. 182–235.

6. An example is Shaykh Mustafa al-Ghayalini, *al-Islam Ruhu al-Madaniyya* (Cairo, n.d. [circa 1926.]) cited in Nazirah Zein ad-Din, "Removing the Veil and Veiling," (Beirut, 1928), reprinted in *Women's Studies Internation Forum* 5, no. 2 (1982).

7. Personal interviews with ʿAsam al-ʿAryan, Cairo, 6 December 1988, and Niʿmat Fouad, Cairo, 24 November 1988; telephone interview with Safinaz Qassim, Cairo, 5 December 1988.

8. The name '*Hawwa*' does not actually appear in the Qurʾan but occurs rather in various *hadith*.

9. Jane Smith and Yvonne Haddad, "Eve."

10. This is admittedly my own interpretation, based on the exegesis of ʿAʾishah abd al-Rahman, but also reflecting the views of many of the Islamist women I interviewed.

11. Smith and Haddad, "Eve."

12. Mahmud Shalabi, *Hayat Adam* (Cairo: 1964), p. 61; and cited in Smith and Haddad, "Eve," p. 143.

13. Smith and Haddad, "Eve," pp. 136–37.

14. al-Rahman, *al-Mafhum al-Islami,* p. 6 cited in Smith and Haddad, "Eve," p. 141.

15. Ibid., p. 142. In Surah Ta Ha, Iblis whispers solely and directly to Adam. Elsewhere, in The Heights, Surah VII: 7:20–25, Iblis tempts *both* Adam and Hawwa. But in the Bible, the serpant approaches "the woman" (Eve), saying, "You will not die if you eat the fruit." Genesis 3:4–6.

16. Mahmoud Mohamed Taha, *The Second Message of Islam*, trans. Abdullahi an-Naim, and introduction (Syracuse, N.Y.: Syracuse University Press, 1987) p. 142, also see pp. 139–45.

17. Abu Ja'far Muhammad b. Jarir al-Tabari, *Tarikh al-Tabari*, ed. Muhammad Abu al-Fadl Ibrahim (Cairo: 1960), 1:108, 1:111–12; Fakhr al-Din al-Razi, *al-Tafsir al-Kabir* (Cairo: 1935), 3:13; Ibn Ishaq Ahmad b. M. Ibrahim al-Tha'labi, *Qasas al-anbiya* (Cairo: n.d.); and in Smith and Haddad, "Eve," p. 139.

18. J. Eisenberg and G. Vajda, "Hawwa," *Encyclopedia of Islam*, edited by B. Lewis, C. Pellat, and J. Schact, (Leiden: E. J. Brill, 1965). Based on Ibn Sa'd, *Tabaqat* 1:116; Ibn Kutayb, *Ma'rif*, ed. 5; 'Ukasha, 15; Ibn Hisham, *al-Tidjan* 8–16; and Nabiah Abbott, *Studies in Arabic Literary Papyri* (Chicago: University of Chicago Press, 1957). Smith and Haddad mention another *hadith* discussed by Shalabi in *Hayat Adam*, p. 108, which promises that on the day of judgment God will reshape all "righteous" women in the image of Hawwa, thus compensating them for the beauty that they lacked on earth. Smith and Haddad, "Eve," p. 143.

19. W. Montgomery Watt, "Khadijah," *Encyclopedia of Islam*, citing Ibn Habib, *Muhabbar* 9–11, pp. 408, 435–55.

20. Watt, "Khadijah"; W. Montgomery Watt, *Muhammad at Medina* (Oxford: Oxford University Press, 1981), pp. 272–73. These matrilineal practices were discussed and perhaps exaggerated by Robertson Smith, *Kinship and Marriage in Early Arabia* (Cambridge at the University Press, 1885).

21. Watt, *Muhammad at Medina;* al-Hibri, "Herstory," pp. 208–9; Subhi Mahmasani, *The Legal Systems in the Arabic States* (Beirut: Dar al-'Ilm lil-Malayin, 1965), pp. 64–65; Smith, *Kinship;* Watt, *Muhammad at Medina*, p. 381; Nawal al-Saadawi also alludes to an early prevailing matriarchy evidenced by woman's freedom to choose the father of her children in one form of polyandry practiced on the Peninsula in "Women and Islam," *Women's Studies International Forum* 5, no. 2 (1982), p. 194, which she bases on al-Isfahani, *al-Aghani* 16:2. Fatima Mernissi discussed the forms of polyandry and the polemics of female influence in "The Effects of Modernization on the Male-Female Dynamics in a Muslim Society: Morocco" (Ph.D. diss., Brandeis University, 1973).

22. Referred to in the *Qur'an*, The Star, Surah 53:19–23: "Have ye seen al-Lat and al-ʿUzzah. And Manat, the third, the other? Are yours the males and His the females? That indeed were an unfair division!" After explaining al-Lat and ʿUzzah's importance to the tribe of Abu Sufyan, al-Saadawi declares: "The important position occupied by some goddesses was symbolic of the relatively higher prestige enjoyed by women in Arab tribal society, and a reflection of the vestiges of matriarchal society that still lived on in some of the tribes." al-Saadawi, "Women and Islam," p. 194.

23. Other respected sources tell us that al-ʿUzzah was worshiped not only in Arabia but at Hira of the Lakhmids, where human sacrifices were made in her name. Abu Sufyan's battle cry was "ʿUzzah is for us and not for you!" al-Tabari, i, 1418. The Syrians worshiped Kawkabta, the goddess of the morning star, who also received human sacrifices and was somehow associated with al-ʿUzzah. Doughty claims that even in the early twentieth century the Arabs of Taif still sought the help of two of the goddesses in cases of illness. Three deities called al-Lat, Hubbal, and al-ʿUzza were enshrined in blocks of stone at Taif. Charles M. Doughty, *Travels in Arabia Deserta* (New York: Random House, 1936). Also see Frants Buhl, "al-ʿUzza" and "al-Lat" in the *Encyclopedia of Islam,* based upon the above sources, and Muhammad Ibn Saʿd, *Kitab al-Tabaqat al-Kabir,* ed. and trans. E. von Sachau (Leiden: Brill, 1905–40); Ibn Hisham, *Kitab Sirat Rasul Allah,* ed. Ferdinand von Wustenfeld (Frankfurt am Main: Minerva, 1961), pp. 55, 145, 206, 839, 871; Gustav Rothstein, *Die dynastie der Lachmiden in [im] al-Hira* (Berlin: Reuther & Reichard, 1894), p. 81, sq. 141; Muhammad ibn ʿUmar Waqidi, *Kitab al-Maghazi* (Berlin: J. Wellhausen, [G. Reimer] 1882), p. 350.

24. In the earlier, disavowed version of the *gharaniq,* Muhammad supposedly recited the opening of The Star, Surah LIII: "Have you thought upon al-Lat and al-ʿUzzah. And Manat, the third, the other?" Then a different form of the verse followed: "They are the exalted birds and their intercession is desired indeed." Worship of the three goddesses could have continued and perhaps entailed the preservation of Meccan power bases and alignments, which would have been detrimental to the unity of the new community.

25. Watt, *Muhammad at Medina,* p. 388; Smith, *Kinship,* p. 102.

26. As they might according to the old matrilineal system, still observed by certain tribes.

27. "When the buried infant shall be asked for what sin she was slain," Qur'an, The Overthrowing, LXXXI:8–9; al-Hibri, "Herstory" p. 212; Qur'an, al-Isra, XVII:31 refers to the killing of children for fear of poverty.

28. al-Hibri, "Herstory," p. 209.

29. Ibid.; Mahmasani, *The Legal Systems*, p. 83.

30. al-Hibri, "Herstory," pp. 210–12.

31. Ijlal Khalifah, *al-Harakah al-Nisa'iyah al-Hadithah: Qisat al-Mar'ah al-'Arabiyah 'ala 'Ard Misr* (Cairo: al-Matbu'ah al-'Arabiyah al-Hadithah, 1973). Goddess-oriented cultures are said to have preceded the male-dominated Indo-European cultures even in Europe, according to Marija Gimbutas, *The Goddesses and Gods of Old Europe* (London: Thames & Hudson, 1974). Some feminists have (correctly or incorrectly) taken her work as evidence that a global pattern of earlier goddess worship was gradually weakened, although vestiges of that tradition remained in popular religion, magic, fertility, and healing rites.

32. Personal interview with Ni'mat Fouad, Cairo, 24 November 1988.

33. Khalifah, *al-Harakah al-Nisa'iyah*, p. 5.

34.   Say I take refuge in the Lord of the Daybreak
From the evil [of that] which he created
From the evil of intense darkness
And from the evil of [female] blowers on knots
And from the evil of the envious one when he envies.

Qur'an, The Daybreak, Surah CXIII:1–5.

35. Lois Beck, "The Religious Lives of Muslim Women," in *Women in Contemporary Muslim Societies*, ed. Jane Smith (London: Associated University Presses, 1980), pp. 27–60.

36. al-Saadawi claims that female circumcision dates back to the Pharaonic kingdoms and that Herodotus mentions the existence of the custom in the seventh century B.C. *The Hidden Face of Eve* (Boston: Beacon Press, 1980), p. 40.

37. Fatima Mernissi, *Le harem politique: Le Prophete et les femmes* (Paris: Albin Michel, 1987), p. 126, discussing al-Jawzi, *Kitab Ahkam an-Nisa'* (Beirut: al-Maktaba al 'Asriya, 1980), and Ibn Taymiyya, *Fatawi 'An al-Nisa'* (Cairo: Maktabat al-'Irfan, 1983).

38. Nabiah Abbott, *Aishah the Best Beloved of Mohammed* (London: Al Saqi Books, 1985), second printing, pp. 20–28.

39. Fatima Mernissi, *Le harem*, pp. 66–81, where a portion of her "inquiry into a misogynist hadith" is a discussion of 'A'ishah's role in the Fitnah and in public life in general.

40. Abbott, *Aishah*, pp. 27, 30–37.

41. Qur'an, The Clans, Surah XXXIII:53.

42. Abbott, *Aishah*, p. 27.

43. Qur²an, Light, Surah XXIV:11–16.

44. Abbott, *Aishah*, pp. 22–23.

45. Al-Bukhari, *al-Jami⁰ as-Sahih*, 67, 83, cited in Watt, *Muhammad at Medina*, pp. 381–82.

46. Watt, *Muhammad at Medina*, pp. 381–82.

47. "He [the Prophet, PBUH] strictly prohibited the women from proceeding on a journey alone without a *mahram* or in the company of a non-*mahram*." S. Abul ²Ala Maududi, citing Ibn ⁰Abbas through al-Bukhari and [Abu] Muslim, *The Meaning of the Qur²an*, vol. 8 (Lahore: Islamic Publications, 1979), p. 137. One should note that Maududi read Arabic in translation.

48. Mernissi, *Le harem*, p. 126.

49. Ibn Sa⁰d, *Tabaqat*, p. 126, in Abbott, *Aishah*, p. 97.

50. Mawardi restricted women from passing judgment in the capacity of *qadi*. Women nonetheless were not restricted from issuing a judgment as a *mufti*.

51. Abbott, *Aishah*, p. 111.

52. Ibid., p. 140.

53. Ibid., pp. 111–65.

54. Imam [sic] Zarkachi, *al-Ijaba li Iradi ma Astradakathu ²Aisha ala-as-Sahada* (Presente par Said al-Afghani, al-Maktab al-Islam, 1980), p. 118. Cited in Mernissi, *Le harem*, p. 75. Other sources have stated that the daughter of the king of Iran who ascended to power during Muhammad's lifetime was the object of this "misogynist hadith" (as in Abbott, *Aishah*, p. 175, from Ibn al-Athi).

55. According to Mernissi, Abu Bakra is not a sound source of *hadith* according to Maliki principles because he was one of four persons who falsely accused [sic] al-Mughira bin Shu²ba of *zina; Le harem*, pp. 80–81. In fact, Ziyad, another of the four witnesses, retracted his testimony. Therefore the case did not hold–which does *not* mean that Abu Bakra bore false witness.

56. Two portions of The Clans, XXXIII:32–33 and 53 are usually referred to; this is from 53:

> And when you ask of them [the wives] anything, ask it of them from behind
> a curtain. That is purer for your hearts and for their hearts. And it is not for

you to cause annoyance to the messenger of Allah, nor that ye should ever marry his wives after him.

Mernissi views this portion of the verse as a separation of public and private space within the Prophet's own house, creating a new concept of personal intrusion. The Islamists often refer to the earlier portion of this Surah (32–33):

> Oh ye wives of the Prophet, you are not like any other women. If you keep your duty, then be not soft of speech, lest he in whose heart is a disease aspire (desire) to you, but utter ordinary speech. And stay in your houses. Bedizen not yourselves with the adornment of the *jahiliyya*.

Mernissi cites Ibn Taymiyya, *Fatawi;* al-Jawzi, *Kitab Ahkam;* Said al-Afghani, *Aicha et la politique* (Beirut: Dar al-Fikr, 1971). The Islamists utilize the traditions of al-Baydawi (d. 1236) and al-Khafaji (d. 1659) regarding the veiling of women.

57. Abbott tells us that ʿAʾishah reportedly said, "Were Muhammad to see what we today see of the women and their behavior or condition, he would prevent them from going to the mosque." Ibn Hanbal VI, p. 69f, cited in Abbott, *Aishah*, p. 93.

58. Abbott, *Aishah*, p. 94.

59. Ibid., pp. 65–66.

60. Asaf Fyzee, *Outlines of Muhammadan Law*, pp. 381–406, cited in Watt, *Muhammad at Medina*, p. 292.

61. Lois Beck, "The Religious Lives of Muslim Women."

62. Farah Azari, "Islam's Appeal to Women in Iran," in *Women of Iran: The Conflict with Fundamentalism* (London: Ithaca Press, 1983).

63. Mernissi, *Le harem*, pp. 242–43. Niʿmat Fouad also chose Sakinah as a symbol of the talent and freedom of Muslim women. Personal interview with Niʿmat Fouad, Cairo, 24 November 1988.

64. Mernissi, *Le harem*, pp. 242–43.

65. Nabiah Abbott, *Two Queens of Baghdad* (London: Al Saqi Books, 1986).

66. Afaf Lutfi al-Sayyid Marsot, *A Short History of Modern Egypt* (London: Cambridge University Press, 1985), p. 25.

67. Judith Tucker, *Women in Nineteenth-Century Egypt.* (London: Cambridge University Press, 1985).

68. Ibid.; Kenneth Cuno disagrees with Tuckers' assessment of the condition of nonelite women in the nineteenth century, because he has reevaluated the sources for the eighteenth and nineteenth centuries upon which Tucker relied (Gran and Baer). I submit that the upper-class propertied women experienced losses in holdings, but that the status of the lower classes relative to later or earlier periods is still open to debate. Kenneth Cuno, "The Origins of Private Ownership of Land in Egypt: A Reappraisal," *International Journal of Middle East Studies* 12, no. 3 (1980); Cuno, (review) *"Women in Nineteenth Century Egypt,"* *Jusur* 2, no. 4 (1988).

69. Muhammad ʿImarah, *Qasim Amin wa Tahrir al-Marʾah* (Beirut: al-Muʾsasah al-ʿArabiyah lil-Dirasat wa al-Nashr, 1980); Margot Badran, "Dual Liberation: Feminism and Nationalism in Egypt, 1870s–1925," *Feminist Issues* 8, no. 1 (Spring 1988); Juan Ricardo Cole, "Feminism, Class, and Islam in Turn-of-the-Century Egypt," *International Journal of Middle East Studies* 13 (November 1981), pp. 387–405.

70. Beth Baron, "The Rise of a New Literary Culture: The Women's Press of Egypt, 1892–1919" (Ph.D. diss., University of California, Los Angeles, 1988), pp. 194–96; Khalifah, *Harakah Nisaʾiyah;* Wafaa Marei, "Female Emancipation and Changing Political Leadership: A Study of Five Arab Countries" (Ph.D diss., Rutgers University, 1978), pp. 61–66.

71. Baron, "New Literary Culture," pp. 129–32; Sarah Graham-Browne, *Images of Women: The Portrayal of Women in Photography of the Middle East: 1860–1950* (New York: Columbia University Press, 1988), pp. 215–17.

72. Margot Badran, "Dual Liberation": Feminism and Nationalism in Egypt,"; Mervat Hatem, "The Enduring Alliance of Nationalism and Patriarchy in Muslim Personal Status Laws: The Case of Modern Egypt," *Feminist Issues* 6, no. 1 (Spring 1986); Graham-Browne, *Images.*

73. Cole associates those debating women's status with an "old" or a "nouveaux" bourgeoisie whose constrasting views of women's proper role stemmed from the tensions of their own social group. Cole, "Feminism, Class, and Islam."

74. al-Sayyid Marsot, *A Short History of Modern Egypt,* p. 93.

75. Different versions of this story exist, attesting to its widespread popularity. Marsot gives two versions: Shaʿarawi was said to have cast her face veil into the sea upon disembarking at Alexandria. Elsewhere the elite women apparently took down a dividing screen at a mixed charity affair. Badran states that Shaʿarawi unveiled along with Nabarawi when stepping off a train

from Alexandria after completing that same ocean voyage. al-Sayyid Marsot, *A Short History of Modern Egypt*, pp. 93–94; Sha³arawi, *Harem Years: The Memoirs of an Egyptian Feminist*, ed. and trans. Margot Badran (New York: The Feminist Press, 1986), p. 7.

76. Badran, *Harem Years*, pp. 20–21.

77. Badran, *Harem Years*, Preface, p. 1.

78. Baron, "New Literary Culture"; Khalifah, *Harakah Nisa³iyah;* Marei, "Female Emancipation."

79. Chafetz and Dworkin, *Female Revolt*, p. 150.

80. Ibid.; Kumari Jayawardena, *Feminism and Nationalism in the Third World* (London: Zed Books, 1986), p. 56, but also see the entire chapters on Egypt and Iran; Sheila Rowbotham, *Women, Resistance, and Revolution.*

81. Badran, *Harem Years*, pp. 129, 137; Thomas Philip, "Feminism and Nationalist Politics in Egypt," in *Women in the Muslim World*, ed. Beck and Keddie, p. 278; Afaf Lutfi al-Sayyid Marsot, "The Revolutionary Gentlewoman," in *Women in the Muslim World*, ed. Beck and Keddie, pp. 268–69.

82. Mervat Hatem, "Egypt's Middle Class in Crisis: The Sexual Division of Labor," *Middle East Journal* 42, no. 3 (Summer 1988) pp. 413–415 provide some evidence. In this article Hatem concentrates on factors leading to the Islamist position on female labor as it affects the middle classes.

83. Hatem, "Enduring Alliance" p. 421.

84. Zeinab Radwan, *Bahth Zahirat al-Hijab bayn al-Jamiᶜyat* (Cairo: National Center for Sociological and Criminological Research 1982). Also cited by Hatem in "Egypt's Middle Class in Crisis."

85. Graham-Browne, *Images*, pp. 221–24.

86. Hussein Ahmad Amin, *al-Gumhuriya*, 18 May 1985. Cited in Nadia Hijab, *Womanpower: The Arab Debate on Women at Work* (London: Cambridge University Press, 1988), p. 33.

87. Zein ad-Din, "Removing the Veil and Veiling."

88. al-Rahman, *al-Mafhum al-Islami.*

89. al-Sayyid Marsot, "Revolutionary Gentlewomen."

90. Jehan Sadat, *A Woman of Egypt* (New York: Simon & Schuster, 1987), p. 309.

91. Mitchell covers the founding of the Muslim Brotherhood. Richard D. Mitchell, *The Society of the Muslim Brothers* (London: Oxford University

Press, 1969); Tariq al-Bishri, *Harakah al-Siyasiyah fi Misr 1945-1952* (Cairo: al-Haya' al-Misriyah lil-Kitab, 1972).

92. al-Sayyid Marsot, *A Short History of Modern Egypt*, p. 89.

93. Afaf Lutfial-Sayyid Marsot, *Protest Movements and Religious Undercurrents in Egypt: Past and Present*, Center for Contemporary Arab Studies Occasional Papers Series (Washington, D.C.: Center for Contemporary Arab Studies, Georgetown University, March 1984), p. 2; Ahmed Goma'a, "Islamic Fundamentalism in Egypt During the 1930s and 1970s," in *Islam, Nationalism, and Radicalism in Egypt and the Sudan*, ed. Gabriel Warburg and U. Kupferschmidt (New York: Praeger, 1983).

94. Crane Brinton, *The Anatomy of Revolution* (New York: Vintage Books, 1965); Samuel P. Huntington, *Political Order in Changing Societies* (New Haven: Yale University Press, 1968); Barrington Moore, *Social Origins of Dictatorship and Democracy: Lord and Peasant in the Making of the Modern World* (Boston: Beacon Press, 1966); or see Elbaki Hermassi and his model of periphery revolutions, in *The Third World Reassessed* (Berkeley: University of California Press, 1980) pp. 41–92.

95. Barrington Moore, in *Social Origins of Dictatorship*, characterized India's political development as just such a postponed revolution, which nonetheless involved political costs, pp. 314–410.

96. Personal interviews with Cairene women, November–December 1988; conversations with Milda and 'Ali Reda.

97. *Iskandaria Leh?*, directed and conceived by Yusuf Shahin, Cairo, 1979.

98. Muhammad Shawqi Zaki, *al-Ikhwan al-Muslimun wa'l Mujtama' al-Misri* (Cairo: 1954), pp. 154–64; Mitchell, *The Society of the Muslim Brothers*, p. 175. Zaki, Mitchell, and others who have recorded snippets of information regarding women in the *Ikhwan* do not mention Zaynab al-Ghazali, but respondents stated that al-Ghazali has been known at a popular level and among political circles for many years.

99. Mitchell, *The Society of the Muslim Brothers*, p. 175, citing Zaki, *al-Ikhwan*, and al-Akhawat al-Muslimat, *al-Risalat al 'Ula* (pamphlet) (Cairo: 1951).

100. Mitchell, *The Society of the Muslim Brothers*, p. 175.

101. Personal interview with Zaynab al-Ghazali, Cairo, 28 November 1988.

102. al-Bahi al-Khuli, *al-Mar*ah bayna al-Bayt wa al-Mujtama*ᶜ* (Cairo: Ikhwan al-Muslimun, 1953), a *risala* commissioned by the Society with Hudaybi's preface); also cited by Mitchell, *Society of the Muslim Brothers* p. 255; Saᶜid Ramadan, *Maᶜalim al-Tariq* (Damascus: 1953), pp. 32–34; and Sayyid Qutb, *al-ᶜAdalat al-Ljtimaᶜiya fi-l-Islam* (3rd ed. Cairo, n.d.) translated by John Hardie in *Social Justice in Islam* (Washington: 1955).

103. Mitchell, *Society of the Muslim Brothers*, pp. 282–83.

104. Ibid., p. 223.

105. Sayyid Qutb, *al-ᶜAlam wa al-Islam* (Cairo: 1951), pp. 57–60; Mitchell, *Society of the Muslim Brothers*, p. 256.

106. Muhammad al-Ghazali, *Min huna naᶜalam* (Cairo: 1954) p. 117ff; also cited in Mitchell, *Society of the Muslim Brothers*, p. 256.

107. Series of conversations with older Syrian, Palestinian, and Lebanese women, Los Angeles, 1984–89.

108. Mervat Hatem, "Through Each Other's Eyes: Egyptian, Levantine-Egyptian, and European Women's Images of Themselves and of Each Other (1862–1920)," *Women's Studies International Forum* 12, no. 2 (1989),

109. Andrea Rugh, *Reveal and Conceal: Dress in Contemporary Egypt* (Cairo: The American University in Cairo Press, 1986).

110. Dr. al-Sayyid Marsot repeated this observation that I remembered hearing in Cairo in 1980 and 1981. Unveiled respondents often made very similar remarks. Personal interviews with fifty Cairene women, November–December 1988.

111. Hudaybi, *al-Mussawar*, 27 November 1953, p. 25.

112. ᶜAbd al-Qadir ᶜAwda, *al-Daᶜwa*, 1 September 1953, p. 3, in Mitchell, *Society of the Muslim Brothers*, p. 258.

113. Mitchell, *Society of the Muslim Brothers*, p. 258, citing *al-Gumhuriya*, 18 March 1954, p. 1.

114. Zaynab al-Ghazali, *Ayyam min Hayati* (Cairo: Dar al-Shuruq, 2nd ed. [1982] [also published in Beirut]); al-Bishri, *Harakat.*

115. Cynthia Nelson, "The Voices of Doria Shafik: Feminist Consciousness in Egypt, 1940–1960," *Feminist Issues* 6, no. 2 (1986), pp. 17–30.

116. Nasser's tight political rein was rationalized by the uncertain internal and external security status of the regime in that period despite his ideological appeal. Under the Sadat regime, films, television stories, and novels

appeared that depicted the low level of human and political rights in the Nasser years, with plots including arrests, detainments, torture, and corruption.

117. Elizabeth Fernea and Robert Fernea, *The Arab World: Personal Encounters* (Garden City, N.Y.: Anchor Press, 1987), pp. 208–9.

118. Ibid.

119. Sawsan el-Messiri, *Ibn al-Balad: A Conception of Egyptian Identity* (Leiden: E. J. Brill, 1978); personal interviews of Cairene women, November–December, 1988.

120. Naguib Mahfouz, *Midaq Alley* (Washington, D.C.: Three Continents Press, 1981).

121. *Li ʾAdam Kifayah al-ʿAdlihi*, featuring Najlah Fathi, Cairo, early 1980s, based on an older story (by Tawfiq al-Hakim) of the *fallaha* who collides with city morals.

122. el-Messiri, *Ibn al-Balad;* Nadia Adel Taher, *Social Identity and Class in a Cairo Neighborhood,* Cairo Papers in Social Science, 9, monograph 4 (Cairo: The American University in Cairo Press, Winter 1986).

123. Janet Abu Lughod, *Cairo: 1,001 Years of the City Victorious* (Princeton: Princeton University Press, 1971); John Waterbury, *Egypt Burdens of the Past, Options for the Future* (London: Indiana University Press, 1978).

124. Nadia Haggag Youssef, *Women and Work in Developing Societies* (Berkeley: University of California, 1974).

125. Nadia Haggag Youssef, "Women in the Muslim World," in *Women of the World,* ed. Lynne Iglitzin (Santa Barbara, Calif.: Clio Press, 1973), p. 203.

126. Ibid.

127. For relevant figures, see chapter 4; based on statistics from the *Yearbook of Labor Statistics* (Geneva: International Labor Office, 1988).

128. Earl Sullivan, *Women in Egyptian Public Life* (Syracuse, N.Y.: Syracuse University Press, 1986), p. 34.

129. Peter Mansfield, *Nasser's Egypt* (Harmondsworth: Penguin Books, 1969), p. 44, cited by Anthony McDermott, *Egypt from Nasser to Mubarak: A Flawed Revolution* (London: Croom Helm, 1988), p. 17.

130. al-Sayyid Marsot, *A Short History of Modern Egypt,* p. 126.

131. Saad Eddin Ibrahim characterized these elements as "anti-regime" or "anti-society" Islamists who contrast with the moderates and other remnants of the Muslim Brothers. Saad Eddin Ibrahim, "Egypt's Islamic Activism in the 1980s," *Third World Quarterly* 10, no. 2 (April 1988), pp. 640–41, 649.

132. Saad Eddin Ibrahim, "Anatomy of Egypt's Militant Islamic Groups: Methodological Note and Preliminary Findings," *International Journal of Middle East Studies* 12 (1981), pp. 423–53.

133. Hamied Ansari, *Egypt, the Stalled Society* (Albany: State University of New York Press, 1986); Leonard Binder, *In a Moment of Enthusiasm: Political Power and the Second Stratum In Egypt* (Chicago: University of Chicago Press, 1978).

134. Muhammad Heikal, *Autumn of Fury: The Assassination of Sadat* (London: Andre Deutsch, 1983), p. 133.

135. Gouda Abdel Khalek, "The Open Door Economic Policy in Egypt: Its Contribution to Investment and its Equity Implications," in *Rich and Poor States in the Middle East: Egypt and the New Arab Order*, ed. Malcolm Kerr and El-Sayed Yassin (Boulder, Colo. Westview Press, 1982), pp. 259–83.

136. Ibid., p. 278.

137. Galal Amin, "External Factors in the Reorientation of Egypt's Economic Policy," in *Rich and Poor*, ed. Kerr and Yassin, pp. 285–319.

138. Heikal, *Autumn of Fury*, pp. 133–35; al-Sayyid Marsot, *Protest Movements*, p. 8.

139. "A sublimation of discontents in a non-political direction." Michael Fischer, *Iran from Religious Disputes to Revolution* (Cambridge: Harvard University Press, 1980), p. 177.

140. Nikki Keddie, *Roots of Revolution: An Interpretive History of Modern Iran* (New Haven: Yale University Press, 1981), pp. 183–85.

141. al-Sayyid Marsot, *Protest Movements*, p. 8.

142. Articles in almost every issue of *al-Daʿwah* throughout 1980 and 1981 discuss the settlement and reaffirm support for Palestinian sovereignty; in particular see vol. 31, August 1981.

143. Emmanuel Sivan, *Radical Islam: Medieval Theology and Modern Politics* (New Haven: Yale University Press, 1985).

144. Jehan Sadat describes the Islamists as "fanatics," concluding that: "Our new opponents were those we had thought our friends." She also

describes how she was repeatedly approached by "well-spoken girls" who tried to convince her to adopt the new Islamic dress. Sadat, *A Woman of Egypt*, pp. 410–16.

145. *Hawwa*, 22 August 1981, cited by Valerie Hoffman-Ladd in "Polemics on the Modesty and Segregation of Women in Contemporary Egypt," *International Journal of Middle East Studies* 19, no. 1 (February 1987), p. 40.

146. *al-Marʾah al-Hadidiyah*. Featuring Najlah Fathi, Cairo, 1985. Although this film was made later in the 1980s, it heightened the already negative portrait of the unveiled woman, elite or middle-class.

147. Sullivan, *Women in Egyptian Public Life*, p. 143 and 125–149.

148. Hijab, *Womanpower;* Mervat Hatem, "Toward the Study of the Psychodynamics of Mothering and Gender in Egyptian Families," *International Journal of Middle East Studies* 19 (1987), p. 291.

149. al-Messiri, *Ibn al-Balad*, p. 96.

150. Elizabeth Taylor, "Egyptian Migration and Peasant Wives," *MERIP Reports* (June 1984), pp. 3–10; Fatma Khafagy, "Women and Labor Migration: One Village in Egypt," *MERIP Reports* (June 1984).

151. *al-Daʾiʿah*, Cairo, 1987. In this film a woman becomes the family provider after their flat collapses and the family goes to live in refugee housing. A nurse, she migrates to work in Saudi Arabia and encounters discrimination as an Egyptian and as a woman. While she is there she sends all her earnings home, but upon returning discovers that her husband has married another woman. She loses her custody of her children and becomes a drug addict, finally avenging herself on her husband. It is popularly thought that the divorce rate among labor migrants has increased, but there are no specific and comprehensive statistics as yet on this phenomenon.

152. Soheir Sukkary-Stolba, "Changing Roles of Women in Egypt's Newly Reclaimed Lands," *Anthropological Quarterly* 58, no. 4 (1985), pp. 182–89.

153. Nadia Khouri-Dagher, "The Answers of Civil Society to a Defaulting State: A Case Study Around the Food Question in Egypt" (Paper presented to the Middle East Studies Association, Baltimore, Maryland, 1987); also, Nadia Khouri-Dagher, "La 'Faillité' de l'Etat dans l'Approvisionnement Alimentaire des Citadins: Mythe ou Realité?" *Egypte—Recompositions, Peuples Méditerranéens*, nos. 41–42 (October 1987–March 1988), published March 1988, dir. Paul Vielle, in conjunction with CEDEJ, (Centre d'études et de documentation, économique, juridique et sociale, Le Caire) pp. 193–210.

154. Khouri-Dagher, "The Answers of Civil Society," p. 19.

155. Unni Wikan, "Living Conditions among Cairo's Poor: A View From Below," *The Middle East Journal* 39, no. 1 (Winter 1985), pp. 23.

156. Khouri-Dagher, "The Answers of Civil Society." *Dallalat* are women who buy and sell legal as well as illegal, blackmarket goods, sometimes items that are supposed to be controlled through the subsidy coupon system.

157. Jehan Sadat was suprised to learn that the personal status reforms were popularly known as "Jehan's laws." Sadat, *A Woman of Egypt.*

158. Fawzi M. Najjar, "Egyptian Laws of Personal Status," *Arab Studies Quarterly* 10, no. 3 pp. 319–344; Sarah Graham-Browne, "After Jihan's Law a New Battle over Women's Rights" *The Middle East* no. 128, pp. 319–44.

159. McDermott, *Egypt from Nasser to Mubarrak,* p. 179.

160. Ibrahim, "Egypt's Islamic Activism."

161. Hijab, *Womanpower,* p. 35.

162. Personal interview with Ingie Roushdie, journalist and activist in legal reform, Cairo, November 1982; Ad Hoc Committee on Women's Status, *The Legal Rights of Egyptian Women: Between Theory and Practice* (in Arabic) (Cairo: 1988).

163. Amina Shafiq, *Al-Marʾah lan Taʿud ila al-Bait* (Cairo: al-Maktabah al-Shaʿabiyah, 1987).

Chapter 4: Studies of Self-Image

1. Michel Foucault, *The Use of Pleasure: The History of Sexuality,* vol. 2 (New York: Vintage Books, 1990), p. 26.

2. Marianne Alireza, "Women of Saudi Arabia," *National Geographic* 172, no. 4 (October 1987), photograph p. 452. The caption reads "A designer veil sports the logo of Yves St. Laurent, reflecting a new worldliness among Saudi women, whose lives have been opened by education and fresh opportunities. Most accept the veil for privacy and protection from male harassment, not as a symbol of oppression, and cling to a tradition that defies Western understanding."

3. Around much of the Mediterranean, married women have often worn black, or black outerwear, especially older women. There is nothing

"Islamic" about this custom, which occurs as often in Greece and Italy as in the Arab Mediterranean. The Qurʾan implies that older women need not cover their *zina* as younger women should, perhaps because they are beyond the years of childbearing.

4. Fadwa el-Guindi, "Veiling Infitah with Muslim Ethic: Egypt's Contemporary Islamic Movement," *Social Problems* 28, no. 4 (April 1981); Zeynab Radwan, "Bahth al-Hijab bayn al-Jamiʿyat" (A Study of the Phenomenon of the Veil among College Students) (Cairo: The National Center for Sociological and Criminological Research, 1982).

5. White-collar workers with low salaries still retain higher status than tradesmen or most blue-collar workers. Their salaries are dependent on their rank and seniority and whether they work for the public or private sector. Public-sector workers work for lower wages. However, some of them supplement their daytime salaries by working at blue-collar jobs at night or driving a cab. Their daughters listed their "official" jobs, because these implied higher status.

6. Willy Jansen, " 'God Will Pay in Heaven.' Women and Wages in Algeria" (Paper presented to the Middle East Studies Association, Baltimore, Maryland, November 1987), especially pp. 5–6.

7. E. W. Lane describes the household division in *Manners and Customs of the Modern Egyptians* (London: East-West Publications, 1981, first printed 1836) p. 172, earlier he comments on the Egyptian personality; Comte de Savary, *Lettres d'Egypte,* vol. 2 (Paris, 1825); personal interview with Ingie Roushdie, Cairo, November 1988.

8. Afaf Lutfi al-Sayyid Marsot, "The Revolutionary Gentlewomen." in Egypt," *Women in the Muslim World,* eds. Lois Beck and Nikki Keddie, (Cambridge, Massachusetts: Harvard University Press, 1978).

9. Afaf Lutfi al-Sayyid commented that women of her mother's generation did not particularly approve of their daughters' employment; nor did another mother and her daughter I interviewed—personal interviews of Mme. and Ms. D., by the author, Cairo, 1 December 1981.

10. Literature, both scholarly and popular, has emphasized arranged marriages and those made against a girl's will, while there is a strong Islamic principle that a young woman must consent to her marriage and may dispute a choice made for her.

11. Personal interview with Ingie Roushdie, Cairo, 30 November 1988.

12. Personal interview with Olfat Kamel, Cairo, 24 November 1988.

13. Fauzi Najjar, "Egypt's Laws of Personal Status," *Arab Studies Quarterly* 10, no. 3 (1989). Veiled and unveiled representatives stood behind the Personal Status Laws, according to Earl Sullivan, *Women in Egyptian Public Life* (Syracuse, N.Y.: Syracuse University Press, 1986), p. 76. Also see Ad-Hoc Committee on Women's Status, *al-Huquq al-Qanuniyah al-Marʾah al-Misriyah: Bayna al-nazariyah wa al-tatbiq,* (Cairo: 1988).

14. John Esposito, *Women in Muslim Family Law* (Syracuse, N.Y.: Syracuse University Press, 1982), pp. 26, 27, 55.

15. *Bidʿah* is a concept used in jurisprudence to indicate a practice, belief, or situation that is inconsistent with the *sunnah* of the Prophet (or with another of the sources of *shariʿah*) and is therefore considered an unacceptable or heretical innovation.

16. Personal interview with Ms. D. S., Cairo, 23 November 1988.

17. Personal interview with Ms. S., Cairo, Cairo University, 2 December 1988.

18. Personal interview with Cherien M., Cairo, 6 December 1988; personal interview with Ingie Roushdie; Mona Hammam, "Women and Industrial Work in Egypt: the Chubra el-Kheima Case," *Arab Studies Quarterly* 1, no. 2 (1980), cited in Nadia Hijab, *Womenpower: The Arab Debate on Women at Work* (Cambridge: Cambridge University Press, 1988).

19. Helmi Tadros, *Social Security and the Family in Egypt, Cairo Papers in Social Science,* vol. 7, monograph 1 (Cairo: The American University in Cairo, 1984), pp. 34, 46–47.

20. Ibid., p. 24.

21. Ibid., p. 24.

22. Personal interview with Ms. A. Cairo, 4 December 1988.

23. Nemat Guenena visited one reading group of this sort and describes her visit in the appendix to her work *The 'Jihad,' an 'Islamic Alternative' in Egypt, Cairo Papers in Social Science,* vol. 9, monograph 2 (Cairo: American University in Cairo, Summer 1986).

24. Personal interviews with Cairene women, Cairo, November–December 1988.

25. Personal interview with Ms. N., Cairo, 6 December 1988. I refer to the Chinese example because earlier in Egypt, Sadat specifically imposed restrictions on a number of topics including *infitah,* the economic opening, the political opposition, and the radical Islamist groups.

26. *al-Ahram,* 11-16 November 1988, *al-Akher Saʿa,* same week.

27. Abd el-Monʿeim Saʿid ʿAly, Cairo, December 1988.

28. The women pointed to just such a miscalculation on the part of Anwar al-Sadat which resulted in his assassination by Khalid al-Islambouli.

29. Personal interview with Djenane Sirry, Cairo, 23 November 1988.

30. Personal interview with Ms. N., Cairo, 6 December 1988.

31. Personal interview with Ms. H., Cairo, 2 December 1988.

32. Fatima Mernissi, "Democracy as Moral Disintegration: The Contradiction between Religious Belief and Citizenship as a Manifestation of the Ahistoricity of the Arab Identity," in *Women of the Arab World,* ed. Nahid Toubia (London: Zed Press, 1988). The same idea is expressed in a more sophisticated manner by Leonard Binder, *Islamic Liberalism* (Chicago: University of Chicago Press, 1988).

33. Esposito mentions the women's right to her own bridewealth (*mahr*) but not the retention of her name. Esposito, *Women in Family Law,* p. 24.

34. Unveiled elite women and unveiled middle-class women made this claim repeatedly, in the interviews and in additional conversations.

35. Andrea Rugh, *Reveal and Conceal, Dress in Contemporary Egypt* (Cairo: American University in Cairo Press, 1986), pp. 108-9, 149-56; Jennifer Scarce, *Women's Costume of the Near and Middle East* (London: Unwin Hyman, 1987).

36. As was previously indicated, the meaning of certain terms is open to interpreation. Qurʾan, Surah XXXIII:59, Surah XXXIII:52, Surah XXIV:31.

37. Scarce, *Women's Costume,* p. 139.

38. Ibid., pp. 122-26.

39. Personal interview with Ms. A., Cairo, 4 December 1988.

40. Valerie Hoffman-Ladd, "Polemics on the Modesty and Segregation of Women in Contemporary Egypt," *International Journal of Middle East Studies* 19, no. 1 (1987), p. 28.

41. Fatima Mernissi, *Beyond the Veil: Male-Female Dynamics in a Modern Muslim Society* (Cambridge: Cambridge University Press, 1975).

42. Fadwa el-Guindi, "Veiling Infitah with Muslim Ethic," pp. 481-2.

43. Ibid., pp. 481-3.

44. Rugh, *Reveal and Conceal,* p. 149.

45. Personal interviews of Cairene women, November–December 1988.

46. For a discussion of *istisham*, see Lila Abu-Lughod, *Veiled Sentiments: Honor and Poetry in a Bedouin Society* (Cairo: American University in Cairo Press, 1986), pp. 107–9, 154–56.

47. *Risalat al-Marʿah al-Muslimah* (Cairo: *Jamaʿah al-Islamiyah*, n.d.) pp. 53–4, cited in Hoffman-Ladd, "Polemics," pp.34–5.

48. *Yearbook of Labor Statistics, 1988* (Geneva: International Labor Office, 1988).

49. Foucault, *The Use of Pleasure*, p. 25.

Chapter 5: Construction of the Virtuous Woman

1. Niʿmat Sidqi, *Tabarruj* (Cairo, 1975), as discussed by Valerie Hoffman-Ladd, "Polemics on the Modesty and Segregation of Women," *International Journal of Middle East Studies* 19, no. 1 (February 1987), pp. 29–31.

2. Zaynab bint Khuzaymah and Zaynab bint Jahsh, the wives of the Prophets, are also historical namesakes. The Prophet received the Verse of the Curtain imposing new restrictions on his wives following his marriage to Zaynab bint Jahsh. Abbott proposes, as do others, that "some of the guests stayed too long at the wedding feast of Zaynab bint Jahsh." At some point "the hands of men guests touched the hands of Muhammad's wives." The Prophet's marital life and privacy was being compromised by his availability to the community, so restrictions were necessary. See W. Montgomery Watt, *Muhammad at Medina* (Oxford University Press, 1981) citing Nabiah Abbott *Aishah the Beloved of Mohammed* (London: Al Saqi Books, 1985; first printing, 1942), pp. 20–29. Zaynab bint Jahsh was said to embody generosity, according to another *hadith* based on a saying of the Prophet's that the wife with the longest "reach" was the most generous. The prophet's daughter was also named Zaynab. Ibn ʿAbbas, cited by Watt, *Muhammad at Medina*, pp. 396–97.

3. The idealization of Zaynab is not restricted to the Shiʿa.

4. Valerie J. Hoffman first gives the year 1936/1356, in "An Islamic Activist: Zaynab al-Ghazali," in *Women and the Family in the Middle East*, ed. Elizabeth Fernea, (Austin: University of Texas at Austin Press, 1986), p. 234. But in the section of *Ayyam min Hayati* that Hoffman translates, al-Ghazali then says it was in 1358 (h.), several months *after* the founding of the A.M.W., that a decision to remain independent of the Brotherhood was

taken; Ibid., p. 238; In my interview with al-Ghazali, she stated that she founded the association in 1938. Personal interview with Zaynab al-Ghazali, Cairo, 28 November 1988.

5. Hoffman, "An Islamic Activist," p. 237.

6. Ibid., p. 236; Zaynab al-Ghazali, *Ayyam min Hayati* (Cairo: Dar al-Shuruq, 1982); personal interview with Zaynab al-Ghazali.

7. Personal interview with Zaynab al-Ghazali; personal interview with Hana Ahmad Shawqi, Cairo, 18 November 1988.

8. Hoffman, "An Islamic Activist," p. 237.

9. Ibid.; personal interview with al-Ghazali.

10. Earl T. Sullivan, *Women in Egyptian Public Life* (Syracuse, N.Y.: Syracuse University Press, 1986), pp. 115–117. Sullivan says that publicly active women have absorbed some "male" attitudes toward service and employment. He defines this male perspective as the belief that merit and honor proceed from a career or public endeavor. Here he cites Aziza Hussein's description of these women as "men in frocks."

11. Ibid., pp. 115–17.

12. Ibid., p. 116.

13. Ni'mat Fouad, *The Project of the Pyramids Plateau: The Most Dangerous Take-Over in Egypt* (World of Books, 1978).

14. Personal interview with Ni'mat Fouad, Cairo, 1 December 1988.

15. Safinaz Qassim was interviewed in "Sword of Islam" (a segment of a five-part series broadcast by the BBC and the Public Broadcast Service in the United States).

16. Personal interviews with fifty Cairene women, November–December 1988. Also from questionnaires distributed in Cairo, November 1988.

17. Afaf Lutfi al-Sayyid Marsot, "Religion or Opposition? Urban Protest Movements in Egypt," *International Journal of Middle East Studies* 16 (1984), pp. 541–52; Emmanuel Sivan, *Radical Islam: Medieval Theology and Modern Politics* (New Haven: Yale University Press, 1985).

18. Personal interview with Zaynab al-Ghazali.

19. Earlier expressions may be found in *al-Da'wah*, all summer issues, 1981, under the editor 'Umar Tilmisani; or in *Liwa al-Islam*, 11 November 1988, pp. 10–11, 14–15.

20. Saad Eddin Ibrahim, "Egypt's Islamic Activism in the 1980s," *Third World Quarterly* 10, no. 2 (April 1988); Nemat Guenena, *The "Jihad," an 'Islamic Alternative' in Egypt, Cairo Papers in Social Science,* vol. 2, monograph 2 (Cairo: The American University in Cairo Press, 1986).

21. Nemat Guenena, *The "Jihad,"* p. 74.

22. Personal interviews with Magdi Ahmad Hussein, A. Shawqi, ʿAsam al-ʿAryan, and corroborative conversation with ʿAbd al-Monʿeim Saʿid ʿAly, Cairo, November–December 1988.

23. Personal interviews with Zaynab al-Ghazali and a member of the editorial staff of *al-Liwa al-Islam;* personal interviews with ʿAsam al-ʿAryan and Hana A. Shawqi, Cairo, December 1988.

24. Ibid.

25. Niʿmat Guenena, *The "Jihad,"* pp. 74–76.

26. Personal interview with Zaynab al-Ghazali.

27. Yvonne Haddad, "Islam, Women, and Revolution in Twentieth-Century Arab Thought," *The Muslim World* 74 (July/October 1984), pp. 152–56.

28. Personal interview with Zaynab al-Ghazali; also see her column 1980 and 1981 in *al-Daʿwah* entitled "The Muslim Woman" (in Arabic).

29. Personal interview with Niʿmat Fouad.

30. Valerie Hoffman-Ladd, "Polemics on Modesty and Segregation;" personal interview with Zaynab al-Ghazali.

31. Personal interview with Zaynab al-Ghazali.

32. Other social movements and states have considered transferring domestic responsibilities to the state in order to free women for productive labor. Such cases include the USSR in the Leninist period and the kibbutz experiment in Israel.

33. *The Meaning of the Glorious Qurʾan.* Trans. and text, Marmaduke Pickthall, Women, IV:34. A. Yusuf Ali translates, "because God has given the one more (strength) than the other. . ."

34. My translation.

35. "to men is allotted what they earn, and to women what they earn."

36. Zaynab al-Ghazali, "al-Mar³ah al-Mu³mina wa al-Mar³ah al-Usriya," *al-Da'wah* (October 1980).

37. Fouad used these examples to illustrate Muslim women's rights to exercise their abilities and talents. Personal interview with Ni'mat Fouad.

38. Personal interview with Zaynab al-Ghazali.

39. As in Abbott's interpretation, Nabiah Abbott, *Aishah the Beloved of Mohammed.*

40. Personal interview with Zaynab at Ghazali.

41. Fatima Mernissi, *Beyond the Veil: Male-Female Dynamics in a Modern Muslim Society* (Cambridge: Cambridge University Press, 1975).

42. Most of the respondents who wore the *niqab* had adopted the *higab* within a year of puberty.

43. Personal interview with Zaynab al-Ghazali.

44. *The Meaning of the Glorious Qur³an.*

45. Ibid.

46. Barbara Stowasser, "The Status of Women in Early Islam," in *Muslim Women,* ed. Freda Hussein (London: Croom Helm, 1984).

47. al-Hibri, "A Study of Islamic Herstory: Or How Did We Ever Get Into This Mess," *Women's Studies International Forum,* 5, No., 2 (1982) Mernissi, *Beyond the Veil.*

48. C. G. Jung, *Psyche and Symbol,* ed. Violet de Laszlo, (Garden City, N.Y.: Doubleday Anchor Books, 1958), pp. 125–26.

49. Ibid., pp. 9–11.

50. Michel Foucault, *The Use of Pleasure: The History of Sexuality,* vol. 2, (New York: Vintage Books, 1990), pp. 29–32.

51. Zaynab al-Ghazali, "'Amal al-Mar³ah . . . wa Ta'limuha," *al-Da'wah,* vol. 30 (September 1980).

52. Ibrahim, "Egypt's Islamic Activism," p. 656.

53. Ibid., pp. 655–56.

54. al-Ghazali, "'Amal al-Mar³ah."

55. Zaynab al-Ghazali, "Al-Mar³ah al-Mu³minah wa al-Mar³ah al-Usriyah," *al-Da'wah,* (October 1980).

56. Ibid.

57. al-Ghazali, *Ayyam min Hayati.*

58. Personal interview with Zaynab al-Ghazali.

59. Ibid.

60. Pickthall's translation is: "And if ye fear that you cannot do justice (to so many) then one only or (the captives) that your right hand possesses." The other reference is to Surah IV, (Women): 129, "Ye will not be able to deal equally between your wives, however much ye wish (to do so). But turn not altogether away (from one) leaving her as in suspense. . . ."

61. Personal interview with Niʿmat Fouad.

62. Personal interviews with veiled women, Cairo, November through December 1988. All respondents signed a form granting permission for the interview and the right to anonymity.

63. al-Ghazali, "ʿAmal al-Marʾah."

64. Personal interview with ʿAsam al-ʿAryan, Cairo, 8 December 1988. Personal interview with Zaynab al-Ghazali.

65. Mervat Hatem, "Towards the Study of the Psychodynamics of Mothering and Gender in Egyptian Families," *International Journal of Middle East Studies* (August 1987), pp. 287–306.

66. Personal interview with ʿAsam al-ʿAryan. Personal interview with Zaynab al-Ghazali.

67. Mernissi, *Beyond the Veil;* Hatem, "Mothering and Gender."

68. Halim Barakat, "The Arab Family and the Challenge of Social Transformation," in *Women and the Family in the Middle East,* ed. Elizabeth Fernea, (Austin: University of Texas Press, 1985).

69. Personal interviews with veiled women, Cairo, November–December 1988.

70. Ad-Hoc Committee on Women's Status, *al-Huquq al-Qanuniyah al-Marʾah al-Misriyah.*

71. Heretofore she did not have the right to the conjugal dwelling for the duration of the custodial period. This issue was hotly debated, due to the housing shortage in Cairo. Some films lampooned this provision as in *Afwah Ayuha al-Qanun,* where a witness lies in court when his wife (who has cuckolded him) dangles the apartment keys knowingly during his testimony. He knows he cannot return to his home unless he obeys his wife. But the *Ikhwan* attacked Dr. Abd al-Munʿim al-Nimr, the theologian and Minister of Religious Endowments, for supporting Law 44. Attacks were also launched at Amina al-Saʿid, the journalist and feminist, for her advocacy of the reforms, charging her with glorifying the West. Samman, *al-ʾItisam,* no. 9 (August

1979), pp. 2, 3. Cited by Fauzi Najjar, "Egypt's Laws of Personal Status," *Arab Studies Quarterly* 10, no. 3 (1988), et passim, p. 343.

72. Najjar, "Egypt's Laws of Personal Status"; Azizah Hussein, "Recently Approved Amendments of Egypt's Law on Personal Status," in *Religion and Politics of the Middle East*, ed. M. Curtis, 1981; Ragai Abdullah, "Case #520 that Stopped the Application of the Personal Status Law," *al-Mussawar*, 9 March 1983. These reforms were popularly known as "Jihan's laws" because she campaigned for them and purportedly pressured Sadat to issue them, which was done without normal legislative review and voting.

73. Personal interview with Zaynab al-Ghazali.

74. Guenena was impressed with the "oversimplified logic" the Islamist women employed in meetings she observed. She also noted the formal and serious tone of conversation. (After a few sessions, she was then discouraged from further attendance.) Nemat Guenena, *"Jihad"*, pp. 76–82.

75. Personal interview with Niʿmat Fouad.

76. Valerie Hoffman-Ladd, "Polemics," pp. 23–50.

77. Sawsan el-Messiri, *Ibn al-Balad: A Conception of Egyptian Identity* (Leiden: E. J. Brill, 1978), 1978), p. 45.

78. Personal interview with Zaynab al-Ghazali.

79. Andrea Rugh, *Family in Contemporary Egypt* (Syracuse, N.Y.: Syracuse University Press, 1984), pp. 70–72.

80. Nayra Atiya, *Khul-Khaal: Five Egyptian Women Tell Their Stories* (Syracuse, N.Y.: Syracuse University Press, 1982), p. 53. Also cited in Rugh *Family in Contemporary Egypt*, pp. 72–73.

81. Personal interview with D. Sirry, 23 November 1988; personal interview with Olfat Kamel, Cairo, 21 November 1988; personal interview with Ingie Roushdie, Cairo, 30 November 1988; personal interview with Fayda Kamel, 25 November 1988.

82. *Hasham* is closely tied to the concept of ʾagl, the social sense and self-control of honorable persons. Just as the possession of ʾagl enables persons to control their needs and passions in recognition of the ideals of honor, so it also allows them to perceive the social order and their place within it. Children, who are said not to have much ʾagl, must be taught to *tahashsham*, [verbal form] (V.); the primary goal of socialization is to teach them to understand social contexts and to act appropriately within them—which means knowing when to *tahashsham*.

Lila Abu-Lughod, *Veiled Sentiments: Honor and Poetry in a Bedouin Society* (Cairo: The American University in Cairo Press, 1986), p. 108. The knowledge of *tahashsham* might not be as strong among urban women, but their concept of *aql* is really very similar to that described above.

83. Personal interview with Niʿmat Fouad.

84. Personal interview with Mme. T., Cairo, 22 November 1988.

85. Informal interview and conversations with H. A. Shawqi, Cairo, 28 November 1988. This remark was made during the interview of Zaynab al-Ghazali to which Mme. Shawqi kindly accompanied me.

86. Fouad Zakaria, "The Standpoint of Contemporary Muslim Fundamentalists," in *Women of the Arab World,* ed. Nahid Toubia (London: Zed Books, 1988), pp. 30–31.

87. Hoffman-Ladd, "Polemics," p. 35.

88. Yvonne Haddad, "Islam, Women, and Revolution," p. 151.

89. Hoffman-Ladd, "Polemics," pp. 29–31.

90. Zakaria, "The Standpoint of Contemporary Fundamentalists," pp. 31–33.

91. Ibid., pp. 31–34.

92. Ibid., p. 32.

93. Ibid., p. 34.

94. For instance, see Sigmund Freud, "Femininity," in *New Introductory Lectures on Psychoanalysis* (New York: W. Norton & Co., 1933), pp. 158–84. For those who discuss "anatomy is destiny," see Simone de Beauvoir, *Le Deuxième Sexe* (Paris: Gallimard, 1981); Sherry B. Ortner, "Woman is to Nature as Man is to Culture," in *Women, Culture, and Society,* ed. M. Rosaldo and L. Lamphere (Stanford, Calif.: Stanford University Press, 1974). Male reduction of woman to her body is carried to its logical apex in Fatna Sabah (pseud.), *Woman in the Muslim Unconscious* (New York: Pergamon Press, 1984).

95. Iqbal Baraka, "The Influence of Contemporary Arab Thought on the Women's Movement," *Women of the Arab World,* ed. Toubia, pp. 52–54.

96. Zaynab al-Ghazali, *Ayyam min Hayati.*

97. H. A. Shawqi, attending interview, Cairo, 28 November 1988.

98. Telephone interview with Safinaz Qassim, Cairo, 5 December 1988.

99. Personal interview with Zaynab al-Ghazali.

100. Fatima Mernissi, *Beyond the Veil*.

101. Fatna Sabah, *Woman in the Muslim Unconscious.*

102. Mernissi, "Democracy as Moral Disintegration:" The Contradiction between Religious Belief and Citizenship as a Manifestation of the Ahistoricity of the Arab Identity," in *Women of the Arab World*, Nahid Toubia, ed., (London: Zed Books, 1988) pp. 36–43.

103. Ibid.

104. Haddad, "Islam, Women, and Revolution," p. 158.

105. Ibid, p. 159.

106. Mahmud Shaltut, *al-Qurʾan waʾl-Marʾah* (Cairo: International Islamic Center for Population Studies and Research, Al-Azhar, n.d., written approx. 1936), from the Academy of Islamic Research of Al-Azhar's version 1956?, pp. 23–24.

107. Rugh, *Family in Contemporary Egypt*, pp. 40–41.

108. Nahid Toubia, "Women and Health in Sudan," in *Women of the Arab World*, ed. Nahid Toubia (London: Zed Books, 1988) pp. 106–8.

Chapter 6: Unveiled Women Reply

1. And whoever is not able to afford to marry free, believing women, let them marry from the believing maids whom your right hand possesses." Women, Surah IV:25.

2. Until recently, the theme was usually of a lower-class woman marrying an upper-class man, as in *Afwah wa Aranib*, starring Fatin Hamama, or in *Intisar ash-Shabab* (1943), featuring Farid el-Atrache and Asmahan. In these stories of ill-fated love, the families typically try to break up the marriages, or one spouse is faithless. Sometimes, the mésalliance occurs in the opposite direction, as in *Dumuʿa bila Khatiʿa*, starring Najlah Fathi—a woman of the rural landed class wants to marry an ordinary doctor, an *effendi*, not of her status, to her uncle's dismay.

3. Nayra Atiya, *Khul-Khaal: Five Egyptian Women Tell Their Stories* (Syracuse: Syracuse University Press, 1982), p. 19.

4. The nouveaux riches have shifted in composition from the early 1970s to the present. They are now composed of some elements of the lower-middle classes and the middle classes. When the *bint al-balad* uses the same term,

she refers to a good and decent man of her own neighborhood and social standing, whose family is honorable.

5. Leonard Binder, *In a Moment of Enthusiasm: Political Power and the Second Stratum in Egypt* (Chicago: University of Chicago Press, 1978); Hamied Ansari, *Egypt: The Stalled Society* (Albany, N.Y.: State University of New York Press, 1986).

6. Afaf al-Sayyid Marsot, "The Revolutionary Gentlewomen in Egypt," in *Women in the Muslim World,* Lois Beck and Nikki Keddie, eds. (Harvard University Press, 1978).

7. Sawsan el-Messiri, *Ibn al-Balad: An Egyptian Concept of Self-Identity* (Leiden: E. J. Brill, 1978), p. 84.

8. Sawsan el-Messiri, "Self-Images of Traditional Urban Women in Cairo," in *Women in the Muslim World,* ed. Beck and Keddie, pp. 530–31.

9. el-Messiri, *Ibn al-Balad,* pp. 86–87.

10. Ibid., p. 93.

11. Ibid, p. 92.

12. In one sense the term *politicized* refers to women's belief that they can affect political outcomes in any way. Secondly, it denotes women's understanding that their personal interactions are affected by their historical and political surroundings, as well as their awareness and understanding of current events.

13. Personal interviews of Egyptian women, Cairo, November–December 1988.

14. Women's participation in voting is also low in many other Third World countries. In Egypt, that situation is related to the relatively high illiteracy rate of women, a factor that is changing.

15. Personal interview with Olfat Kamel, Cairo, 21 November 1988.

16. Jehan Sadat, *A Woman of Egypt,* (New York: Simon and Schuster, Inc., 1987), p. 310.

17. Ibid., p. 330. Sadat describes the confrontation that followed Qaddhafi's presentation to the women of the Union, when Amina el-Said rose and responded, "Perhaps you have forgotten, Mr. President, that at the time of the Prophet women were sharing the burden of the struggle and fighting side by side with men. How can you say after so many centuries that women no longer have equal footing?" Sadat, *A Woman of Egypt,* pp. 334–36.

18. Earl Sullivan, *Women in Egyptian Public Life* (Syracuse, N.Y.: Syracuse University Press, 1986), pp. 72–76, but also pp. 65–67.

19. Ibid., pp. 76–77.

20. Ibid., p. 77.

21. For statistics on preferred ages for marriage, see Helmy Tadros, *Social Security and the Family in Egypt, Cairo Papers in Social Science,* vol. 7, monograph 1 (Cairo: The American University in Cairo Press, 1984), p. 29.

22. Many young women were therefore considering part-time employment or careers in areas that would permit a hiatus of a few years and assured rehiring. In Egypt, graduates of public universities enter a graduate placement system. They may wait several years to be hired, and they may end up being posted to a job not particularly relevant to their academic degree or interests.

23. Yvonne Haddad, "Islam, Women, and Revolution," in Twentieth-Century Arab Thought," *The Muslim World,* 74, (July/October 1984), pp. 148–49. Not only does working reduce fertility, but also it creates competitiveness between partners and destroys the woman's meekness and delicacy if she aspires to share "equal burdens with man"; *Risalat al-Mar³ah al-Muslimah* (Cairo: Jama'a al-Islamiyya, n.d.), pp. 53–54, cited in Hoffman-Ladd, "Polemics on the Modesty and Segregation of Women in Contemporary Egypt." *International Journal of Middle East Studies,* 19, (1987), pp. 34–35; also see Barabara Stowasser, "Liberated Equal or Protected Dependent? Contemporary Religious Paradigms on Women's Status in Islam," *Arab Studies Quarterly,* 9, No. 3, (Summer 1987), p. 276.

24. Women, Surah IV:32. Implicit in this statement is the notion that wealth is unequally distributed, as is the ambition or talent for acquiring that wealth. Men and women may be richer than other men or women, but women may also excel over men and earn greater fortunes than they. Hence, in line 34, men would not be dominant over women, as implied in the word *qawamun,* because they would not be spending their wealth on women.

25. W. Montgomery Watt, "Khadija" in *Encyclopedia of Islam;* also Masud al-Hasan, *Daughters of Islam* (Lahore: The Lion Art Press, n.d.).

26. Wafaa Abou-Negm Marei, "Female Emancipation and Changing Political Leadership: A Study of Five Arab Countries," (Ph.D. diss., Department of Political Science, Rutgers University, 1978), pp. 93–94.

27. Ibid.

28. Ibid., pp. 94–98. Also see Nadia Youssef, *Women and Work in Developing Societies,* (Berkeley: University of California, 1974).

29. Marei, "Female Emancipation," pp. 95–98; Youssef, *Women and Work.*

30. When women work in education or in the health care fields, their presence is enclosed, in a sense. They remain within the hospital or school and do not really encounter great numbers of the general public.

31. Personal interview with Ms. U., Cairo, 2 December 1988.

32. *Zīna* is meant in this case to imply sexual attractions. The term has been taken to mean the entire female body except for the face and hands. The early interpreters of the Qurʾan regarded this term as merely implying adornment, jewelry, or bodily decoration; it later came to "mean natural beauty." Hoffman-Ladd, "Polemics," p. 29.

33. Praise came in the form of affectionate terms, such as *ya shatra*, said to other women on redonning or arranging their *higab* or *niqab*, or one woman said, "See Zaynab here has worn the *niqab* for ten years, may God keep her and preserve her." Then, another girl hugged Zaynab.

34. Not unlike the Chinese principle of *yin* and *yang*; also see Simone de Beuvoir's *Le Deuxième Sexe* (Paris: Gallimard, 1981).

35. Personal interviews with Mrs. A., Los Angeles, California, August 1988, and in Cairo, November 1988.

36. Halim Barakat, "The Arab Family and the Challenge of Social Transformation," in *Women and the Family in the Middle East,* Elizabeth Fernea, ed. (Austin, Texas: University of Texas Press, 1985), pp. 28–48.

37. More of the older women, those over fifty, in my data listed parental opposition to their plans, and expressed regret over that opposition, than did younger women.

38. Safia Mohsen, "New Images, Old Reflections: Working Middle-Class Women in Egypt," in *Women and the Family,* ed. Fernea, p. 59.

39. Ibid., pp. 57–58.

40. Andrea Rugh, *Family in Contemporary Egypt* (Syracuse, N.Y.: Syracuse University Press, 1984), especially "Ties," pp. 89–107.

41. Divorced women are described as loose or immoral because they are seen as sources of temptation for married or single men. They are considered sexually frustrated and therefore more likely to pursue an illicit arrangement. Before the reforms of the Personal Status Laws, divorced women could lose their home or apartment, along with their older children. If they did not

return to their parents' homes, they would be strangers in a new building or area. Also see Mohsen, ''New Images,'' p. 76.

42. Mohsen, ''New Images''; and Ad Hoc Committee on Women's Status, *The Legal Rights of Egyptian Women: Between Theory and Practice* (Cairo: 1988).

43. Mohsen, ''New Images,'' p. 62.

44. Although Mohsen says that upper-class men and women may now plan their household budget together, ibid., p. 60.

45. Mohsen, ''New Images,'' p. 71.

46. Personal interview with Olfat Kamel, Cairo, 21 November 1988. Personal interview with Jeanette Kamel Saad, Cairo, 2 December 1988.

47. al-Sayyid Marsot, ''Revolutionary Gentlewomen''; personal interview with Jeanette Kamel Saad, Cairo, 2 December 1988. Mme. Saad is one of several women I spoke to who is deeply involved in charitable work, and she has worked administratively with hospitals and various training and educational programs for years.

48. The smaller number of veiled women who did stress the *jawhar* of their religion seemed to be unusually perceptive in their other responses as well.

49. Personal interview with Djenane Sirry, Cairo, 23 November 1988. Personal interview with Ingie Roushdie, Cairo, 30 November 1988.

50. Mohsen, ''New Images,'' pp. 67–68.

51. Fadwa El-Guindi, ''Veiling Infitah with Social Ethic: Egypt's Contemporary Islamic Movement,'' *Social Problems* 28, (April 1981).

52. Sawsan el-Messiri, ''Self Images of Traditional Urban Women,'' pp. 526, 529, 530. For another description of the clothing of *bint al-balad,* see Rugh, *Reveal and Conceal: Dress in Contemporary Egypt* (Cairo: The American University in Cairo Press, 1986), pp. 104–13.

53. el-Messiri, ''Self-Images,'' pp. 526, 532; Andrea Rugh, ''Women and Work: Strategies and Choices in a Lower-Class Quarter,'' *Women and Family in the Middle East,* ed. Fernea, pp. 276–77, 282–83. A woman may also work as a *dallala,* a shopper, or as a *ballana,* one who bathes other women and serves as a depilator.

54. el-Messiri, ''Self-Images,'' p. 527. The *muᶜallima* may also take on the functions of community leader and mediator while working as a merchant, butcher, or coffeehouse keeper.

55. el-Messiri, "Self-Images," pp. 535–36.

56. Unni Wikan, "Living Conditions among Cairo's Poor—A View from Below," *The Middle East Journal* 39, no. 1 (Winter 1985), p. 9.

57. Evelyn Early, "Catharsis and Creation: The Everyday Narratives of Balady Women of Cairo," *Anthropological Quarterly* 58, no. 4 (October 1985), p. 179.

58. el-Messiri, "Self-Images," pp. 534–35.

59. Rivka Yadlin, "Militant Islam in Egypt: Some Sociocultural Aspects," in *Islam, Nationalism, and Radicalism,* ed. Gabriel Warburg and Uri Kupferschmidt (New York: Praeger, 1983), p. 172.

60. "In the early 1970s people used to say 'Egypt has become a country of school certificates, what is needed is a *shahada* (diploma) above all.' Now they say: 'It's the technicians who excel. It's practical work not education that pays.' And they are right if money is the issue." Unni Wikan, "Living Conditions among Cairo's Poor," p. 14.

61. Ibid. Wikan upholds the gains of the lower classes despite statistical evidence. She argues that statistics cannot correctly gauge the perceptions of the poor toward their own economic circumstances.

Chapter 7: Dreaming the Myth, and Veiling It

1. Val Moghadam, "Women, Work, and Ideology in Iran," *International Journal of Middle East Studies* 21 (Summer 1989) holds that ideology to be flexible as well.

2. C. G. Jung, *Psyche and Symbol,* Violet S. de Laszlo, ed. (Garden City, N.Y.: Doubleday Anchor Books, 1958) and p. 123.

3. Ibid.

4. Michel Foucault, *The Use of Pleasure: The History of Sexuality,* Vol. 2 (New York: Vintage Books, 1990), pp. 25–26.

5. Ibid., p. 27.

6. Personal interview with ʿAsam al-ʿAryan, Cairo, 6 December 1988.

7. Hamied Ansari, "The Islamic Militants in Egyptian Politics," *International Journal of Middle East Studies* 16, no. 1 (March 1984); Saad Eddin Ibrahim, "Anatomy of Egypt's Militant Islamic Groups: Methodological Note and Preliminary Findings," *International Journal of Middle East Studies,* 12, (1981); Nemat Guenena, *The "Jihad" An "Islamic Alternative" in*

Egypt, Cairo Papers in Social Science, 9, Monograph 2, (Cairo: The American University in Cairo Press, 1986); Leonard Binder, *Islamic Liberalism* (Chicago: University of Chicago Press, 1988).

8. Yvonne Haddad, "Islam, Women, and Revolution in Twentieth-Century Arab Thought," *The Muslim World,* Vol. 74, Nos. 3–4 (July/October 1984).

9. Fadwa El-Guindi, "Veiling Infitah with Muslim Ethic: Egypt's Contemporary Islamic Movement," *Social Problems,* 28, No. 4 (April 1981); Valerie Hoffman-Ladd, "Polemics on the Modesty and Segregation of Women in Contemporary Egypt," *International Journal of Middle East Studies* 19, No. 1 February 1987).

10. The term *Westoxification* was used before, during, and after the Iranian revolution to describe the Western intellectual, material, psychological, and political infection of the Middle East.

11. C. G. Jung, *Psyche and Symbol,* p. 26.

12. Nira Yural-Davis, "The Jewish Collectivity," in *Women in the Middle East* (London: Zed Books, 1987), a *Khamsin* publication, pp. 60–93.

BIBLIOGRAPHY

Arabic Sources

(*Note: The apostrophe will now indicate the letter ʿain [as well as the hamzah] to concord with the most common spellings of these materials.)

Books or Chapters in Books

Abduh, Shaykh Muhammad. "Hijab al-Nisaʾ min al-Jahat al-Diniyah." In *Fi Qadhaya al-Marʾah*. Beirut: Muʾsasah Nasr al-Thaqafah, 1980. Originally appeared in Amin, Qasim. *Tahrir al-Marʾah*, Cairo: 1928.

Ad-Hoc Women's Status Research Group. *al-Huquq al-Qanuniyah lil Marʾah al-Misriyah bayna al-Nazariyah wa-al-Tatbiq*. Cairo, 1988.

Afifi, Abdallah. "Huriyah al-Marʾah wa Hurmat Raʾyahah fi Islam." In *Fi Qadhaya al-Marʾah*. Beirut: Muʾsasah Nasir al-Thaqafah, 1980.

al-Afghani, Saʾid. *al-Islam wa-l-Marʾah*. Dimashq: Dar al-Fikr, 1964.

——— . *ʾAʾishah wa-al-siyasa*. Beirut: Dar al-Fikr, 1971.

Amin, Qasim. *Qasim Amin wa Tahrir al-Marʾah*, edited by Muhammad ʾImarah. Beirut: al-Muʾsasah al-Arabiyah lil-Dirasat wa al-Nashr, 1980.

al-Bahi, Muhammad. *al-Islam wa Ittijah al-Marʾah al-Muslimah al-Muʾasarah*. Cairo: 1979.

al-Bishri, Tariq. *al-Harakah al-Siyasiyah fi Misr 1945–1952*. Cairo: al-Hayaʾ al-Misriyah lil-Kitab, 1972.

al-Bukhari. *Sahih al-Bukhari*. edited by Muhammad Khan. Gujranwala Cantt., Pakistan, 1971. Vols. 1–7.

al-Ghayalini, Shaykh Mustafa. *al-Islam Ruhu al-Madaniyya*. Cairo, n.d. (1920s).

al-Ghazali, Muhammad. *Min Huna Naʾalam*. Cairo: 1954.

al-Ghazali, Zaynab. *Ayyam min Hayati*. Cairo and Beirut: Dar al-Shuruq, n.d. (2nd edition, 1982).

——— . *Nahw Baʾth Jadid*. Cairo: Dar al-Shuruq, 1987.

Hanafi, Hassan. *al-Turath wa al-Tajdid: Mawqifna min al-Turath al-Qadim*. Beirut: Dar al-Tanwir, 1981.

Ibn Hisham. *Kitab Sirat Rasul Allah,* edited by Ferdinand von Wustenfeld. Frankfurt am Main: Minerva, 1961.

al-Husaini, Ishak Musa. *The Muslim Brethren*. Beirut: Khayat [Freres], 1956.

Abu al-Khair, Abd al-Rahman. *Dhikrayati maʾ Jamaʾat al-Muslimin: al-Takfir wa-l-Higrah*. Kuwait: 1980.

Khalifah, Ijlal. *Al-Harakah al-Nisaʾiyah al-Hadithah: Qisat al-marʾah al-ʾarabiyah ʾala ʾard misr*. Cairo: al-Matbuʾah al-ʾArabiyah al-Hadithan, 1972.

Mahmasani, Subhi. *The Legal Systems in the Arab States.* Beirut: Dar al-ʾIlm lil-Malayin, 1965.

Mahmud, Zaki Nagib. *Shuruq min al-Gharb.* Cairo: Dar al-Shuruq, 1982.

Musa, Nabawiyya. *al-Marʾah wa al-ʾAmal.* Alexandria: al-Matbaʾah al-Wataniyah, 1920.

Qutb, Sayyid. *al-ʾAlam waʾl-Islam.* Cairo: 1951.

————. *Fi Zilal al Qurʾan.* Beirut: Dar al-Shuruq, 1974.

————. *Maʾalam ʾala al-Tariq.* Cairo: Dar al-Shuruq, 1982.

Rashid Rida, Muhammad. "Kilmah fi al-Hijab." In *Fi Qadhaya al-Marʾah.* Beirut: Muʾasasah Nasir al-Thaqafah, 1980.

————. "Wa Tarbiyat Nisaʾ al-Muslimin." In *Fi Qadhaya al-Marʾah.*

————. "Al-Talaq fi Islam." (Originally from *Nidaʾ al-Jins al-Latif.* Cairo: 1351) in *Fi Qadhaya al-Marʾah.* Beirut: Muʾasasah Nasr al-Thaqafah, 1980.

Ibn Saʾd, Muhammad. *Kitab al-Tabaqat al-Kabir,* edited by E. Sachau. Leiden: Brill, 1905–1940.

Salim Latifah, Muhammad. *al-Marʾah al-Misriyyah wal-Taghyir al-Ijtimaʾi 1919–1945.* Cairo: al-Hayʾah al-Misriyyah al-ʾAmmah lil-Kitab, 1984.

al-Shaʾarawi, Muhammad Mutawalli. *al-Marʾah kama Aradaha Allah.* Cairo: 1980.

Shafiq, Amina. *al-Marʾah: Lan Taʾud ila al-Bait.* Cairo: Dar al-Thaqafa al-Jadidah, 1987.

Shalabi, Mahmud. *Hayat Adam.* Cairo: Maktabat al-Qahirah, 1964.

Shaltut, al-Shaykh Mahmud. *al-Qurʾan wa-al-Marʾah.* 2nd ed. Cairo: International Islamic Center for Population Studies and Research, Al-Azhar, 198?.

Sharif, Hashim. *Al-Marʾah al-Muslimah bayna Haqiqat al-Sharʾiah wa Zif al-Abatil,* Cairo: Dar al-Maʾrafah al-Jamaʾiyah, 1987.

Tabari, Abu Jaʾfar Muhammd b. Jarir. *Tarikh al-Tabari,* edited by Muhammad Abu al-Fadl Ibrahim. Vol. 1. Cairo: 1960.

Ibn Taymiyya. *Fatawi ʾan Nisaʾ.* Cairo: Maktabat al-ʾIrfan, 1983.

Zaki, Muhammad Shawqi. *al-Ikhwan al-Muslimun waʾl Mujtamaʾ al-Misri.* Cairo: 1954.

Periodical Literature, and Papers

Abdulla, Ragai. "Case #520 that Stopped the Application of the Personal Status Law." *al-Mussawar,* 9 March 1983.

Abdulʾaziz Abu Zayd, ʾUla. "al-Islam wa al-Siyasat al-Kharajiya al-Misriyah fi Fitrah Hukm Husni Mubarak." A paper presented at the Second Conference on Political Research, Cairo University, 3–5 December 1988.

al-Bakri, Khamis. "Religious Dissident Describes His Arrest, Imprisonment." *al-Nur,* 12 January 1983.

al-Daʾwah. Vol. 28, nos. 44, 45; vol. 29, nos. 46, 47, 48, 49; vol. 30, nos. 50, 51, 1980; vol. 31, nos. 63, 64, 1980–81. Cairo.

Fahmi, ʾAli. "Masculine and Feminine in Egypt: Differences and Roles." *al-Fikr,* vol. 2, no. 6, March 1985.

al-Ghazali, Zaynab. "Wahdat al-Muslimin Dharuratan." *al-Liwa al-Islam,* 11 November 1988.

————. "ʾAmal al-Marʾah . . . wa Taʾlimuha." *al-Daʾwah*, vol. 30, no. 51, September 1980.

al-Ghazali, Zaynab. "al-Marʾah al-Muʾminah wa al-Marʾah al-ʾUsriyah." *al-Daʾwah*, October 1980.

Hamid, Dunya. "The Mosques for Praying and the Universities for Studying." *Uktubir*, vol. 5, no. 255, 13 September 1981.

Hassan, Zaynab. "The Working Woman and the Problem of Returning Home." *Al-Musawwar*, no. 3063, 24 June 1983.

al-Jiyar, Sawsan. "Women's Oppression Law—The House, the Second Wife, Alimony." *Ruz-al-Yusuf*, vol. 60, issue 2974, 10 June 1985.

al-Khuli, Bahi. *al-Marʾah bayna al-Bayt wa al-Mujtamaʾ*. Cairo: Ikhwan al-Muslimun, 1953.

Abu al-Majd, Sabri. "Invocation to Complete the Dialogue in Abu Zaʾbal Prison." *al-Musawwar*, no. 2999, 2 April 1982.

Qassim, Safinaz. "In Defense of the Egyptian Women." *al-Musawwar*, no. 3060, 3 June 1983.

Radwan, Zeinab. *Bahth Zahirat al-Hijab bayn al-Jamiʾyat*. Cairo: National Center for Sociological and Criminological Research, 1982.

Roushdie, Ingie. "Madtha Qadam al-Mujtamʾa lil-Marʾah?" *al-Ahram*, 2 February 1984.

Saʾid Aly, Abd al-Munʾim. "Al-ʾAwdah ila al-Sif: Misr wa al-Watan al-Arabi, 1978–1988." A paper presented to the Second Conference on Political Research, Cairo, 3–5 December 1988.

Salab, Ihab. "Men and Women in the Labor Market." *al-Ahram al-Iqtisadi*, no. 801, 21 May 1984.

al-Sibaei, Iqbal. "Nominating Women: Is it Forbidden or Permitted Religiously?" *Ruz al-Youssef*, 14 May 1984.

al-Sidqi, Niʾmat. *al-Tabarruj*. Cairo: 1975.

Zurayk, Huda. "Dawr al-Marʾah fi al-Tanmiyah al-Ijtimaʾiyyah al-Iqtisadiyyah fi al-Buldan al-ᶜArabiyah." *al-Mustaqbal al-ᶜArabi* 109 (1988).

English Sources

Books, Chapters in Books, and Monographs

Abadan-Unat, Nermin. *Women in the Developing World: Evidence from Turkey.* Vol. 22, book 1. Monograph Series in World Affairs, University of Denver: 1986.

Abbott, Nabiah. *Aishah the Beloved of Mohammed.* 2nd ed. London: Al Saqi Books, 1985.

————. *Studies in Arabic Literary Papyri.* Chicago: University of Chicago Press, 1972.

————. *Two Queens of Baghdad.* London: Al-Saqi Books, 1986.

Abdalla, Ahmed. *The Student Movement and National Politics in Egypt, 1923–1973.* London: al-Saqi Books, 1985.

Abdel-Khalek, Gouda. "The Open Door Economic Policy in Egypt: A Search for Meaning, Interpretation, and Implication." *Cairo Papers in Social Science,* monograph 3. Cairo: The American University in Cairo Press, March 1979.

Abdel-Fadil, Mahmoud. *Development, Income Distribution, and Social Change in Rural Egypt: 1952-1970.* London: Cambridge University Press, 1975.

Abu Lughod, Janet. *Cairo: 1,001 Years of the City Victorious.* Princeton: Princeton University Press, 1971.

Abu Lughod, Lila. *Veiled Sentiments: Honor and Poetry in a Bedouin Society.* Cairo: The American University in Cairo Press, 1987.

Adams, Richard, *Development and Social Change in Rural Egypt.* Syracuse, N.Y.: Syracuse University Press, 1986.

Adel Taher, Nadia. *Social Identity and Class in a Cairo Neighborhood. Cairo Papers in Social Science,* vol. 9, monograph 4. Cairo: American University Press, Winter 1986.

Ahmed, Leila. "Early Feminist Movements in Turkey and Egypt." In *Muslim Women,* edited by Freda Hussein. London: Croom Helm, 1984.

Amin, Galal. "External Factors in the Reorientation of Egypt's Economic Policy." In *Rich and Poor States in the Middle East: Egypt and the New Arab Order,* edited by Malcolm Kerr and El-Sayed Yassin. Boulder, Colo.: Westview Press, 1982.

Andors, Phyllis. *The Unfinished Liberation of Chinese Women 1949-1980.* Bloomington, Ind.: Indiana University Press, 1983.

Ansari, Hamied. *Egypt, The Stalled Society.* Albany: State University of New York Press, 1986.

Antonius, Soraya. "Fighting on Two Fronts: Conversations with Palestinian Women." In *Third World Second Sex,* edited by M. Davies. London: Zed Press, 1983.

Atiya, Nayra. *Khul-Khaal: Five Egyptian Women Tell Their Stories.* Syracuse, N.Y.: Syracuse University Press, 1982.

Ayubi, Nazih. "Implementation Capability and Political Feasibility of the Open Door Policy in Egypt." In *Rich and Poor States in the Middle East: Egypt and the New Arab Order,* edited by M. Kerr and E. Yassin. Boulder Colo.: Westview Press, 1982.

Azari, Farah. "Islam's Appeal to Women in Iran." In *Women of Iran: The Conflict with Fundamentalism,* edited by Farah Azari. London: Ithaca Press, 1983.

Baraka, Iqbal. "The Influence of Contemporary Arab Thought on the Women's Movement." In *Women of the Arab World,* edited by Nahid Toubia. London: Zed Books, 1988.

Badran, Margot, and Miriam Cooke. *Opening the Gates: A Century of Arab Feminist Writing.* Bloomington: Indiana University Press, 1990.

Barakat, Halim. "The Arab Family and the Challenge of Social Transformation." In *Women and the Family in the Middle East,* edited by Elizabeth Fernea. Austin: University of Texas Press, 1985.

Bates, Daniel, and Amal Rassam. *Peoples and Cultures of the Middle East.* Englewood Cliffs, N.J.: Prentice-Hall, 1983.

Beinin, Joel, and Zachary Lockman. *Workers on the Nile.* Cambridge: Cambridge University Press 1990.

Bellamy, James A. "Sex and Society in Islamic Popular Literature." In *Society and* the Sexes in Medieval Islam. Edited by Afaf Lutfi al-Sayyid Marsot. Malibu, Calif.: Undena Publications, 1979.

Bianchi, Robert. Unruly Corporatism: Associational Life in Twentieth-Century Egypt. Oxford: Oxford University Press, 1989.

Binder, Leonard. Islamic Liberalism. Chicago: University of Chicago Press, 1988.

————. In a Moment of Enthusiasm: Political Power and the Second Stratum in Egypt. Chicago: University of Chicago Press, 1978.

Boserup, Rose. Woman's Role in Economic Development. London: George Allen & Unwin, 1971.

Botman, Salma. "Women's Participation in Radical Egyptian Politics 1939–1952." In Women in the Middle East, edited by (Khamsin) London: Zed Books, 1987.

Boudiba, Abdelwahab. Sexuality in Islam, translated by Alan Sheridan. London: Routledge & Kegan Paul, 1985.

Chodorow, Nancy. "Family Structure and Feminine Personality." In Woman, Culture, and Society, Michelle Rosaldo and Louise Lamphere. Stanford, Calif.: Stanford University Press, 1974.

Chafetz, Janet S. and Anthony G. Dworkin. Female Revolt: Women's Movements in World and Historical Perspective. Totowa, N.J.: Rowmen & Allenheld, 1986.

Coulson, Noel J. "Regulation of Sexual Behavior under Traditional Islamic Law." In Society and the Sexes in Medieval Islam. Edited by Afaf Lutfi al-Sayyid Marsot. Malibu, Calif.: Undena Publications, 1979.

Cromer, Earl of. Modern Egypt. Vols. 1 and 2. London: MacMillan & Co. 1908.

Davis, Fanny. The Ottoman Lady: A Social History from 1718 to 1918. New York: Greenwood Press, 1986.

Davis, John. "The Sexual Division of Labour in the Mediterranean." In Religion, Power, and Protest, edited by E. Wolf. 1984.

Dessouki, Ali E. Hillal. "The New Arab Political Order: Implications for the 1980s." In Rich and Poor States in the Middle East: Egypt and the New Arab Order, Malcolm Kerr and El Sayyid Yassin. Boulder, Colo.: Westview Press, 1982.

Didar, Fawry. "Palestinian Women in Palestine." In Women of the Mediterranean, edited by Monique Gadant. London: Zed Books, 1986.

Doane, Mary Ann. The Desire to Desire. Bloomington: Indiana University Press, 1987.

Donovan, Josephine. "Feminism and Marxism," "Feminism and Freudianism," and "Feminism and Existentialism." In Donovan, Josephine. Feminist Theory: The Intellectual Traditions of American Feminism. New York: Ungar, 1985.

Dorsky, Susan. Women of 'Amran: A Middle Eastern Ethnographic Study. Salt Lake City: University of Utah Press, 1986.

Doughty, Charles M. Travels in Arabia Deserta. New York: Random House, 1936.

Drucker, Alison. "The Influence of Western Women on the Anti-Footbinding Movement 1840–1911." In Women in China: Current Directions in Historical Scholarship, edited by Richard W. Guisso and Stanley Johannesen. Youngstown, N.Y.: Philo Press, 1981.

Early, Evelyn. "Fatima: A Life History of an Egyptian Woman from Bulaq." In Women and the Family in the Middle East, edited by E. Fernea. Austin: University of Texas Press, 1985.

Eccel, Chris. *Egypt, Islam, and Social Change: Al-Azhar in Conflict and Accommodation.* Berlin: Klaus Schwarz Verlag, 1984.

El Guindi, Fadwa. "The Egyptian Woman: Trends Today, Alternatives Tomorrow." In *Women in the World,* edited by L. Iglitzin and R. Ross. Santa Barbara, Calif.: ABC-Clio Press, 1986.

El-Messiri, Sawsan. *Ibn al-Balad: A Conception of Egyptian Identity.* Leiden: E. J. Brill, 1978.

———. "Self-Images of Traditional Urban Women in Cairo." In *Women in the Muslim World,* edited by Lois Beck and Nikki Keddie. Cambridge: Harvard University Press, 1978.

Engels, Frederick. *The Origins of the Family, Private Property, and the State.* New York: International Publishers, 1969.

Esposito, John. *Women in Muslim Family Law.* Syracuse, N.Y.: Syracuse University Press, 1982.

Farah, Madelain. *Marriage and Sexuality in Islam.* Salt Lake City: University of Utah Press, 1984.

Fernea, Elizabeth. "Libya: The Family in Modern Islamic Society." In *Change and the Muslim World,* edited by Philip Stoddard, David Cuthell and Margaret Sullivan, Syracuse, N.Y.: Syracuse University Press, 1981.

Fernea, Elizabeth, and Basima Bezirgan. *Middle Eastern Muslim Women Speak.* Austin: University of Texas Press, 1977.

Fernea, Elizabeth, and Robert Fernea. *The Arab World: Personal Encounters.* Garden City, N.Y.: Anchor Books, 1987.

Fluehr-Lobban, Carolyn. "The Political Mobilization of Women in the Arab World." In *Women in Contemporary Muslim Societies,* edited by Jane Smith. Lewisburg, Penn.: Bucknell University Press, 1980.

Fischer, Michael. *Iran from Religious Dispute to Revolution.* Cambridge: Harvard University Press, 1980.

Fouad, Nemat. *The Project of the Pyramids Plateau: The Most Dangerous Take-Over in Egypt.* World of Books, 1978.

Foucault, Michel. *The Use of Pleasure: The History of Sexuality.* Vol. 2. New York: Vintage Press, 1990.

Freud, Sigmund. "Femininity." In *New Introductory Lectures on Psychoanalysis.* New York: W. Norton, 1933.

Gadant, Monique. "Fatima, Ouardia, and Malika, Contemporary Algerian Women." In *Women of the Mediterranean,* edited by M. Gadant. London: Zed Books, 1984.

Gadon, Elinor. *The Once and Future Goddess.* New York: Harper & Row, 1989.

Geertz, Clifford. *The Interpretation of Cultures.* New York: Basic Books, 1973.

———. *Islam Observed.* Chicago: University of Chicago Press, 1968.

Gerner, Debbie. "Roles in Transition: The Evolving Position of Women in Arab-Islamic Countries." In *Muslim Women,* edited by Freda Hussein. London: Croom Helm, 1985.

Giacaman, Rita and Muna Odeh. "Palestinian Women's Movement in the Israeli-Occupied West Bank and Gaza Strip." In *Women of the Arab World: The Coming Challenge,* edited by Nahid Toubia. London: Zed Books, 1988.

Gilligan, Carol. "In a Different Voice: Women's Conceptions of Self and of Morality." In *The Future of Difference,* edited by Hester Eisenstein and Alice Jardine. New Brunswick, N.J.: Rutgers University Press, 1987.

Gimbutas, Marija. *The Goddesses and Gods of Old Europe.* London: Thames & Hudson, 1974.

Ginat, Joseph. *Women in Muslim Rural Society: Status and Role in Family and Community.* New Brunswick, N.J.: Transactions Books, 1982.

Goitein, S. D. "The Sexual Mores of the Common People ." In *Society and the Sexes in Medieval Islam,* edited by Afaf Lutfi al-Sayyid Marsot. Malibu, Calif.: Undena Publications, 1979.

Goldberg, Ellis. *Tinker, Tailor, and Textile Worker: Class and Politics in Egypt 1930–1952.* Berkeley, Calif.: L.A. Press, 1986.

Goma'a, Ahmed. "Islamic Fundamentalism in Egypt during the 1930s and 1970s." In *Islam, Nationalism, and Radicalism in Egypt and the Sudan,* edited by Gabriel Warburg and Uri Kupferschmidt. New York: Praeger, 1983.

Graham-Brown, Sarah. *Images of Women: The Portrayal of Women in Photography of the Middle East 1860–1950.* New York: Columbia University Press, 1988.

Guenena, Nemat. *The 'Jihad': An 'Islamic Alternative' in Egypt. Cairo Papers in Social Science,* vol. 9, monograph 2. Cairo: The American University in Cairo Press, Summer 1986.

Hale, Sondra. "The Politics of Gender in the Middle East." In *Gender and Anthropology,* edited by Sandra Morgen. Washington D.C.: American Anthropological Association, 1989.

Hall, Marjorie and Bakhita A. Ismail. *Sisters under the Sun: The Story of Sudanese Women.* London: Longman, 1981.

Hanafi, Hassan. *Religious Dialogue and Revolution.* Cairo: Anglo-Egyptian Bookshop, 1977.

Harris, Christina. *Nationalism and Revolution in Egypt: The Role of the Muslim Brotherhood.* The Hague: Mouton, 1964.

Heikal, Muhammad. *Autumn of Fury: The Assassination of Sadat.* London: Andre Deutsch, 1983.

Hermassi, Elbaki. *The Third World Reassessed.* Berkeley: University of California Press, 1980.

Hetata, Sherif. *The Net.* London: Zed Books, 1986.

Heyworth-Dunne, J. *An Introduction to the History of Education in Modern Egypt.* London: Frank Cass, 1968.

Hill, Enid. *Mahkama! Studies in the Egyptian Legal System.* London: Ithaca Press, 1979.

Hijab, Nadia. *Womanpower: The Arab Debate on Women at Work.* Cambridge: Cambridge University Press, 1988.

Hoffman, Valerie. "An Islamic Activist: Zaynab al-Ghazali." In *Women and the Family in the Middle East,* edited by E. Fernea. Austin: University of Texas Press, 1985.

Hussein, Aziza. "Recently Approved Amendments to Egypt's Law on Personal Status." In *Religion and Politics in the Middle East,* edited by M. Curtis. Boulder, Colo.: Westview Press, 1981.

Huston, Perdita. *Third World Women Speak Out.* Washington D.C.: Overseas Development Council, 1979.

Ibrahim, Saad Eddin. "Oil, Migration, and the New Arab Social Order." In *Rich and Poor States in the Middle East: Egypt and the New Arab Order*, edited by M. Kerr and S. Yassin. Boulder, Colo.: Westview Press, 1982.

Issawi, Charles. *The Economic History of the Middle East 1800–1914*. Chicago: University of Chicago Press, 1966.

———. *An Economic History of the Middle East and North Africa*. New York: Columbia University Press, 1982.

Jaggar, Alison, and Paula Rothenberg Struhl, eds. *Feminist Frame-Works: Alternative Accounts of the Relations between Women and Men*. New York: McGraw-Hill, 1978.

Jameelah, Maryam. "Al-Ikhwan al-Muslimun." In *Islam in Theory and Practice*, Lahore: Muhammad Yusuf Khan, 1967.

Jayawardena, Kumari. *Feminism and Nationalism in the Third World*. London: Zed Books, 1986.

Jung, C. G. *Psyche and Symbol*, edited by Violet S. de Laszlo. New York: Anchor Books, 1958.

Keddie, Nikki R., with a section by Yann Richard. *Roots of Revolution: An Interpretive History of Modern Iran*. New Haven and London: Yale University Press, 1981.

Kepel, Gilles. *Muslim Extremism in Egypt: The Prophet and Pharaoh*. Berkeley: University of California Press, 1985.

Kerr, Malcolm, and El Sayed Yasin, eds. *Rich and Poor States in the Middle East: Egypt and the New Arab Order*. Boulder, Colo.: Westview Press, 1982.

Lakhdar, Lafif. "Why the Reversion to Islamic Archaism?" In *Forbidden Agendas*. London: Zed Press, 1984.

Landecker, Werner S. *Class Crystalization*. New Brunswick, N.J.: Rutgers University Press, 1981.

Lane, Edward William. *An Account of the Manners and Customs of the Modern Egyptians*. The Hague and London: East-West Publications, 1978. Reprint of 1895 edition.

Mabro, Robert and Samir Radwan. *The Industrialization of Egypt: Policy and Performance*. Oxford: Clarendon Press, 1976.

MacKinnon, Catharine. "Feminism, Marxism, Method, and the State: An Agenda for Theory." In *The Signs Reader: Women, Gender, and Scholarship*, edited by Elizabeth Abel and Emily K. Abel. Chicago: University of Chicago Press, 1983.

Mahjoube, Abdolrahmane. "The Inner Revolution of a Khomeyni Activist." In *Women of the Mediterranean*, edited by Monique Gadant. London: Zed Books, 1984.

Makhlouf, Carla. *Changing Veils: Women and Modernisation in North Yemen*. Austin: University of Texas Press, 1979.

Mahfouz, Naguib. *Midaq Alley*. Washington D.C.: Three Continents Press, 1981.

Mansfield, Peter. *The British in Egypt*. Holt, Rinehart & Winston, 1972.

March, Kathryn, and Rachelle Taqqu. *Women's Informal Associations in Developing Countries: Catalysts for Change?* Boulder, Colo.: Westview Press, 1986.

Macleod, Arlene. *Accomodating Protest: Working Women, the New Veiling and Change in Cairo*. New York: Columbia University Press, 1991.

Martin, Emily. *The Woman in the Body: A Cultural Analysis of Reproduction.* Boston: Beacon Press, 1987.

Masud-ul-Hasan. *Daughters of Islam.* Lahore: Lion Art Press Ltd., n.d.

al-Maududi, S. Abul ʾAla. *The Meaning of the Qurʾan.* Bilingual text. Lahore: Islamic Publications Ltd. 1979.

Mayer, Ann, ed. *Property, Social Structure, and Law in the Modern Middle East.* Albany: State University of New York Press, 1985.

McDermott, Anthony. *Egypt from Nasser to Mubarak: A Flawed Revolution.* London: Croom Helm, 1988.

Mernissi, Fatima. "Democracy as Moral Disintegration: The Contradiction between Religious Belief and Citizenship as a Manifestation of the Ahistoricity of the Arab Identity." In *Women of the Arab World,* edited by Nahid Toubia. London: Zed Books, 1988.

———. *Beyond the Veil: Male-Female Dynamics in a Modern Muslim Society.* Cambridge: Cambridge University Press, 1975.

Mikhail, Mona N. *Images of Arab Women: Fact and Fiction.* Washington, D.C.: Three Continents Press, 1981.

Mitchell, Richard P. *The Society of the Muslim Brothers.* London: Oxford University Press, 1969.

Mitchell, Timothy. *Colonising Egypt.* Cambridge: Cambridge University Press, 1988.

Mohsen, Aisha, and Noor Baʾabad (interviews). "Building a New Life for Women in South Yemen" In *Third World Second Sex,* edited by Miranda Davies. London: Zed Press, 1983.

Mohsen, Safia. "New Images, Old Reflections: Working Middle Class Women in Egypt." In *Women and the Family in the Middle East,* edited by E. Fernea. Austin: University of Texas Press, 1985.

Musallam, Basim. *Sex and Society in Islam: Birth Control before the Nineteenth Century.* Cambridge: Cambridge University Press, 1983.

Nowaihi, Mohammed. "Changing the Law on Personal Status within a Liberal Interpretation of the Sharia." In *Law and Social Change in Contemporary Egypt,* edited by Cynthia Nelson and Klause Kock. *Cairo Papers in Social Science,* vol. 2, no. 4. Cairo: The American University in Cairo Press, 1979.

O'Brien, Mary. "Production and Reproduction." In *The Politics of Reproduction.* Boston: Routledge & Kegan Paul, 1981.

Ortner, Sherry B. "Is Female to Male as Nature is to Culture?" In *Women, Culture and Society,* edited by Michelle Rosaldo and Louise Lamphere. Stanford, Calif.: Stanford University Press.

Oweiss, Ibrahim, ed. *The Political Economy of Contemporary Egypt.* Washington D.C.: Center for Contemporary Arab Studies, Georgetown University, 1990.

Philip, Thomas. "Feminism and Nationalist Politics in Egypt." In *Women in the Muslim World,* edited by Lois Beck and Nikki Keddie. Cambridge: Harvard University Press, 1978.

Porret, Evelyn. "Fatnah and her Village in Fayoum." In *Women of the Mediterranean,* edited by Monique Gadant. London: Zed Books, 1986.

Rahman, Fazlur. "Roots of Islamic Neo-Fundamentalism." In *Change and the Muslim World*, edited by P. Stoddard, D. Cuthell, and M. Sullivan. Syracuse, N.Y.: Syracuse University Press, 1981.

Rassam, Amal. "Toward a Theoretical Framework for the Study of Women in the Arab World." In *Social Science Research and Women in the Arab World*. (UNESCO). Paris and London: Frances Pinter, 1984.

Ridd, Rosemary, and Helen Callaway, eds. *Women and Political Conflict*. New York: New York University Press, 1987.

Rishmawi, Mona. "The Legal Status of Palestinian Women in the Occupied Territories." In *Women of the Arab World*, edited by N. Toubia. London: Zed Press, 1988.

Rosaldo, Michelle. "Woman, Culture and Society: A Theoretical Overview." In *Women, Culture, and Society*, edited by Michelle Rosaldo and Louise Lamphere. Stanford: Stanford University Press, 1974.

Rosenthal, Franz. "Fiction and Reality: Sources for the Role of Sex in Medieval Muslim Society." In *Society and the Sexes in Medieval Islam*, edited by Afaf Lutfi al-Sayyid Marsot. Malibu, Calif.: Undena Publications, 1979.

Rossanda, Rossana. "A Feminine Culture." In *Women of the Mediterranean*, edited by Monique Gadant. London: Zed Books, 1986.

Rowbotham, Sheila. *Women, Resistance, and Revolution: A History of Women and Revolution in the Modern World*. New York: Vintage Books. 1974.

Rugh, Andrea. *Family in Contemporary Egypt*. Syracuse, N.Y.: Syracuse University Press, 1986.

———. *Reveal and Conceal: Dress in Contemporary Egypt*. Cairo: American University in Cairo Press, 1986.

———. "Women and Work: Strategies and Choices in a Lower-Class Quarter of Cairo." In *Women and the Family in the Middle East*, edited by E. Fernea. Austin: University of Texas Press, 1985.

Sa'adawi, Nawal. "The Political Challenges Facing Arab Women at the End of the Twentieth Century." In *Women of the Arab World*, edited by Nahid Toubia. London: Zed Press, 1988.

———. *God Dies By the Nile*. London: Zed Books, 1985.

———. *Woman at Point Zero*. London: Zed Books, 1983.

———. *The Hidden Face of Eve: Women in the Arab World*. Boston: Beacon Press, 1982.

Sabagh, Georges. "Migration and Social Mobility in Egypt." In *Rich and Poor States in the Middle East: Egypt and the New Arab Order*, edited by Malcolm Kerr and El-Sayyed Yassin, Boulder, Colo.: Westview Press, 1982.

Sabbah, Fatna. *Woman in the Muslim Unconscious*. New York: Pergamon Press, 1984.

Sabban, Rima. "Lebanese Women and Capitalist Cataclysm." In *Women of the Arab World*, edited by Nahid Toubia. London: Zed Press, 1988.

Sadat, Jehan. *A Woman of Egypt*. New York: Simon & Schuster, 1987.

Said, Edward. *Orientalism*. New York: Pantheon Books, 1978.

Salem, Norma. "Islam and the Legal Status of Women in Tunisia." In *Muslim Women*, edited by Freda Hussein. London: Croom Helm, 1985.

al-Sanabary, Nagat. "Continuity and Change in Women's Education in the Arab

States." In *Women and the Family in the Middle East*, edited by E. Fernea. Austin: University of Texas Press, 1985.

Sanasarian, Eliz. *The Women's Rights Movement in Iran*. New York: Praeger, 1982.

al-Sayyid Marsot, Afaf Lutfi. *A Short History of Modern Egypt*. Cambridge and N.Y.: Cambridge University Press, 1985.

——— . *Egypt in the Reign of Muhammad Ali*. Cambridge: Cambridge University Press, 1984.

——— . *Protest Movements and Religious Under-Currents in Egypt: Past and Present*. Center for Contemporary Arab Studies, Occasional Papers Series. Washington, D.C.: Georgetown University, March 1984.

——— . "The Changing Arab Muslim Family." In *Islam: The Religious and Political Life*, edited by M. Kelly. 1984.

——— . "The Revolutionary Gentlewoman in Egypt." In *Women in the Muslim World*, edited by Lois Beck and Nikki Keddie. Cambridge: Harvard University Press, 1978.

Scarce, Jennifer. *Women's Costume of the Near and Middle East*. London: Unwin Hyman, 1987.

Schimmel, Annemarie. "Eros—Heavenly and Not So Heavenly—in Sufi Literature and Life." In *Society and the Sexes in Medieval Islam*, edited by Afaf Lutfi al-Sayyid Marsot. Malibu, Calif.: Undena Publications, 1979.

Scholch, Alexander. *Egypt for the Egyptians! The Socio-political Crisis in Egypt, 1878–1882*. London: Ithaca Press, 1981.

Seibert, Ilse. *Woman in Ancient Near East*, translated by Marianne Herzfeld. Leipzig: Editions Leipzig, 1974.

Shaaban, Bouthaina. *Both Right and Left Handed: Arab Women Talk About Their Lives*. London: The Women's Press, 1988.

Shaalan, Thaira. "Yemenite Women: Employment and Future Challenges." In *Women of the Arab World*, edited by N. Toubia. London: Zed Press, 1988.

Sha'arawi, Huda. *Harem Years: The Memoirs of an Egyptian Feminist*, translated and edited by Margot Badran. New York: Feminist Press, 1986.

Sharabi, Hisham. *Neopatriarchy: A Theory of Distorted Values in Arab Society*. New York: Oxford University Press, 1988.

——— . *Arab Intellectuals and the West: The Formative Years, 1875–1914*. Baltimore: Johns Hopkins Press, 1970.

Sharara, Yolla. "Women and Politics in Lebanon." In *Third World Second Sex*, edited by Miranda Davies. London: Zed Press, 1983.

Shariati, Ali. *Marxism and Other Western Fallacies: An Islamic Critique*. Berkeley: University of California Press, 1980.

Sivan, Emmanuel. *Radical Islam: Medieval Theology and Modern Politics*. New Haven, Conn.: Yale University Press, 1985.

——— . *Interpretations of Islam Past and Present*. Princeton: Darwin Press, 1985.

Smith, Jane, ed. *Women in Contemporary Muslim Societies*. London: Associated Universities Press, 1980.

——— . "The Experience of Muslim Women: Considerations of Power and Authority." In *The Islamic Impact*, edited by Haddad, Haines, and Findley. Syracuse N.Y.: Syracuse University Press, 1984.

Smith, W. Robertson. *Kinship and Marriage in Early Arabia.* Cambridge at the University Press, 1885.

Smock, Audrey, and Nadia Youssef. "Egypt: From Seclusion to Limited Participation." In *Women: Roles and Status in Eight Countries,* edited by Janet Giele and Audrey Smock. New York: John Wiley & Sons, 1977.

el-Sokkari, Myrette Ahmed. *Basic Needs, Inflation, and the Poor of Egypt. Cairo Papers in Social Science,* vol. 7, monograph 2. Cairo: The American University in Cairo Press, 1984.

Springborg, Robert. *Mubarak's Egypt: Fragmentation of the Political Order.* Boulder, Colo.: Westview 1989.

Staudt, Kathleen, and Jane Jaquette, eds. *Women in Developing Countries: A Policy Focus.* New York: Haworth Press, 1983.

Stowasser, Barbara. "The Status of Women in Early Islam." In *Muslim Women,* edited by Freda Hussain. London: Croom Helm Ltd., 1984.

Sullivan, Earl. *Women in Egyptian Public Life.* Syracuse, N.Y.: Syracuse University Press, 1986.

Sullivan, Earl. "Women and Work in Egypt." In *Women and Work in the Arab World,* edited by Earl Sullivan and Karima Korayem. *Cairo Papers in Social Science.* vol. 4, no. 4. Cairo: The American University in Cairo Press, December 1981.

Tadros, Helmi. *Social Security and the Family in Egypt. Cairo Papers in Social Science.* vol. 7, monograph 1. Cairo: The American University in Cairo Press, 1984.

Taha, Mahmoud Mohamed. *The Second Message of Islam,* translated and introduced by Abdullahi an-Naim. Syracuse, N.Y.: Syracuse University Press, 1987.

Tripp, Charles, and Roger Owen, eds. *Egypt Under Mubarrak.* London: Routledge, 1990.

al-Torki, Soraya, and Camillia El-Solh, eds. *Arab Women in the Field: Studying Your Own Society.* Syracuse, N.Y.: Syracuse University Press, 1988.

Toubia, Nahid. "The Social and Political Implications of Female Circumcision." In *Women and the Family in the Middle East,* edited by Elizabeth Fernea. Austin: University of Texas Press, 1985.

————. "Women and Health in Sudan." In *Women of the Arab World: The Coming Challenge,* edited by Nahid Toubia. London: Zed Books, 1988.

Trotsky, Leon. *Women and the Family.* New York: Pathfinder Press, 1970.

Tucker, Judith. *Women in Nineteenth Century Egypt.* Cairo: The American University in Cairo Press, 1986.

Walker, Carolyn Bynum. "On the Complexity of Symbols." In Walker, *Gender and Religion.* Boston: Beacon Press, 1986.

Wallerstein, Immanuel. "The Rise and Future Demise of the World Capitalist Systems: Concepts for Comparative Analysis." In Wallerstein, *The Capitalist World Economy.* New York: Cambridge University Press, 1979.

Waterbury, John. "Egypt, Islam, and Social Change." In *Change and the Muslim World,* edited by P. Stoddard, D. Cuthell, and M. Sullivan. Syracuse, N.Y.: Syracuse University Press, 1981.

————. *The Egypt of Nasser and Sadat: The Political Economy of Two Regimes.* Princeton, N.J.: Princeton University Press, 1983.

———— . *Egypt: Burdens of the Past, Options for the Future.* Bloomington and London: Indiana University Press, 1978.

Watt, W. Montgomery. *Muhammad at Medina.* Oxford: Oxford University Press, 1981.

Wikan, Unni. *Behind the Veil in Arabia: Women in Oman.* Baltimore: Johns Hopkins University Press, 1982.

Williams, John A. "Veiling in Egypt as a Political and Social Phenomenon." In *Islam and Development,* edited by John Esposito. Syracuse, N.Y.: Syracuse University Press, 1980.

Yadlin, Rivka. "Militant Islam in Egypt: Some Sociocultural Aspects." In *Islam, Nationalism, and Radicalism,* edited by G. Warburg and U. Kupferschmidt. New York: Praeger, 1983.

Youssef, Nadia. "The Status and Fertility Patterns of Muslim Women." In *Women in the Muslim World,* edited by L. Beck and N. Keddie. Cambridge: Harvard University Press, 1978.

———— . "Women in the Muslim World." In *Women of the World,* edited by L. Iglitzin. Santa Barbara, Calif.: Clio Press, 1973.

———— . *Women and Work in Developing Societies.* Berkeley: University of California, 1974.

Yural-Davis, Nira. "The Jewish Collectivity." In *Women of the Middle East, Khamsin* publication, London: Zed Books, 1987.

Zakaria, Fouad. "The Standpoint of Contemporary Muslim Fundamentalists." In *Women of the Arab World,* edited by Nahid Toubia. London: Zed Books, 1988.

Periodicals and Papers

Abu-Lughod, Lila. "The Romance of Resistance: Tracing Transformations of Power through Bedouin Women." *American Ethnologist* 17, no. 1 (February 1990).

———— . "Bedouins, Cassettes, and Technologies of Public Culture." *Middle East Report* no. 159, vol. 19, no. 4 July–August, 1989.

———— . "A Community of Secrets: The Separate World of Bedouin Women." *Signs* 10, no. 4 Summer 1985.

Ahmed, Leila. "Feminism and Feminist Movements in the Middle East. A Preliminary Exploration: Turkey, Egypt, Algeria, People's Democratic Republic of Yemen." *Women's Studies International Forum* 5, no. 2 (1982).

Ansari, Hamied. "Mubarak's Dilemma: The Contradictions of Two Regimes." *Current History* January 1985.

———— . "The Islamic Militants in Egyptian Politics." *International Journal of Middle East Studies* 16, no. 1 (1984). pp. 123–144.

Ata, A. W. "Impact of Westernizing and Other Factors on the Changing Status of Muslim Women." *The Islamic Quarterly* 30, no. 4 1986.

Badran, Margot. "Dual Liberation: Feminism and Nationalism in Egypt, 1870s–1925." *Feminist Issues* 8, no. 1 Spring 1988.

Baffoun, Alya. "Women and Social Change in the Muslim Arab World." *Women's Studies International Forum* 5, no. 2 (1982).

Bahonar, Muhammad. "Islam and Women's Rights." *Al-Tawhid* 1, no. 2, 1984.

Baron, Beth. "Women's Nationalist Rhetoric and Activities in Early Twentieth Century Egypt." Paper presented to the Middle East Studies Association, Baltimore, Maryland, November 1987.

Bauer, Janet. "Sexuality and the Moral Construction of Women in an Islamic Society." *Anthropological Quarterly* 58, no. 3 (July 1985).

Bowen, Donna, "Muslim Juridical Opinions Concerning the Status of Women as Demonstrated in the Case of ʾAzl." *Journal of Near Eastern Studies* 40, no. 4.

Charrad, Mounira. "State, Civil Society and Gender: Examples from the Maghreb." Paper presented to the Social Science Research Council, Joint Committee on the Near and Middle East. Aix en Provence: 25–27 March 1988.

Cole, Juan Ricardo. "Feminism, Class and Islam in Turn-of-the Century Egypt." *International Journal of Middle East Studies* 13, November 1981.

Cuno, Kenneth. "The Origins of Private Ownership of Land in Egypt: A Reappraisal." *International Journal of Middle East Studies* 12, no. 3 (1980).

Danforth, Sandra. "The Social and Political Implications of Muslim Middle Eastern Women's Participation in Violent Political Conflict." *Women and Politics* 4, no. 1 (Spring 1984).

Dorph, Kenneth. "Islamic Law in Contemporary North Africa: A Study of the Laws of Divorce in the Maghreb." *Women's Studies International Forum* 5, no. 2 (1982).

Early, Evelyn. "Catharsis and Creation: The Everyday Narratives of Baladi Women of Cairo." *Anthropological Quarterly* 58, no. 4 (October 1985).

Ebeid, Joan. "Women at the Centre of Social Change: The Egyptian Case." *British Society for Middle East Studies Bulletin* 12 (1985).

El Guindi, Fadwa. "Veiling Infitah with Muslim Ethic: Egypt's Contemporary Islamic Movement." *Social Problems* 28, no. 4 (April 1981), pp 465–85.

Faruqi, Lois. "Women in a Quranic Society." *al-Tawhid* 1, no. 5 (1984).

———. "Islamic Traditions and the Feminist Movement: Confrontation or Cooperation?" *Islamic Quarterly* 27, no. 3 (1983).

Gadalla, Saad, James McCarthy, and Oona Campbell. "How the Number of Living Sons Influences Contraceptive Use in Menoufia Governorate, Egypt." *Studies in Family Planning.* Social Research Center, American University in Cairo, vol. 16, no. 3, May–June 1985.

Gaffney, Jane. "The Egyptian Cinema: Industry and Art in a Changing Society." *Arab Studies Quarterly* 9, no. 1 (Winter 1987).

Gerber, Haim. "Social and Economic Position of Women in an Ottoman City, Bursa, 1600–1700." *International Journal of Middle East East Studies* 12, no. 3 (November 1980).

Ghoussoub, Mai. "Feminism—or the Eternal Masculine—in the Arab World." *New Left Review* no. 161 (Spring 1987).

Goldberg, Ellis. "Bases of Traditional Reaction: A Look at the Muslim Brothers." *Peuples Mediterraneens* 14 (1981).

Haddad, Yvonne. "Islam, Women and Revolution in Twentieth-Century Arab Thought." *The Muslim World* 74, nos. 3–4 (July/October 1984).

Hale, Sondra. "State Ideology, Islamic Fundamentalism and the Sexual Division of Labor—A Marxist-Feminist Anthropological Inquiry, Sudan." Paper presented to the Middle East Studies Association, Beverly Hills, California, November 6, 1988.

———. "The Wing of the Patriarch: Sudanese Women and Revolutionary Parties." *Middle East Report* 16, no. 1 (1986).

Hamed, Osama. "Egypt's Open Door Economic Policy: An Attempt at Economic Integration in the Middle East." *International Journal of Middle East Studies* 13 (1981).

Hammam, Mona. "Women and Industrial Work in Egypt: The Chubra al-Kheima Case." *Arab Studies Quarterly* 2, no. 1 (1980).

Hanafi, Hassan. "The Relevance of the Islamic Alternative in Egypt." *Arab Studies Quarterly* 4, nos. 1–2 (Spring 1982).

Hatem, Mervat. "Through Each Other's Eyes: Egyptian, Levantine-Egyptian, and European Women's Images of Themselves and of Each Other (1862–1920)." *Women's Studies International Forum* 12, no. 2 (1989).

———. "Egypt's Middle Class in Crisis: The Sexual Division of Labor." *Middle East Journal* 42, no. 3 (Summer 1988).

———. "Toward the Study of the Psychodynamics of Mothering and Gender in Egyptian Families." *International Journal of Middle East Studies* 19, no. 3 (August 1987).

———. "The Enduring Alliance of Nationalism and Patriarchy in Muslim Personal Status Laws: The Case of Modern Egypt." *Feminist Issues* 6, no. 1 (Spring 1986).

Hendricks, Bertus. "The Legal Left in Egypt." *Arab Studies Quarterly* 5 (1983).

al-Hibri, Azizah. "A Study of Islamic Herstory: Or How Did We Ever Get Into this Mess?" *Women's Studies International Forum* 5, no. 2 (1982).

Hoffman-Ladd, Valerie. "Polemics on the Modesty and Segregation of Women in Contemporary Egypt." *International Journal of Middle East Studies* 19, no. 1 (February 1987).

Howard-Merriam, Kathleen. "Egypt's Other Political Elite." *Western Political Quarterly* 34, no. 1 (1981).

Ibrahim, Barbara Lethem. "Family Strategies: A Perspective of Women's Entry to the Labor Force in Egypt." *International Journal of Sociology of the Family* 11, no. 2 (July–December 1981).

———. "Social Change and the Industrial Experience: Women as Production Workers in Urban Egypt." Ph.D. diss., Department of Sociology, Indiana University, 1980.

Ibrahim, Saad Eddin. "Egypt's Islamic Activism in the 1980's." *Third World Quarterly* 10, no. 2 (April 1988).

———. "Anatomy of Egypt's Militant Islamic Groups: Methodological Note and Preliminary Findings." *International Journal of Middle East Studies* 12, no. 4 (1980).

Jennings, R. C. "Women in Early Seventeenth Century Ottoman Judicial Records: The Shariᵖa Court of Anatolian Kayseri." *Journal of the Economic and Social History of the Orient* 18 (1975).

Joseph, Suad. "Women and Politics in the Middle East." *Middle East Report* , no. 138, vol. 16, no. 1 (January/February 1986).

——— . "Working-Class Women's Networks in a Sectarian State: A Political Paradox." *American Ethnologist* 10, no. 1 (February 1983).

Jowkar, Forouz. "Honor and Shame: A Feminist View from Within." *Feminist Issues* 6, no. 1 (Spring 1986).

Keddie, Nikki R. "Problems in the Study of Middle Eastern Women." *International Journal of Middle East Studies* 10 (April 1979).

Khafagy, Fatma. "Women and Labor Migration: One Village in Egypt." *Merip Reports*, no. 124 (June 1984).

Khouri-Dagher, Nadia. "The Answers of Civil Society to a Defaulting State: A Case Study Around the Food Question in Egypt." A paper presented to the Middle East Studies Association, Baltimore, Maryland, November 1987.

Larson, Barbara. "The Status of Women in a Tunisian Village: Limits to Autonomy, Influence, and Power." *Signs* 9, no. 3 (Spring 1984).

Lawson, Fred H. "Rural Revolt and Provincial Society in Egypt 1820–1824." *International Journal of Middle East Studies* 13, no. 2 (1981).

Marshall, Susan. "Paradoxes of Change: Culture Crisis, Islamic Revival, and the Reactivation of Patriarchy." *Journal of Asian and African Studies* 19, nos. 1–2 (1984).

Mayer, Ann. "Libyan Legislation in Defense of Arabo-Islamic Mores." *The American Journal of Comparative Law* 28, no. 2 (Spring 1980).

Mernissi, Fatima. "Muslim Women and Fundamentalism." *Middle East Report*, no. 153, vol. 18, no. 4 (July–August 1988).

——— . "Professional Women in the Arab World: The Example of Morocco." *Feminist Issues* 7, no. 1 (Spring 1987).

——— . "Virginity and Patriarchy." *Women's Studies International Forum* 5, no. 2 (1982).

——— . "The Effects of Modernization of the Male-Female Dynamics in a Muslim Society: Morocco." Ph.D. diss., Brandeis University, Department of Sociology, 1973.

Miller, Judith, and Marie Colvin. "Behind the Veil." *Savvy*, January 1988.

Moghadam, Val. "Women, Work, and Ideology in the Islamic Republic." *International Journal of Middle East Studies* 20 (1988).

——— . "Problems in Middle East Women's Studies: The View from Marxist-Feminist Sociology." Paper presented to the Middle East Studies Association, Beverly Hills, California, November 1988.

Momeni, Jamshid. "Divorce in the Islamic Context," *Islamic Culture* 60, no. 2 (April 1986).

Moustafa, Saad Moustafa. "Man and Woman in Islam," parts 1 and 2. *al-Azhar*, 60, parts 5 and 6, (January and February 1988).

Naficy, Mejid. "Khomeini and Sexuality." Paper presented to the Middle East Studies Association, Baltimore, Maryland, November 1987.

Najjar, Fauzi. "Egypt's Laws of Personal Status." *Arab Studies Quarterly* 10, no. 3 (1988).

Nelson, Cynthia. "The Voices of Doria Shafik: Feminist Consciousness in Egypt, 1940–1960." *Feminist Issues* 6, no. 2 (Fall 1986).

Olson, Emelie. "Muslim Identity and Secularism in Contemporary Turkey: 'The Headscarf Dispute.' " *Anthropological Quarterly* 58, no. 4 (October 1985).

Philip, Thomas. "Women in the Historical Perspective of an Early Arab Modernist (Gurgi Zaidan)." *Welt des Islams* 18 (1977).

Sa'adawi, Nawal. "Woman and Islam." *Women's Studies International Forum* 5, no. 2 (1982).

Sabagh, Georges, and Iman Ghazalla. "Arab Sociology Today: A View From Within." *Annual Review of Sociology* 12 (1986).

Safwah, Safiyyah Muhammad. "The State of Sudanese Women under What is Called the Laws of the Islamic Shar'iah." *al-Dustur* 14, iss. 348, 12 November 1984.

Sayigh, Rosemary. "Roles and Functions of Arab Women: A Reappraisal." *Arab Studies Quarterly* 3, no. 3 (Autumn 1981).

Schimmel, Annemarie. "Women in Mystical Islam" (Azizah al-Hibri, guest ed.) *Women's Studies International Forum* 5, no. 2, (1982).

Shadid, Mohammed. D. "The Muslim Brotherhood Movement in the West Bank and Gaza." *Third World Quarterly* 10, no. 2 (April 1988).

Smith, Jane, and Yvonne Haddad. "Eve: Islamic Image of Woman" (Azizah al-Hibri, guest ed). *Women's Studies International Forum* 5, no. 2 (1982).

Stillman, Yedida Kalfon. "Female Attire of Medieval Egypt: According to the Trousseau Lists and Cognate Material from the Cairo Geniza." Ph.D. diss., Department of Oriental Studies, University of Pennsylvania, 1972.

Stowasser, Barbara. "Liberated Equal or Protected Dependent? Contemporary Religious Paradigms on Women's Status in Islam." *Arab Studies Quarterly* 9, no. 3 (Summer 1987).

Sukkary-Stolba, Soheir. "Changing Roles of Women in Egypt's Newly Reclaimed Lands." *Anthropological Quarterly* 58, no. 4 (October, 1985).

Suleiman, Michael. "Changing Attitudes Toward Women in Egypt: The Role of Fiction in Women's Magazines." *Middle Eastern Studies.* 14, no. 3, 1978.

Taylor, Elizabeth. "Egyptian Migration and Peasant Wives." *Merip Reports* no. 124, vol. 14, no. 5 (June 1984).

Tucker, Judith. "Insurrectionary Women: Women and the State in Nineteenth Century Egypt." *MERIP* no. 138, vol. 16, no. 1 (January/February 1986).

———. "Problems in the Historiography of Women in the Middle East: The Case of Nineteenth Century Egypt." *International Journal of Middle East Studies* 15 (1983) pp. 321–336.

Viorst, Milton. "A Reporter At Large: Man of Gamaliya." *The New Yorker,* 2 July 1990, pp. 32–53.

Widad, Marcos. "The New Family Law in Egypt." *CEMAM Reports,* (1981).

Wikan, Unni. "Living Conditions Among Cairo's Poor—A View From Below." *Middle East Journal,* vol. 39, no. 1, Winter 1985. pp. 7–26.

Youssef, Nadia. "A Woman-Specific Strategy Statement: The Case of Egypt." Aid Bureau of Program and Policy Coordination Report, Cairo, 1980.

Zein Ed-Din, Nazirah. "Removing the Veil and Veiling" (1928). *Women's Studies Internat'l Forum* 5, no. 2 (1982).

Zuhur, Sherifa. "Self-Image of Egyptian Women in Oppositionist Islam." Ph.D. diss., Department of History, University of California, Los Angeles, 1990.

———— . "Revealing Reveiling: Body and Morality Concepts in Traditional and Current Islamic Covering." A paper presented to the American Ethnological Society, Atlanta, Georgia, 26 April 1990.

———— . "Why False Consciousness?" A paper presented to the Berkshire Conference on Women's History, New Brunswick, New Jersey, 9 June 1990.

French and Other Languages:

Books and Articles

de Beauvoir, Simone. *Le deuxième sexe*. Paris: Gallimard, 1981.

Commission des Sciences et des Arts. *Descriptions de l'Egypte*. Vols. 18–21. Paris: 1809–1825 (illustrated and text versions).

Contu, Giuseppe. "La donne comuniste e il movimento democratico femminile in Egitto fino al 1965." *Oriente Moderno* 55, 5–6 (1975).

Echavarri, Luis, trans., edited and introduced by Gustave von Grunebaum. *Los Suenos y las sociedades humanas*. Buenos Aires: Editorial Sudamericano, 1964.

Fenerci Mehmed Albumu. *Osmanli Kiyafetleri*, edited by Ilhami Turan. Istanbul: Vehbi Kocvakfi, 1986.

Hussein, Mahmoud. *La lutte des classes en egypte, de 1945 à 1968*. Paris: Maspero, 1969.

Kepel, Gilles. "Les groupes Islamistes en Egypte: Flux et reflux 1981–1985." *Politique Etrangere* 51, no. 2 (1986).

Khayat-Bennai. *Le monde arabe au feminin*. Paris: Editions l'Harmattan, 1985.

Mernissi, Fatima. *Chahrazade n'est pas Marocaine: Autrement, elle serait salariée!*. Casablanca: Éditions le Fennec, 1988.

———— . *Le harem politique: le Prophete et les femmes*. Paris: Albin Michel, 1988.

———— . *Le Maroc raconte par ses femmes*. Rabat: Societé Marocaine des Éditeurs Reunis, 1984.

———— . *Sexe, ideologie, et islam*. Paris: Tierce, 1983.

Minces, Juliet. *La femme dans le monde arabe*. Paris: Mazarine, 1980.

Mirel, Pierre. *L'Egypte des ruptures: l'ere Sadate, de Nasser a Moubarak*. Paris: Sindbad, 1982.

Peuples Méditerranées (nos. 42–42) in conjunction with CEDEJ, dir. Paul Vielle. *Egypte—Recompositions*. Paris: 1988.

Savary, Comte de. *Lettres sur l'Egypte*. Vols. 1–3. Paris: 1825.

Shafik, Doria Razai. *La femme et le droit religieux de l'Egypte contemporaire*. Paris: 1960.

Tillion, Germaine. *Le harem et les cousins*. Paris: Editions du Seuil, 1966.

Vial, Charles. *Le personnage de la femme dans le roman et la nouvelle en Egypte de 1914 à 1960*. Thesis, University of Paris III, 28 January 1974.

Zenie-Ziegler, Wedad. *La face voilée des femmes d'Egypte*. Paris: Mercure de France, 1985.

Periodicals (collected)

Revue de la Presse Egyptienne, no. 31, 2ème trimestre. Cairo: Centre de documentation et d'études economiques, juridiques et sociales (1988).

Interviews

al-ʿAryan, ʿAsam. Personal interview with the author, Cairo, 6 December 1988.
Fouad, Niʿmat. Personal interview with the author, Cairo, 24 November 1988.
al-Ghazali, Zaynab. Personal interview with the author, Cairo, 28 November 1988.
Kamel, Fayda. Personal interview with the author, Cairo, 25 November 1988.
Kamel, Jeanette Saad. Personal interview with the author, Cairo, 2 December 1988.
Kamel, Olfat. Personal interview with the author, Cairo, 21 November 1988.
Qassim, Safinaz. Telephone interview with the author, Cairo, 5 December 1988.
Roushdie, Ingie. Personal interview with the author, Cairo, 30 November 1988.
Sirry, Djenane. Personal interview with the author, Cairo, 23 November 1988.
Shawqi, Hana Ahmad. Personal interview with the author, Cairo, 18 November 1988.
Personal interviews with fifty (anonymous) Cairene women, November–December 1988.

INDEX

Activism, female, 20; despite centrality of the family, 89–90, 92–95;
and Islamists, 95, 127–128; and
Zaynab al-Ghazali's view, 89–90.
See also Political activism and
participation
Age: general factors of 13, 18; and
Islamist identification, 61–62, 130;
and middle aged and older women,
64–65; and older women's dress,
116; and power of mother-in-laws,
97; and Third Worldism, 83; and
younger women, 61, 62, 64, 83;
and younger women's environment, 108
Ahistoricity, 10, 27; and Islamists, 75,
106d; versus flexibility of women's
image, 108
ʿAʾishah bint Abu Bakr, 34–38; and
affair of the slander, 35; and the
fitnah, 36, 37; under ʿUmar's rule,
36; role in public affairs, 36, 90;
and virginity, 37
Alimony and Islamists, 97
Amin, Qasim, 10, 40; Islamist views
of, 42
Anomie. *See* Social anomie
Arabian peninsula and women
in the pre-Islamic era, 4, 27, 31,
32, 33
Archetypes: effect of, 7; and gender
issues, 131; and historical synthesis,
133–134; and Jung, 92, 126; and
linkages for veiled women, 126; and
new virtuous female image, 127;
and Yvonne Haddad's study, 104.
See also Historical models
Association of Muslim Women,
45, 46

Barakah: and parental influence, 117;
of the Prophet, 92; of women
through veiling, 92
Beauty: female and the *hijab*, 90–91
Bint al-balad: definition of, 8, 9; and
hijab, 123; and *ibn al-nas*, 110; and
image of unveiled woman, 124; as
muʿalimat, 122; and Nasserist period, 122–123; and religiosity, 123;
and social mobility, 122; and work,
121–122
Bint al-dhawwat, 109–110; and importance of children to, 113–114. *See
also Bint al-nas* and Elite women.
Bint al-nas, 110–111
Bint al-Shatti (ʿAʾishah abd al-
Rahman), 43
Birth control: and foreign conspiracies, 88–89; and *Ikhwan's* position
on, 46; and survey attitudes, 68–70;
versus redistribution of resources,
87–88; and unveiled women, 114.
See also Family, planning
Brideprice, *See Mahr*
al-Bukhari, restrictions of women, 5
Burqa (traditional face-veil), 9, 77.
See also Veiling

Children; value of, 113–114; socializa-
tion of, 64, 96, 119; young wom-
en's views of, 68–69
Childcare: costs of, 69, 94; and un-
veiled women, 119
Circumcision, female, 21, 34, 106
Class divisions. *See* Socioeconomic
class; divisions
Complementary of the sexes, 15
Copts and Islamist state, 73, 87

201